THE GREEKS AND THEIR HISTORIES

In this concise but stimulating book on history and Greek culture, Hans-Joachim Gehrke continues to refine his work on 'intentional history', which he defines as a history in the self-understanding of social groups and communities – connected to a corresponding understanding of the other – which is important, even essential, for the collective identity, social cohesion, political behaviour, and cultural orientation of such units. In a series of four chapters, Gehrke illustrates how Greeks' histories were consciously employed to help shape political and social realities. In particular, he argues that poets were initially the masters of the past, and that this dominance of the aesthetic in the view of the past led to an indissoluble amalgamation of myth and history and lasting tension between poetry and truth in the genre of historiography. The book reveals a more sophisticated picture of Greek historiography, its intellectual foundations, and its wider social-political contexts.

HANS-JOACHIM GEHRKE is Professor Emeritus of Ancient History at the University of Freiburg (Breisgau). He was Professor and Visiting Scholar at several German and European universities, and President of the German Archaeological Institute. He is the editor of *Making Civilisations* (2020).

CLASSICAL SCHOLARSHIP IN TRANSLATION

Series editors
RENAUD GAGNÉ, UNIVERSITY OF CAMBRIDGE
JONAS GRETHLEIN, RUPRECHT-KARLS-UNIVERSITÄT HEIDELBERG

Classical Scholarship in Translation provides English translations of some particularly notable and significant scholarship on the ancient Greek and Roman worlds and their reception written in other languages in order to make it better known and appreciated. All areas of classical scholarship are considered.

Recent titles in the series:
The Greeks and Their Histories: Myth, History, and Society
HANS-JOACHIM GEHRKE

The Hera of Zeus: Intimate Enemy, Ultimate Spouse
VINCIANE PIRENNE-DELFORGE AND
GABRIELLA PIRONTI

THE GREEKS AND THEIR HISTORIES

Myth, History, and Society

HANS-JOACHIM GEHRKE

Albert-Ludwigs-Universität Freiburg, Germany

Translated by Raymond Geuss, University of Cambridge

Shaftesbury Road, Cambridge CB2 8EA, United Kingdom

One Liberty Plaza, 20th Floor, New York, NY 10006, USA

477 Williamstown Road, Port Melbourne, VIC 3207, Australia

314–321, 3rd Floor, Plot 3, Splendor Forum, Jasola District Centre, New Delhi – 110025, India

103 Penang Road, #05–06/07, Visioncrest Commercial, Singapore 238467

Cambridge University Press is part of Cambridge University Press & Assessment,
a department of the University of Cambridge.

We share the University's mission to contribute to society through the pursuit of
education, learning and research at the highest international levels of excellence.

www.cambridge.org
Information on this title: www.cambridge.org/9781009011150

DOI: 10.1017/9781009022279

Preface and English translation © Cambridge University Press & Assessment 2023

First published in 2014 as Hans-Joachim Gehrke: *Geschichte als Element antiker Kultur* ©
Walter de Gruyter GmbH Berlin Boston. All rights reserved.

*This work may not be translated or copied in whole or part without the written permission of the
publisher (Walter De Gruyter GmbH, Genthiner Straße 13, 10785 Berlin, Germany).*

This publication is in copyright. Subject to statutory exception and to the provisions
of relevant collective licensing agreements, no reproduction of any part may take
place without the written permission of Cambridge University Press & Assessment.

First published 2023
First paperback edition 2025

A catalogue record for this publication is available from the British Library

ISBN 978-1-316-51978-3 Hardback
ISBN 978-1-009-01115-0 Paperback

Cambridge University Press & Assessment has no responsibility for the persistence
or accuracy of URLs for external or third-party internet websites referred to in this
publication and does not guarantee that any content on such websites is, or will
remain, accurate or appropriate.

Contents

Foreword by Jonas Grethlein — *page* vii
Preface to the German Edition — xi
Preface — xv
Note on Abbreviations — xvii

Introduction — 1

1 The Locus of Intentional History: Reference-Group – Producers – Media — 10

2 Greek Myths As a History of the Greeks: Motifs – Forms – Structures — 42

3 Greek Historiography between Past and Present — 73

4 Greek Historiography between Fiction and Truth — 95

Concluding Perspectives — 133

References — 138
Index — 161

Foreword

Jonas Grethlein

Ranke famously declared that it is the task of the historian to reconstruct the past 'how it actually was' and he identified Thucydides as the 'father of all true history'. Both his understanding of history and his esteem for Thucydides are representative of the nineteenth century, a century in which historiography blossomed into a leading discipline. The ideas of historicism soon came under fire – Nietzsche fiercely polemicised against the anaemia of antiquarianism while historians like Lamprecht challenged the inordinate focus on the political history of the state – but its premises were to have a lasting impact on approaches to antiquity and its relation to the past. For a long time, scholars concentrated on ancient historians, envisaging them as the predecessors of modern historians. If non-historiographic forms of memory came into view, they were considered chiefly as steps in a development that would ultimately lead to the emergence of historiography.[1]

The past decades, however, have seen a mounting interest in the various forms and media of memory. To give a few examples: Loraux (1981) examined funeral speeches as the semi-official history of Athens; Bowie (1986) made a case for historical elegy, which was corroborated by the discovery of the 'New Simonides'; Chaniotis[2] investigated inscriptional records of the past; Alcock (2002) considered the role of ruins and other material remains; Higbie (2003) explored the commemorative function of votives in her study of the Lindian chronicle. Inquiries into the memory of particular events – for example, Jung (2006) on the battles of Marathon and Plataea and Luraghi (2008) on the construction of the Messenian past – also addressed a wide range of media.

---

[1] For example, Deichgräber, Karl (1952, 7–56); Gomme, A. W. (1954) *The Greek Attitude to Poetry and History*, Berkeley; Châtelet, François (1962) *La naissance de l'histoire*, Paris; Mazzarino, Santo (1966) *Il pensiero storico classico*, Rome.

[2] Chaniotis, Angelos (1988) *Historie und Historiker in den griechischen Inschriften*, Stuttgart.

Despite this widening of the scope, the privileging of historiography, explicit or implicit, has proven tenacious. It is tangible even in Boedeker's masterful and far-reaching survey of representations of the Persian War in the fifth century BC when she speaks of 'the paradox that historiography itself develops late in a city so rich in memorials of its great past deeds'.[3] Is it a paradox? Should we not rather ask why historiography emerged in an already crowded field of memory?

It is one of the merits of Gehrke's *The Greeks and Their Histories* that it provides a conceptual grid that allows us to examine various commemorative media in their own right as well as reassess historiography. Gehrke advances what he calls 'an etic perspective on an emic (intentional) state of affairs', that is, a reconstruction in our terms of how the Greeks viewed their past (and not the examination of the correctness of their memories). While the framework is thus set by Berger's and Luckmann's sociology of knowledge, which tackles the structures of plausibilities forged in a society, the broad focus is inspired by Halbwachs' concept of *mémoire collective* and its reception by Assmann. More specifically, Gehrke resuscitates the notion of 'intentional history', coined by the anthropologist Mühlmann (1938) in the analysis of ethnic identities and later made fruitful for the study of history by Wenskus (1961). 'Intentional history' signifies the memories of the past that help define the identity of a group. The heuristic value of this term is that it sidelines the question of whether ancient records of the past are reliable or not and instead addresses their significance and functions for the groups that remembered the past.

Kant observed that while 'intuitions without concepts are blind', 'thoughts without content are empty'. The richness of the material that Gehrke unfolds before the eyes of the reader is another merit of *The Greeks and Their Histories*. Bringing together sources that belong to the domains of different disciplines, he discusses inscriptions as well as oral traditions, examines pictorial records of the past together with poetry and oratory, and is sensitive to the importance of rituals. The numerous examples presented in the course of his study provide compelling evidence for the agonistic structure of Greek memory, for its deep roots in specific contexts and the close entwinement of the past with the present. Gehrke's familiarity with the full range of sources and his impressive command of scholarship yield a unique survey of the important functions that the past served in ancient Greece and the multitude of forms in which it was evoked.

---

[3] Boedeker, Deborah (1988) *Democracy, Empire, and the Arts in Fifth-Century Athens*, Cambridge, MA, 185–6.

Gehrke's book also substantiates a key hope attached to the series Classical Scholarship in Translation. The series aims not only to make the books selected for translation better known in the anglophone world but also to give readers access to the traditions to which the books are indebted. Gehrke's thinking, for example, is influenced by his mentor Heuß and his interest in how the Greeks envisaged the world. He also draws on other works that have received little attention in anglophone scholarship, for example, Prinz's (1979) investigation of ancient Greek foundation myths and the articles of Strasburger (1982/1990) on memory and historiography. Of course, new questions have surfaced, and new approaches have been ushered in, but, for example, Strasburger's reassessment of Hellenistic historiography and his argument that the experiential accounts by Agatharchides and others, instead of being a deterioration of methodological standards, need to be taken seriously as a form of mimesis, still read fresh.

The argument of Gehrke itself illustrates the boundaries between national traditions of scholarship. In the second half of the book, Gehrke turns to historiography, which he also considers as a form of intentional history, without, however, ignoring what distinguishes the reports of Herodotus & Co. from other forms of memory. One of the links between historiographic and non-historiographic memory on which Gehrke elaborates is rhetoric. Given the salience of rhetoric in the ancient world, this emphasis is not surprising, but it is noteworthy that Gehrke does not reference the works of Woodman, which, while being discussed controversially, were key for directing the focus of anglophone scholars on the rhetorical nature of ancient historiography. The comparison is illuminating -Woodman pushes his argument far, contending 'that there is no theoretical basis whatsoever for the view that classical historiography resembles its namesake. Historiography was regarded by the ancients as not essentially different from poetry: each was a branch of rhetoric, and therefore historiography, like poetry, employs the concepts associated with, and relies upon the expectations generated by, a rhetorical genre.'[4] Gehrke, on the other hand, does not see rhetoric and truth necessarily at loggerheads – he sees, of course, the danger of neglecting the truth in order to dazzle the reader, but, aware of the close relation between experience and narrative, he notes that narrative is an indispensable means of representing the past and its careful crafting has the capacity of making it present to readers.

---

[4] Woodman, A. J. (1988) *Rhetoric in Classical Historiography*, London, x.

It is also interesting to compare the different angles: whereas Woodman starts with a close reading of Thucydides' methodological reflections and then goes on to discuss Cicero's comments on history, Gehrke zooms in on Isocrates and the influence he is said to have had on Ephorus and Theopompus. Isocrates is not an author with whom many classicists sympathise, but Gehrke takes him seriously and aligns his meditations on truth and representation with those of Thucydides. I wonder if the prominence of Isocrates in Gehrke's argument is incidental. Gehrke calls Isokrates 'a great teacher and educator', a label that several generations of students and scholars would unhesitatingly assign to Gehrke himself. I also suspect that Isocrates' pragmatism resonates with Gehrke, who, besides his illustrious scholarly career, was also active in the highest circles of academic politics in Germany, for example as a member of the senate of the Deutsche Forschungsgemeinschaft and as the president of the Deutsches Archäologisches Institut.

Thucydides concedes that his account of the Peloponnesian War 'will seem less entertaining; but if those, who wish to view *to saphes* of the things which took place and of those which one day, given human nature, are destined to take place again in more or less the same fashion, should judge my work useful, that will be enough' (1.22.4). Woodman (1988: 23–8) contests that *to saphes* here means 'complete accuracy' (Lesky) or 'the truth' (Dover) and instead ties it to the rhetorical category of *enargeia* – Thucydides lays claim not to truthfulness but to graphic quality. Gehrke also discusses the vivid presentation to which ancient historians aspired, but he does not see it necessarily conflict with the goal of truthfulness. I suspect that he would hear both sides in Thucydides' reference to *to saphes*.

Gehrke's own prose is vivid and vigorous. He not only exposes his theory in an unassuming and direct manner, making his claims tangible through examples, but also writes in an unusually engaging style. Thanks to the translation of the philosopher Raymond Geuss, his meditation on the significance of history in ancient Greece can now also be appreciated by anglophone readers. Whether they raise their eyebrows when they encounter some positions – for example that the impact of the shift from orality to literacy should not be overestimated – or wish to extend Gehrke's approach to the Imperial period, which is not addressed but has become one of the foci of (not only) anglophone scholarship – *The Greeks and Their Histories* is bound to enrich the ongoing discussion about the 'grip of the past' in ancient Greece.

Preface to the German Edition

This book is an interim report on work-in-progress, in the sense that in it I try to give a preliminary summing up of the results of the reflections on history that have engaged me for many decades. This has been a collaborative venture of research, teaching, and conversation, involving many other scholars, which has been conducted in a wide variety of formats, some rather informal but some more strictly institutionalised. I have derived much inspiration from the other participants in this process.

I think here especially of the Graduate Collegium 'Ancient Presents and Their Pasts', initiated by Volker Michael Strocka in Freiburg, the Special Research Programme 'Identities and Alterities', which I planned, organised, and moderated for a period of time (also in Freiburg), and the European Network for the Study of Ancient Greek History, which provided an especially congenial and multi-faceted milieu for work in this area and constantly threw up new ideas for further research. It was in the context of the European Network that, together with Lyn Foxhall (Leicester) and Nino Luraghi (Princeton), I was able to organise a conference specifically focused on the topic of intentional history.

One high point in the history of my reflections on this subject was the very fruitful academic year I spent in 2012/2013 as Professor for the Cultural History of the Ancient World at the Munich Centre for Ancient Worlds (MZAW) at the University there. In my seminars with doctoral candidates, and also in numerous conversations I had with students and colleagues from Munich and elsewhere, I found myself reaching out to make connections that I would otherwise have found it hard to envisage.

The series of public lectures I was invited to give in Munich on the topic of 'History as an element in (ancient) culture' provided an opportunity to formulate my views, to see them subjected to discussion, and to develop them further in the light of criticism. After several further rounds of criticism by colleagues in Munich and revisions which, I hope, have made them more substantial and better grounded, these lectures finally took the form of this opusculum. The small difference between the title of these lectures and that of the book, and the greater length and level of annotation of the latter, indicate the changes that have taken place between the time of the original lectures and this written version. It was precisely the intellectual richness of the environment in Munich that allowed me to impose my problems and concerns on many of my conversational partners and thus to remain focused on the ancient world. I did not, consequently, get as far in treating this history as I had originally planned. I succumbed once again to the fascination of the study of this period and hope the reader can feel something of that fascination in the text.

My special thanks then go to the colleagues at the Munich Centre for the Study of Ancient Worlds (MZAW), who were kind enough to accept me as one of their own for a while, and who then made my time there so marvellously pleasant and productive. I would also like to thank the doctoral students in my two seminars, whose seminar presentations and contributions to the discussion, often as a response to things I said, gave me more food for thought than they probably realised. 'Off to new frontiers' was the inscription on the card that accompanied the gift which they very generously presented to me on the occasion of my leaving.

I would like to return the sentiment. I am very grateful to the following helpful members of the staff of the Centre: Isabella Wiegand, Sandra Zerbin, and Nicole Schüler. They seemed always to have time to provide assistance, even of the most varied kind, not to mention the interesting conversations that often ensued (with or without coffee, which, as far as I could tell, never seemed to run out). My time at the MZAW had one further, and highly gratifying, result: In June 2013 and January 2014, two workshops took place in Freiburg on 'Ancient Historiography and Conceptions of the Past'. The participants in these two workshops were chiefly younger scholars from Munich and Freiburg, but also from many much more far-flung places. This led to the founding of the 'International Network historiai'.

Portions of the following text have been presented on different occasions in various places: in 2010, at a meeting of the contributors to the Protestant–Catholic commentary on the New Testament in Frankfurt; in Heidelberg, at an event to celebrate Tonio Hölscher; in 2012, at the Princeton Department of Classics; in Vienna, at a conference organised by Walter Pohl and Helmut Reimitz for the Research Group 'Visions of Community'; at the Free University of Berlin, in the context of a Colloquium of the Excellence Cluster TOPOI; and, in 2013, at the École Normale Supérieure in Paris. May I take this opportunity to thank all those who invited me to speak and all those who helped me with tips, references, and suggestions in the various discussions. Finally, the production of the book has gone remarkably smoothly. Christian Kunze contributed to illustrations, and Serena Pirrotta (in addition to the other members of the de Gruyter team) were ideal editors. My thanks to them all.

Preface

It came as something of a surprise to me when the slim volume containing some guest lectures I gave at the University of Munich during the academic year 2012/2013 was received with such enthusiasm. The attempt that I made in these lectures to place Greek historiography in the wider context of the ways in which ancient society in general conceived of the past was a bit of an experiment for me, and so I was extremely pleased when readers seemed to think that I was on the right track. I take this to be a confirmation of the potential fruitfulness of this line of enquiry. That is one of the reasons I am especially glad that this *opusculum* will now appear in English and, consequently, be more easily accessible to an international readership. I have taken the opportunity provided by the translation to correct a few accidental oversights in the text and to take account of some of the recent literature.

I have several people to thank for organising the translation and for the way in which it was carried out. In the first instance, I should like to thank the editors of the new Cambridge University Press series 'Classical Scholarship in Translation', Renaud Gagné and Jonas Grethlein, who originally took the initiative for this project and pursued it with great energy. I must thank Jonas Grethlein for writing a Foreword to this work, and I must also thank Raymond Geuss, who worked assiduously to produce a brilliant translation of my sometimes rebarbative German text. The intense exchanges with him, which went far beyond the discussion of specific formulations and verbal nuances, were a particular intellectual pleasure, especially during a winter in which a pandemic was raging.

Mark Marsh-Hunn, who has been such a great help to me in so many ways during the past few years, displayed his usual precision and conscientiousness in reading the proofs and especially in making the index. Two editors of Cambridge University Press oversaw the editorial and production sides of the publication, Michael Sharp and Katie Idle, as well as Adam

Bell of Ambb Editorial, and it was a great relief for me to know that this meant that the work was in the best possible hands.

Finally, I wish to thank the officers of the Gerda Henkel Foundation, who authorised a substantial grant that made possible the translation and publication of the book.

I am very grateful to these people and to all those who helped to bring the book to publication. I hope that their efforts have not been in vain.

Note on Abbreviations

The abbreviations are used according to: *Der Neue Pauly (DNP): Enzyklopädie der Antike.* Edited by Hubert Cancik and Helmuth Schneider, vol. I, Stuttgart 1996 (English version: *Brill's New Pauly: Encyclopaedia of the Ancient World.* Edited by Hubert Cancik, Helmuth Schneider, and Christine F. Salazar, vol. I, Leiden 2002; New Pauly Online https://referenceworks.brillonline.com/browse/brill-s-new-pauly).

Introduction

History in the broadest sense has always been my central concern, and in what follows I try to give an interim report about how far I have come in my reflections about it. History is not merely one object of scientific study among others, but in the sense in which I am interested in it, it is something that has the power to shape collective and individual human life; one might even say that it is a vital elixir that invigorates individuals and groups. Because of the role it plays in human existence, I think of history as more than just one science among many, but as an element of culture. I use this term in the sense that has become usual in recent discussion in the field of the cultural sciences, to refer to 'meanings, modes of perception, and ways of making sense of things',[1] that is to the interpretative schemata individuals and groups of all types use and the imaginative space they inhabit. Humans, after all, do constantly try to comprehend the things that directly affect them; in particular, they make a concerted effort to make sense of those features of their world and experience that seem initially the hardest to understand and the least accessible. My subject is the particular way in which, in the context of this general project of understanding the world, they have made sense of their past. To be more precise, I wish to focus on the Greeks, or, to be even more precise, I wish to look at those groups and individuals who called themselves 'Hellenes' and whom we may call the 'Greeks'. This particular focus is in part a consequence of my own special expertise and my own personal inclination, but only in part, because I shall argue that the Greek case has exemplary value.

There is a fundamental, categorical distinction that can be made between two different senses of the past and two correspondingly different ways of relating to it. This is a difference between two ideal types, one

---

[1] Daniel 2002, 17. On the general range of senses in which the concept of 'culture' can be used, see Gotter 2000.

which was very clearly formulated and emphasised by scholars such as Alfred Heuß and Reinhart Koselleck. However, it was foreshadowed in the writings of Jacob and Wilhelm Grimm in their Preface to *Deutsche Sagen* (*German Legends*) and it emerged fully into the light in the second of Friedrich Nietzsche's *Unzeitgemäße Betrachtungen* (*Untimely Meditations*).[2] On the one side there stands history as living memory, *memoria*. It is something transmitted down the generations and bound up with the existence of a particular community. Memory in this sense is what is understood by a community to be the recollection of its own past, as constituting, one might say, part of its own tradition.

The Brothers Grimm expressed this notion of history in an especially vivid and emphatic way:

> Therefore nothing that can properly be called 'history' can be incorporated into the life of a people, except through the mediation of legend; the people will remain indifferent to an event that is spatially and temporally far away, unless it satisfies this condition, or, if people do briefly accept it, they will quickly drop it from their memory. In contrast to this, how firmly we see a people hold fast to its own inherited, traditional legends. No matter where a people roams, its legends move with it, at an appropriate distance, and remain connected to its most familiar concepts. Their own legends can never bore people because they are not for them a mere empty game that one can take up or abandon as one wishes, rather they seem to be a necessity which belongs to their way of living, which is self-evident, which also, to be sure only comes to expression on the right occasion, and then only with the kind of solemnity that is demanded in dealing with serious matters . . . .
> A scent of legend and song gradually surrounds any feature of a landscape that seems unusual to the human senses and which history invokes, just as the distant sky takes on a blue hue or and a fine, delicate dust settles slowly on fruit and flowers.

Nietzsche speaks in this connection of 'antiquarian history', but contemporary treatments of this aspect of history remain deeply dependent on Maurice Halbwachs' (1997) notion of '*mémoire collective*', or at any rate they start from this concept. Halbwachs connected memory and history, as forms of remembrance, each to its own collective subject. History in his sense is particularly significant because it creates forms of orientation: orientation about origins, ancestry, about spatial location and the possession of land, about who belongs and who is foreign. Consequently, there is

---

[2] Grimm 1865, VIIf.; Nietzsche cited in Rossmann 1969, 328–55; Heuß 1959, 1984; Koselleck 1979; 2000. See also Le Goff 1977/1988 and Straub 1998b, 12f., who come to similar conclusions although starting from very different points of departure.

a very close connection between the subject who remembers and the object remembered; they refer to the same thing, the group or community that is in question. At the same time there is a plurality of such groups and communities constituted by memory, so that one must speak in the plural of *memoriae*.[3]

The telling of stories is an elementary form of this and plays an especially important role in constituting such a memory.[4]

An awareness of this aspect of history has stimulated much intensive research recently and has proved to be of interest far beyond the confines of professional historians. Two variants or versions of this approach have been particularly influential. First of all there is the programme of studying 'sites of memory' (*lieux de mémoire*), which Pierre Nora originally developed and which has been widely received and imitated.[5] The second variant is the one centred around Jan Assmann's distinction between 'communicative' and 'cultural' memory.[6] Several further large and fruitful bodies of research have gradually accumulated along these two lines of enquiry. Thus, for instance, it is quite normal nowadays to speak of 'cultures of remembrance'[7] or of the 'politics of history', and in the study of ancient civilisations one can see similar developments.[8]

This, then, is the first of the two ways of dealing with the past, and opposed to it stands another approach which undoes the connection between subject and object. This second approach lays claim in a more or less emphatically expressed way to objectivity or at any rate to freedom from prejudice, and so those who adopt this approach characteristically speak of 'history' in the singular. They aspire to attain 'scientific' status for their results, and this leads them to commit themselves to forms of investigation that stay close to the agreed-on facts of the matter and to

---

[3] Reinhart Koselleck has particularly underlined this point.
[4] The comments of Stierle 1979, 92f. still set the standard for discussion in this area. On the theoretical background, the relevant chapters of Rüsen 1990/2012 are of fundamental importance; see also below (p. 43f).
[5] Nora 1984–1992; various successor projects with wide-ranging ambitions have attempted to extend Nora's approach to countries and cultures other than that of France (see for instance François and Schulze 2001; Markschies and Wolf 2010). See also Stein-Hölkeskamp and Hölkeskamp 2006, 2010 for a similar treatment of antiquity.
[6] Assmann 1992; see also A. Assmann and Friese 1998; A. Assmann 1999.
[7] One might mention in this context the special research project at the University of Giessen with this name.
[8] See the large number of recent and very recent works that adopt this approach, including quite a few dissertations, for instance in particular Alcock 2002; Higbie 2003; Jung 2006; Grethlein 2006a; Kühr 2006; Clarke 2008; Luraghi 2008; Hartmann 2010; Franchi and Proietti 2012; Osmers 2013; Steinbock 2013; Boschung, Busch, and Versluys 2015; Zingg 2016; Hübner 2019; Giangiulio, Franchi, and Proietti 2019; Pohl and Wieser 2019; Schröder 2020.

intersubjectively recognised rules of methodology and argumentation. This is the perspective of the modern historian (at least the professional historian); it attained its present shape in the 'saddle-time'[9] around 1800. The basic features of this way of looking at history have been described repeatedly, in particular when treating those developed forms of historism or neo-historism that celebrated Leopold von Ranke as their heroic founder.[10] This is what Nietzsche calls the 'critical' way of dealing with the past.[11] What is emphasised here is precisely the distance between the object of investigation – a group that is remembering – and a subject who is conducting research according to his/her own principles and lights. One can see this difference very clearly in the sober book which Edward Hallett Carr (1961) devoted to the question 'What is history?', a book that is still very much worth reading. However, from the point of view of those who take history to be a form of 'collective memory', efforts like those of the historians and of Carr must be considered to have missed the point; they are, from this point of view, instances of the 'loss of history'.[12]

The first approach has long preoccupied me, since I first began to ask how the Greeks themselves saw and tried to understand their own past.[13] The second approach is that of my profession, that of the historian. In my capacity as a historian, I decided to study the first approach. Nonetheless, from the very beginning[14] I have made it my goal never to separate in a complete and categorical way the two approaches, despite the need to distinguish them in principle. I understand the difference between the two as a difference between two ideal types (in the sense of Max Weber), that is, as a distinction that brings out abstractly different properties of the two approaches, despite the fact that these approaches can in reality overlap and vitally complement each other in a number of different ways. This is particularly important to see because the mode of proceeding that is used by the modern historical sciences is also the way in which modern (in any case, modern 'Western') societies try to make sense of their own past. The subject and the object of history would then, as the Enlightenment proposed, be humanity *tout court*, something it is important to keep in mind in an era of globalisation. Things were, however, originally very different in the nineteenth century, that time of revolution and Romanticism, when the nation state was just beginning to come into existence.

---

[9] Koselleck 1979. [10] See now Evans 1997; the classic treatment is still Meinecke 1936.
[11] Nietzsche 1980. [12] Heuß 1959, 1984.
[13] This was during my activities within the Research Training Group 'Ancient presents and their relation to the past' at the University of Freiburg in 1990–6.
[14] Gehrke 1994.

Introduction

This is the reason why I have not made any attempt to position 'scientific' history next to, or even apart from, traditional cultures of remembrance, nor do I claim that it, in sharp contrast to saga and myth, is 'history without further qualification'. Rather, I would like, as it were, to integrate the two ideal types, and so I quite deliberately call both of them forms of 'history'. I would like to put the social, or, more precisely, the socio-cultural function of the various ways of treating the past at the centre of attention and to concentrate on that part of history (in its various modes) which is relevant for the identity of social groups, whether they be large or small. This is the most important function of history in its social context, because each group has an existential need for its own appropriate past, for a history, a form of remembering, which is shared by its members and cultivated by them, a 'cultural memory'. A group needs this in order to be able to persist beyond the span of the biological life of the individuals who constitute it at any given time, and that means in order to exist in time at all as a group which has an identity.

This is particularly true if one makes a further assumption that I think is unavoidable, namely that social groups with a strong sense of belonging, such as tribes or nation states are not primarily strictly biological organisms, but rather the end results of complicated social processes. All human societies are characterised by processes of experiencing, perceiving, attributing, and identifying, which take place in a context that is structured by the contrast between Self and Other, identity and alterity. Social groups with this sense of belonging arise and maintain themselves in existence when these fluid processes congeal, and especially when they become fixed and rigid.[15] So we are required to take account of events that are primarily located in the consciousness (in Wilhelm Dilthey's sense[16]) of agents, even though the agents are not always clearly aware of them as such.

---

[15] These are the conceptual foundations of the Collaborative Research Centre 'Identity and Alterities. The Function of Alterity in the Constitution and Construction of Identity', which I originally initiated because of what I learned in the Research Training Group mentioned above and which I moderated at the University of Freiburg in 1997–2003. On this, see Fludernik and Gehrke 1999, Gehrke 2001, and especially Eßbach 2002. In the context of the Excellence-Cluster 'TOPOI. The Formation and Transformation of Space and Knowledge in Ancient Societies and Beyond' at the Freie and the Humboldt University in Berlin, I had the opportunity to pursue different aspects of this topic again. This was in Cross Sectional Group V (2009–12), see Gehrke et al. 2011. These collaborative research projects allowed me to modify the emphasis of some of my work, and what I learned in them has had significant influence on Chapter 2 of this book. One way in which this is true is that collective identity here is construed in a way that is similar to the notion of *ethnic identity* which one finds in the work of Jonathan Hall (1997, 19), namely as 'socially constructed and subjectively perceived'. However, my concept of collective identity is much broader and more encompassing than one connected to the notion of ethnicity *strictu senso* (see now also Gruen 2013).

[16] 'Consciousness' for Dilthey is a totalising concept, see Dilthey 1983, 44–9, 64–8, 93–5.

However, the events in question are the result of cultural processes, not fixed genetic dispositions. They are not biologically determined for members of a specific ethnic group, but rather they are driven and guided by intentions. In his book *Methodik der Völkerkunde* (*The Methods of Anthropology*) the ethnologist and anthropologist Wilhelm Mühlmann (1938) used the notion of 'intentionality' with reference to ethnic identities.[17] By using 'intentionality', an explicitly non-racist concept, as his central concept, he departed significantly from the view that was fashionable and politically acceptable during the National Socialist era.[18] In particular, following the example of Husserl's phenomenology, Mühlmann took the ethnographically relevant 'intentional data' to be the 'expression' of the way in which a population understood itself.[19]

Since Mühlmann's time, this concept of intentionality has proved its empirical value in history and ethnology (or social anthropology) and it has been shown that it can be used effectively to track the development and constitution of collective identities far beyond the domain of the ethnic. So I shall now call that body of conceptions of the past which are relevant for the kinds of collective identity that I have just mentioned 'intentional history'.[20] Contributions to intentional history include such items as the collective forms of remembrance in traditional societies, but also highly systematic, scientific undertakings like the exceptionally sober and reliable *Monumenta Germaniae Historica*, which in its initial phase subscribed

---

[17] Reinhard Wenskus' (1961) dissertation *Stammesbildung und Verfassung* (*The Formation of Tribes and the Constitution*) drew my attention to the work of Mühlmann.

[18] Mühlmann's general relation to the Nazis in the 1930s is a very highly controversial topic. See for example Rössler 2007 or Haller 2012, 169–72.

[19] On this point see Mühlmann 1938, 108–12, 124–60, 227–40. At a crucial place in his argument, Mühlmann cites the Russian ethnographer Sergej Michailovich Shirokoghorov (*Psychomental Complex of the Tungus*, London, 1935, 13), who claims that an ethnos is a group 'with more or less similar cultural complexes, speaking the same language, believing in a common origin, possessing group consciousness and practicing of endogamy', and he adds

> The ethnos is the unit within which cultural assimilation takes place, and only the existence of such processes of assimilation allows one to conclude that an ethnos is present. An ethnos is a dynamic state of equilibrium which is dependent on the following factors: the size of the population, the type of cultural assimilation practiced, and the nature of the territory. It is actually better to construe an ethnos in terms of 'processes' rather than as a 'unity' (1938, 229).

Mühlmann (1938, 235) takes race to be a biological fact true of individuals and he 'emphasises that differences between races cannot be mapped in a one-to-one way onto differences in culture' (236).

[20] On this concept see further Gehrke 1994, 2000, 2004, 2005a, 2010; Foxhall, Gehrke, and Luraghi 2010; on 'contextualisation' see also Proietti 2012a; 2012b; for further attempts to apply this concept see, for instance, Dillery 2005; Backhaus 2007/2009.

to the motto created by Johann Lambert Büchler (1785–1858): *sanctus amor patriae dat animum* ('Sacred love of the fatherland is what gives it its character').[21]

Intentional history, then, designates those conceptions of history, or, rather, more precisely and more generally, those conceptions of the past, which define the identity of a group and are characteristic of it. This is intended to be true of a wide spectrum of human associations, from groups of agriculturalists, with a rudimentary internal social organisation, to nations and complex cultures. Following Dilthey[22] we could say that these include: 'families, composite associations, nations, epochs, historical movements and developmental sequences, social organisations, cultural systems and other subdivisions of the human race'. Dilthey's list of items is part of a modern set of tools for describing and analysing historical phenomena, that is, this toolbox is something used by the modern discipline of history, which aspires to be a science. This set of conceptual instruments serves to give us a better understanding of the various different processes and properties that characterise intentional history. That is, the items on the list refer, from a modern, scientific point of view, to those elements in conceptions of the past that, in the conscious view of the social groups and individual actors in question (that is, according to their own intentions), were essential for the way they thought about themselves and, consequently, for their identity. If necessary, these intentions could have been articulated by the agents to which they are ascribed. So, this set of conceptual tools represents an etic perspective on an emic (intentional) state of affairs. On the interpretation being given here, which emphasises the human propensity to 'make sense of the world', the agents who are the objects of analysis, be they individuals or groups, are specifically asserted to have had their own set of ideas, and, in the cases that interest us, their own ideas about their history. The best-case scenario is that our analysis eventually gives us an understanding of those ideas and perhaps permits a reconstruction of their genesis. It is, of course, perfectly possible that, for the human individuals and groups who are the objects of our investigation, many aspects of their situation will have seemed to them to be explicable in a very different way from the way we are inclined to explain them. Coming to a correct understanding is, however, always fraught with the possibility of non-understanding or misunderstanding.

Peter L. Berger and Thomas Luckmann (1966) have spoken in this context of 'reification'. What we, from our perspective and using the categories and

---

[21] Fuhrmann 1996. [22] Dilthey 1983, 250.

methods which we normally use, consider to be a construct, a product of the creativity of the community in question, is for the members of that community a fixed magnitude, an incontrovertible fact, a certainly and firmly held truth, a given physical fact. This is particularly true of intentional history. Many ethnically defined groups, who are still habitually called 'tribes', understand themselves as constituting a community of those who have a common biological descent. From a contemporary scientific point of view that might be highly dubious. But given that the actors themselves firmly believed this to be their own history – they 'reify' their past in this way – this history was for them a fact and a part of the 'recipe knowledge' (Berger and Luckmann 1966) that gave them their orientation in the world. To that extent, we must also take this reification seriously and make it an object of our analysis; doing this is part of what it means to deal with 'intentional history'. This is also relevant for the distinction between myth and history. We have developed clear criteria for distinguishing between these two. However, what we classify as myth, and thus as historically dubious, implausible, or fictive, can be just what the agents involved take, from their emic perspective, to be history *simpliciter* – they can take it, in fact, to be *their* history in the sense in which the Brothers Grimm used that term in the quotation I cited above.

This connection that exists between a group and its use of the past tense is the systematic basis for the approach to intentional history that I would like to develop here. This approach is an etic and analytic one, which, however, concentrates its attention on emic conceptions and takes them very seriously. The result is that people's conceptions of the past, too, can come to be understood as part of a culture, that is, as part of the horizon of interpretations and organising principles that, as shown above, is characteristic of the given society. This makes the tension between the historical and the modern, the emic and the etic even more complex, because, as is well known, Greek culture has, in manifold, convoluted ways, become part of our own culture. In this book, I shall try to understand Greek culture historically, that is, on its own terms and as something *sui generis*, not merely as a precursor or an *exemplum* for us. In various places in my discussion, it will emerge, without any need on my part to make it explicit, that all this also affects us, even if only indirectly; this, however, is something that is true of any investigation in the cultural sciences.

The nature of my subject – history as an element in the culture of the ancient Hellenic world – leads me to divide the following discussion into two clear parts. The first part will contain a treatment of the mechanisms of intentional history that were in operation in the Greek world. I shall be specifically interested in trying to answer the question of how the process of 'understanding of themselves in history' actually functioned for the Greeks.

This will also give me the opportunity of using this example to give slightly more systematic structure to the reflections about intentional history that I have made at various points. For the sake of clarity, I shall distinguish between, on the one hand, the 'vehicles' and 'media' of intentional history, and, on the other, the structure and forms of such history. This will be the subject of the first two chapters.

If one attempts to tie intentional history very closely to what Halbwachs called *mémoire collective*, one is very quickly confronted with a problem: How can any individual at all take 'a step out of' the flux which is his or her tradition, that is, to what extent is any kind of independent comprehension of the past possible? How is it possible to have an even partially independent form of memory? Paul Ricœur (2004, 190–2) criticises Halbwachs exactly on this point, and explicitly affirms the 'autonomy of historical knowledge vis-à-vis the phenomenon of human memory' (210). He makes it clear that this is not an expression of his own modern prejudice, but that he is merely taking up again an ancient Greek view by placing a citation of the first sentence of Herodotos' history at the start of one of his sections as its motto. The second part of my book then will investigate the role that Greek historiography had against the backdrop of, and in the context of, the intentional history, or the intentional histories, of the Greeks. The main focus here is on a question the Greeks themselves asked, the question of truth (*alētheia*). This question takes the particular form it does because Hellenic historiography eventually comes to drape itself in the cloth of rhetoric, especially in those cases in which written history aspired to have an effect on a broad public and thus was particularly closely linked with intentional history.

CHAPTER I

The Locus of Intentional History
Reference-Group – Producers – Media

There is one particular feature in the way in which intentional histories are formulated that is immediately striking and repeatedly draws attention to itself, and that is the grammatical form which members of a group use in such histories to refer to the group itself; they not infrequently use the first-person plural and they do so in a very broad way. They will characteristically do this even when referring to events that occurred in the deep past and at a great geographical distance from the place where they live, and in which, therefore, they could not really be or have been directly involved. Thus, someone might say: 'We just lost at football to the Argentine team', meaning by 'we' the national team of whatever the speaker's particular nation is. Individuals will do this even if they were not members of that team and 'belonged' to it only in a highly indirect way, by virtue of being members of the relevant nation, or, as we should add now, as residents of the territory of that nation who identify with it (or with its football players). Or, to take another example, think of the use of 'we' in the discussions that were conducted about whether or not there was a 'distinctive way' (*Sonderweg*) that Germany took to arrive at modernity which was very different from that followed by the paradigmatic Western European societies. People in Germany would say 'We Germans have always gone our own way (*Sonderweg*)' or 'We Germans never had a *Sonderweg*'. Similarly, 'We Germans are guilty for, or at least ought to feel ashamed of, the criminal acts perpetrated during the National Socialist regime.' Comparable uses of the first-person plural are widespread in other countries, too, and often give rise to requests for forgiveness (presented with appropriate rituals) that are made by contemporary representatives of some groups for the sometimes past (mis)deeds committed long ago by members of other groups.[1]

---

[1] A slightly different but equally characteristic example of this use of 'we' can be found in the address that the Prime Minister of Turkey, Recep Tayyip Erdoğan, gave on 27 February 2010 in the Hall of Congress in Istanbul before an audience of 2,160 people (according to official figures) comprising

Those who offer apologies and ask forgiveness accept it that others ascribe to them their history, that is, the things that members of their group did in the past. This is an extreme form of diachronic identification and collective identity, and as such it is at the core of intentional history.

Greek authors proceed in the same way in the texts that are crucial for their intentional history. One can see this clearly as early as the archaic epoch, when Mimnermos of Kolophon (second half of the seventh century BC), refers to events in the deep past of his community, and says, with a specific allusion to the so-called Ionian Migration:[2] 'When from the lofty city of Neleian Pylos *we* came on shipboard to the pleasant land of Asia ... and sat down at lovely Kolophon, whence went *we* forth ... and ... took Aiolian Smyrna' (italics added).[3] According to the Spartan Tyrtaios, who was active at about the same time, 'Kronos' Son Himself, Zeus ... hath given this city [sc. *Sparta*] to the children of Herakles, with whom *we* came into the wide isle of Pelops from windy Erineüs' (italics added).[4] And, in another passage, Tyrtaios speaks of 'our king ... Theopompus, through whom we took spacious Messenè'.[5] Although he says 'we' in all these cases, Tyrtaios was not himself present at any of these events, which took place, as he says himself, in the time of 'the fathers of our fathers'.[6]

This last reference to 'the fathers of our fathers' seems prima facie to place the action being described two generations in the past,[7] which is a span that could in principle be encompassed by the memory of a human individual, but in the two previous cases the lapse of time between the era in which the author lived and that of the past occurrences in question is significantly longer. Both of these past events concern the conquest and occupation of land, and each is thus historically of particular importance for Spartan identity. If one consults the Spartan king-lists, the gap is one of

---

Turkish citizens living abroad and citizens of other countries who were, however, of Turkish ancestry. Here, Prime Minister Erdoğan said:

> Even if history and fate have scattered us to different places, our hearts are one and beat as one. Our aspirations, goals, and our fates are one. We are all brothers and sisters. We are children of the same tribe. When the nose of one of our brothers in Solingen bleeds, we feel it in our hearts on five continents. When the tears of one innocent person fall on the ground in Sarajevo, it burns in all our hearts at the same time (Cited in *Frankfurter Allgemeine*, 19 March 2010, p. 6).

[2] See p. 54f.   [3] Fr. 9 IEG; translation J. M. Edmonds (Loeb).
[4] Fr. 4, 12–15 IEG; translation J. M. Edmonds (Loeb).
[5] Fr. 5, 1f IEG; translation J. M. Edmonds (Loeb).
[6] Fr. 5, 6 IEG; translation J. M. Edmonds (Loeb). For further discussion of these texts, see Grethlein 2010, 56–8; on Tyrtaios, see also Nafissi 2010, 97.
[7] 'The fathers of our fathers' could, of course, simply stand for 'our ancestors' in a very general sense (see, for instance, Luraghi 2003, 110f and Grethlein 2010, 52 note 13), but that is not relevant here.

about ten generations, and if one then calculates the time elapsed by the methods that would have been used by Greeks of the later period, this would amount to about 300 years. So, this is a 'we' which reaches far back into the past, and its use indicates very clearly that what we have here is an explicit instance of intentional history.

In the context of a discussion of the identificatory 'we', the formulation one finds in the third of the above examples is typical: 'the fathers of our fathers' (*pateres hēmeterōn paterōn*). This points very concretely to the basis of the identification and is the foundation of the group identity that is expressed by the use of 'we'. The group is construed as a collection of people related by descent, and in accordance with the prevailing structural features of the society at that time, the descent is reckoned patrilineally. The appeal to 'the ancestors' (*progonoi*) in this context was common among the Greeks, not only in the early period, but also for centuries after that, as is documented over and over again by the occurrence of this or a similar formula. It is, for instance, particularly frequent in honorific inscriptions. A regular feature of such inscriptions is their emphasis on the achievements of the ancestors of the individual being honoured, even before his own meritorious deeds are mentioned, as if what the ancestors did – 'achievements coming down from the forefathers' – had marked out in advance the path on which the individual himself then simply took a few further steps. Here, too, 'forefathers' refers to the whole community, particularly the polis.

A good example of this are the honours given by the Polis Chaleion in Western Locris, which was at that time a member of the Aitolian League, to the poet Aristodama of Smyrna.[8] Aristodama is singled out and honoured by being awarded the right of citizenship in Chaleion, on the grounds that she, in her poems, devoted 'appropriate' (*axios*) attention to the Aitolian tribe (*ethnos*) and 'invoked the ancestors of our polis'. Here, the possessive pronoun of the first-person singular is explicitly related to the polis and directly connected with the ancestors. The honours given to the poet and her closest relatives were some of the highest the city could award, which demonstrates in a very vivid way how important her poetic presentation of their own past – and of the larger political unit which they had joined (the Aitolian League) – was to the citizens of the city. It is true that in the poems (*poiēmata*) of Aristodama, the past was the object of literary treatment; we would probably say she produced a form of fiction, or even perhaps myth, but for the community of Chaleion, which passed an official decree

---

[8] IG IX I²3, 740; see also the very similar IG IX 2, 62 from Thessalian Lamia.

honouring her in the Assembly, what she had written was *their* history. They believed what was being sung when Aristodama's poems were performed and took it to be their own history. To the extent to which that really was the case, what was in fact a product of poetic creation, came to be, as Peter L. Berger and Thomas Luckmann would have put it, 'reified'.

In this context one might also speak of an identificatory circle; we are us, because we always have had our history here in this place, the history that we believe is true, that is, which is true for us, and as such also binding on us, and gives us an orientation in the world. Through strengthening certain components and giving more shape to this circular process, intentional history makes an essential contribution to creating what Otto Bauer (1881–1938) long ago called a 'community of fate', a concept he formulated in order to try to get away from something he was particularly keen to avoid: a substantivist notion of the collective or of the process of socialisation, such as those often embodied in the idea of the 'nation'.[9] I am attempting something similar here by using the concept of intentionality.

Friedrich Nietzsche also endowed this 'we' with the power of speech and gave it a very penetrating voice in the second of his Untimely Meditations, *On the Use and Abuse of History for Life*, when he describes the 'antiquarian man', who, as we have seen, stands for the way of looking at the world that we have called that of intentional history:[10]

> The history of his city becomes for him the history of his self ... Here one could live, he says to himself, for here one can live and will be able to live, for we are tough and not to be uprooted over night. And so, with this 'We', he looks beyond the ephemeral, curious, individual life and feels like the spirit of the house, the generation, and the city. Occasionally he will greet the soul of his people as his own soul even across the wide, obscuring and confusing centuries; and power of empathy and divination, of scenting an almost cold trail, of instinctively reading aright the past however much it be written over, a quick understanding of the palimpsests, even polypsests – these are his gifts and virtues. With them Goethe stood before the memorial of Erwin von Steinbach [the first architect of the cathedral of Strasbourg]; in the tempest of his emotions the historical cloudcover spread between them tore, and for the first time he saw the German work again 'exerting his influence out of a strong robust German soul'.[11] Such a sense and disposition guided the Italians of the Renaissance and reawakened in their poets the ancient

---

[9] See Langewiesche 2008, 63–6. [10] Cited following Rossmann 1969, 344.
[11] The reference is to Goethe's essay 'Von deutscher Baukunst', which is dedicated to the departed spirit (*divis manibus*) of Erwin von Steinbach. The quotation is found near the end of this short essay.

Italic genius to a 'wondrous reverberation of the ancient lyre',[12] as Jacob Burckhardt puts it.[13]

Given, then, the importance of the reference-group, the question immediately arises of how any group comes to have its own history. How does it produce one? Who produces it for the group? In the last case discussed, the poet who was honoured by Chaleion came herself from a different polis, she was, as it were, a foreigner. However, in the previous cases the poets, although they were artists and thus, in some sense, experts in the deployment of the creative imagination, were able, when speaking in their own authorial voices as 'I', also to use the first-person plural, 'we', because they themselves really belonged to the community in question (Kolophon in one case, or Sparta in the other). This shows that the reference-group and the 'producer of history' need not be identical, and also that there can be a medium in which remembrance is cultivated and passed down that is outside the bounds of what we would strictly call the genre of 'written history'. Certainly, it demonstrates that this kind of memory need not depend on the existence of a profession of 'writers of history' in the strict sense of that term.[14]

To be sure, we can observe that specialisation occurs in certain societies in which some individuals or groups come to concentrate on memory, recollection, and similar phenomena and on the passing of things down from one generation to the next. This is particularly true for information deemed to be important. This specialisation can be observed both in Greece and in other comparable cultures. There were people with skills that can only be described as 'professional', who retained certain bits of knowledge over long periods of time; they did this partly because they had naturally retentive memories and had in addition trained this ability to a high level, and partly because they had access to and could use various media, in particular, writing. The 'recipe knowledge' of the society was preserved and passed on by these experts. This was primarily a case of retaining and transmitting elementary religious knowledge, especially knowledge of rituals and also legal knowledge, two things that in traditional societies were in any case thought to be essentially connected to each other and to belong together.

In Greece, it was people called 'rememberers' (*mnēmones/mnāmones*) who were responsible, as it was sometimes said, 'for divine and human affairs' and who, as '*archives vivantes*', functioned as the bearers of memory

---

[12] Jacob Burckhardt, *Die Cultur der Renaissance in Italien*, 4th ed., Leipzig, 1885, Vol. I, 286.
[13] Nietzsche 1980, 19.   [14] See also Le Goff 1988, 113.

for the community.¹⁵ As their name indicates, their main resource was their own memory (*mnēmē*) but they retained their function – at any rate, for a time – even after the introduction of writing. One should not underestimate what the human memory itself is capable of, even without recourse to external aides. Think of the Indian Brahmans who operated in an environment that was completely oral and dependent on the mastery of sophisticated mnemonic techniques and yet were able to learn lengthy sacred texts by heart and transmit them orally and without any change. The body of material they mastered included not only the texts themselves, but also an apparatus of explanations, interpretations, and commentaries, which eventually then came to be considered sacred in its own right.¹⁶ Something like this seems also to have been true of the druids who are mentioned by Caesar,¹⁷ and, in China, comparable specialists existed from an early period, although there the general use of writing was established very quickly. This led in China to the development of the classical example of a society of the written word, so exactly the opposite of what happened in the Indian case. The consequence of this early adoption of literacy was that in China the idea of history and that of literacy came virtually to coincide. The main corpus of written texts comprised official documents and chronologies, although they stood together with texts that were addressed to the gods, so that the general ambiance was one of something recognisably sacred.¹⁸

These examples show that it would be a mistake to exaggerate the difference between oral and literate societies, if one's concern is whether the society has an effectively functioning system for preserving and passing on what one knows. What the examples show before all else, though, is that the domain on which societies are focused when it comes to remembering and to the transmission of knowledge to the next generation is, in the first instance, that of the sacred and that which has to do with religion. In addition, then, they were keen, in general, to preserve the knowledge of sets of rules that had to be followed strictly, even if these rules were not what we would call rules of religion, but rather rules of law. This was the reason why exact repetition and precision were important. For the community as a whole, these were existential issues concerning its relation to the gods or, at any rate, its own internal order. These objects of remembrance are, as

---

¹⁵ On these figures, see, for instance, Gehrke 1997, 45f with further references; the concept of a 'living archive' comes from the French legal scholar Rodolphe-Madeleine Dareste (1824–1911).
¹⁶ On this issue see in the first instance Falk 1993, especially 321–4; Michaels 2013, especially 28–30.
¹⁷ Caes. Gall. 6, 14; on the interpretation of this passage, see Maier 2012, 171f.
¹⁸ On this phenomenon see Le Goff 1988, 235.

it were, the system of inner cogs and gears that keep the society running and in order. The specialists in remembering and the passing on of the legacy of the past thus had a primarily practical function and a very concrete role in ensuring the functioning and therefore also the very survival of the group.

However, memory specialists sometimes, perhaps even often, have nothing to do with the stories and tales, the myths and sagas that we so frequently encounter in intentional history. This is true despite the fact that the sacred and the details of various rituals were often intimately interwoven with the very fabric of the narrative in myths, particularly in Greece. One might even try to distinguish societies and culture according to the extent to which these primarily religious-legal experts, who, in some cases, were able to become a caste or form of separate group of political functionaries, officials, or mandarins, were able to cultivate those forms of memory that were relevant for the group and keep them under control.

In Greece, in any case, there was a distinct, genuine, and thus probably also aboriginal separation between these 'mnemonic' specialists and the specialists who were responsible for narrative, because they were the bearers of another kind of memory, 'mytho-historical memory'. The second group, that of the 'tellers of tales', were the servants of the daughters of memory (Mnemosyne), the Muses. In Hesiod, the Muses were also of some importance for the legal order: not, however, because they were responsible for the recollection of the rules themselves, but because they gave to the 'kings', in their role as judges, good judgement and a winning way of expressing themselves.[19] However, it was in the first instance the poets who were kissed by the Muses. They were, as Marcel Detienne (1967) puts it, the 'Masters of Truth'.

In Greece, it was culturally decisive that the poets were the ones who created and transmitted intentional history.[20] Homer and Hesiod – or whoever the author(s) were who were later referred to by these names – laid the foundations of this in their archetypical narratives in the epic metre, hexameter, and in a genre that could very early – as we can see from the case of Hesiod's didactic poem 'Works and Days' – become an object of playful

---

[19] As Primavesi 2009, 105–12, especially 110, has shown at length with reference to Hesiod *erg.* 81–93.
[20] Leopold von Ranke's observations about Serbian 'folk-poetry' (1844) contain references to an interesting modern parallel to the Greek case: 'It is worth noting that only by being expressed in poetry, did the history of the nation become a national treasure and come to be preserved as the object of living remembrance.' This is poetry as intentional, and thus living, history. Clark 2012, 23 has used this example to show what powerful effects such history can have in the modern world. (I take over the reference to this important passage in Ranke from Clark's book.)

variation.²¹ As we shall soon see, Greek epic already ascribed to time a crude but definite structure, and epic concepts had, in general, important consequences for religion, too, particularly for conceptions of the various divinities and of their relation to humans, because the gods were always present and, as it were, acting in collaboration with humans in the epic narratives and in the myths. These myths were taken to be not just stories, but history. This is one of the reasons Herodotos could later claim that, for the Greeks, it was Homer and Hesiod who gave the gods their form.²² The world also had an order which revealed itself in the 'catalogues' that were such an important part of epic poetry, such as the catalogues of the various Greek and Trojan contingents in the *Iliad*. These catalogues reflect the close connection that existed between communities and particular geographic localities. In a parallel way in the *Odyssey*, the world as it would be experienced by seafarers is very vividly presented, but it is also turned into something like the stuff of fairy tales, with the consequence that the incredible becomes plausible.²³

The significance of these Homeric texts was, however, even greater than this suggests, in that the two Homeric epics became the foundational texts of Greek culture, texts that again and again served as a benchmark, not least in the realm of aesthetics, for everything from literature to the visual arts. Artists returned repeatedly to these monumental works, imitated them, produced variations on them, tried to surpass them: *imitatio* took the form of *variatio* and *aemulatio*. In addition, these epics played an essential role in Greek education and gave the Greeks a general orientation in life. So much so that Plato (*rep.* 10.606e) calls Homer the educator of Greece. The epics contained very particular ideas about the origin of the cosmos, the gods, and humans, and then about the different sorts of humans and the different sorts of Greeks who existed. The 'different sorts of Greeks' was the topic of the various 'catalogues of women' that were attributed to Hesiod. Together with the stories about some later events that we think actually happened, such as the Persian Wars, these epic tales, which were constantly varied, but so constantly repeated that they were omnipresent, constituted a single mytho-historic space. The intentional history of the Greeks was composed, then, to a significant extent, of individual events

---

²¹ On Homer and Hesiod, see the relevant passages in Zimmermann 2011, 7–123, which were written by Michael Reichel, Luigi Enrico Rossi, Andrea Ercolani, and Antonios Rengakos.
²² On this point, compare Gehrke 2013a, especially 81–4.
²³ On this, see principally, Visser 1997; Kullmann 2002; on the *Odyssey*, see Hölscher 1989, 141–58; on the (pseudo-)Hesiodic catalogues of women, see 46, 51f. In the following chapters we shall see how important the tension between reality and invention is.

and constellations of events, some of which we classify as belonging to the world of myth and some to history. We would correspondingly call some of this material 'historical' and some 'unhistorical'. It is important to keep in mind that this distinction did not exist for the Greeks, or at any rate, as we shall see, was drawn by them in a different way.

Later, and I shall discuss this further in Chapter 3, there appeared on the scene a different, more rationalist approach to this whole mytho-historical space: a scientific and philosophical, and thus more intellectualist, way of writing history. This approach was based on the new ideas of the Ionian thinkers. It, too, was concerned with the truth (*alētheia*) but this was a truth that could stand up to rational and critical scrutiny by the thinking individual, and, by surviving such scrutiny, show that it was well-founded. In addition, claims had to be based on research (*historiē*). The person who had the decisive word to say was the man who was knowledgeable. This person was now not necessarily a poet, but a sage, a philosopher, an intellectual, or a historian. What people in all of these roles actually did was very similar, and the connection of all of them with the realm of the poetic was still extremely intimate. The sentence with which Hekataios of Miletos (c. 560–480 BC) began his work on history (called *genealogiai*[24]) sums up this kind of new historical thinking: 'Hekataios of Miletus reports the following (*hōde mytheitai*): I write what seems to me to be true (*alēthea*), for the stories of the Greeks (*logoi*) are many and ridiculous (*polloi kai geloioi*)'.[25]

This rational-critical option was even further strengthened by Herodotos and Thucydides, and entered into the intentional history of the Greeks, so that now historians, too, became producers of intentional history, although this approach was not as dominant as we might tend to assume. Hellenistic inscriptions about claims to the ownership of property and conflicts that arise from competing claims often use historical arguments. This is one of the ways in which intentional history takes on a concrete form.[26] These inscriptions cite as 'witnesses' to the past again and again, however, 'poets and historians'. These two categories of people constituted, then, for the Greeks, in the final analysis, the 'professionals' in matters historical. Even as late as the period of the Roman Empire, the

---

[24] It is characteristic that other titles, such as *historiai* (*Researches*) or *hērōologiai* (*Stories of Heroes*) are also recorded, see K. Meister DNP V 1998 (*s.v.* Hekataios) 266.
[25] FGrH 1 F1.
[26] An international legal disagreement between Priene and Samos is a particularly clear example of this. See IPriene 37, and further discussion in Gehrke 1994, 256 A.42.

stories of poets about the deeds of heroes are cited as legally relevant confirmations of the status of a polis in imperial decisions.[27]

This state of affairs had significant consequences for intentional history. On the one hand, the rules of a certain aesthetic and intellectual discourse came to be dominant. We would say that these rules were followed and enforced with enormous professionalism. Although they had, in essence, nothing at all to do with conceptions of history, they had a direct effect on them. On the other hand, the competitiveness with which individuals cultivated art or wisdom was very pronounced, and this is another aspect of the same rule-governed structure that can be observed in these discourses and which has already been mentioned. The agonal character of Greek culture, which, since the time of Jacob Burckhardt, has become proverbial, is particularly in evidence here. One might even say that the first commandment was to surpass one's colleague or predecessor, even if he was one's teacher. *Polloi mathētai kreissones didaskalōn* ('Many pupils are better than their teachers') was a proverbial expression among the Greeks.[28] This was clear even for Cicero: 'There has never been a poet or speaker who considered another to be better than he is.'

It was this conjunction of rules and *agon* which brought it about that the Greeks constantly and unceasingly produced very different versions of their own history. This was a built-in consequence of the system and one that was actually actively encouraged by it. Even Hekataios, at the very start of the tradition, polemicised against the large number of 'stories' the Greeks told. And, in fact, no one version was at all like another. The number and variety of accounts was enormous even synchronically, as poets and thinkers who were contemporaries competed against each other, but there was also great variation diachronically. Stories were not merely accepted and passed on, but they were creatively and critically transformed and imaginatively developed.[29]

This meant that historical narration had a rather 'partial character' and was concerned more with '*réconstruction générative*'[30] than with a literal and quasi-mechanical reproduction of the past or with attaining some kind of unitary total view of what happened. This kind of approach gives rise to

---

[27] SEG LI 641. LVI 565; compare on this general issue Knoepfler 2006.
[28] TrGF adespota 197 = Cic. fam. 9.7.2. The following quotation can also be found in Cic. Att. 14.20.3 *nemo umquam neque poeta neque orator fuit quemquam meliorem quam se arbitraretur*. On competitive aspects of the art of poetry, see also Bowie 2010, 81.
[29] Jan Assmann (1992, 280–5) has coined the very apt term '*hypolepsis*' for this process.
[30] See the observation of the anthropologist Jack Goody, as cited in LeGoff 1988, 114. On this aspect of early Greek poetry see also Svenbro 1976, 18–44.

stories rather than history, stories that are subject to further creative elaboration in the process of being told and retold. This process started with the *aoidai* and *rhapsodes* of the epic poems.[31] This does not mean that one could not accept these versions of the past as history and thus as giving an account of the 'true' past. It was perfectly possible to accept something flexible and make it fixed, without thereby becoming inflexible; there was, after all, no agency or institution in the society which had the monopoly of power that would have enabled it to impose definitive fixity in this domain. There is an inconsistency here that is difficult for us really to imagine, but which we must simply recognise and accept.[32]

The social structures of society and its norms were essential for permitting the development of the system of rules that governed the culture of memory in Greece. A certain openness in social life was an important factor, in addition, of course, to its striking competitivity. Early Greek communities had a relatively flat hierarchical structure, so that there was little political or religious control of cultural life (Gehrke 2013a). This meant that the aesthetic and intellectual domains could develop in relative freedom and form something like a distinct subsystem[33] in the society. At any rate, these domains enjoyed the most extensive autonomy in codifying their own internal set of rules and the way these rules were implemented. The basic features of the society that have just been mentioned – its openness, the competitiveness that animated it at all levels, and its relative lack of hierarchy – were what ensured that this would be the case: unity was not an object of aspiration, nor was it even possible; a canon that was

---

[31] On this issue, see the very enlightening contribution of Burkert 1987/2001. I cannot here enter into the debates about the relation of orality and writing in Homer. The two polar opposite positions are represented by, for instance, Kullmann 1992 and Nagy 2009. On the state of the discussion, see Rengakos in Rengakos and Zimmermann 2011, 167–9 and Michael Reichel in Zimmermann 2011, 47–50. South Slavic poetry, which is often cited in the oral-poetry research, was in fact already discussed in connection with Homer by Leopold von Ranke (1844, 65f. n1):

> If one notices a rather less productive poetic talent at work in some parts of the Homeric poems, we would like to draw from this the conclusion, which is supported by the experience of collecting Serbian songs, that at the moment of transition from oral presentation to writing sometimes only less talented rhapsodes were available for some of the cantos than for the others. One must not imagine that a singer is simply someone who declaims [a pre-given text]; he is supposed to reproduce the poem which has come down to him from the tradition, using his own poetic power.

This is precisely *réconstruction générative*.

[32] In contrast, they may well have been more coherent when dealing with individual groups and for their own internal purposes, cf. Kowalzig's (2007, 22) reference to the remarks of the anthropologist Stephen Hugh-Jones (1979, 252–60).

[33] 'Subsystem' in the sense in which Niklas Luhmann uses the term (see Luhmann 1977, 29–53) or a 'field' to use Pierre Bourdieu's expression.

binding on everyone did not exist, rather, it was at best (or at worst) something that could perhaps be developed. On the other hand, the situation was not one of complete chaos, because there were rules that were recognised; it is just that they were self-imposed rules. *Mutatis mutandis* this was a world that Goethe might have been describing when he wrote in 1797: 'The literary world has the peculiarity that nothing in it is destroyed, without something new arising, something new of the same type.'[34] For this reason alone, such things as variations on familiar themes, *topoi*, and set-pieces play such an important role in cultural life.

This, in turn, meant that that which ran against the current, the deviant, and the disparate were also always possible, even within the work of a single author. Depending on where he was performing or who was commissioning him, an author could draw on completely different strands of tradition and enunciate very different ways of orienting oneself in the world of action. Good instances of this variability are to be found in the ancient corpus of *epinikia*. In drama, a certain ambivalence about these potential shifts in orientation was even specially cultivated and intensified, even to the point of generating tragic conflict. Whatever position was expressed in one place or another of a poet's oeuvre could, by interpreting and modifying it appropriately, be presented as history. Appropriating the work of poets in this way was particularly tempting because they were assumed to be particularly inspired and to have the power of inspiring others. So if a tragedy of Euripides contained a new version of the genealogy of Macedonian kings, which conformed to the ideas that King Archelaos had about the close kinship between Greeks and Macedonians, this could partly 'lay the foundation' for a new history.[35] The general point here is that this plurality of Greek intentional history, which was deeply anchored in its very nature, meant that it was unsuited for making effective propaganda – as otherwise might be expected – because the means were always ready at hand to refute or relativise any given claim.

When we think of history and its effect on people, we immediately think of readers as the potential audience. This is an expectation that Thucydides formulated in an explicit way, and one that is, in general, of great importance for the diachronic and hypoleptic treatment of history. Even in Thucydides' lifetime, though, literature, particularly literature of a mythic-historical

---

[34] Johann Wolfgang von Goethe, letter to Karl Ludwig Knebel, Jena, 2 March 1797 in Goethe and Knebel 1851, 143.

[35] On Euripides' *Archelaos* in general see Harder 1985; on its political significance and reception, see the reflections by Hammond in Hammond/Griffith 1979, 10–13. See also Borza 1990, 171–72; Roisman 2010, 157 with further references.

character, was usually performed, as it always had been, orally. It continued to take the form of a specific oral performance, despite the increasing participation in the practice of reading. We can still make a distinction between the oral and the written, but this distinction should not be made too strictly, as if there was a great divide here[36] with an abyss between the two sides, and an associated implication that we should subsume the gap under the paradigm of progress.[37] The reality is that the oral and the written co-existed in parallel. This was particularly true in Greece.

Even if literature was composed using the help of written notes, it was, for a very long time, always presented orally. The episode with Demodokos in the *Odyssey*[38] was the model. He entertains the guests at a feast with songs – songs about the gods, but also tales of contemporary heroes. Some of the tales later became part of the intentional history of the Greeks. In this passage in Homer's epic, we find a literary reflection of the original context in which intentional history arose. The festive banquet, and then, even more importantly, the symposium were, in fact, the essential *loci* for this kind of song, and thus, eventually, for literature in general. It is true, to be sure that the symposium was part of the life of an elite that was in the process of constituting itself, and to that extent a matter only for a selected group of society.[39] However, it was precisely this elite that gave this type of poetry a very prominent and socially influential home. The Homeric epics show us, in virtually every line, the close connection between life and literature.

One reason for this was that literature had an essential social function to discharge, as we can see in the episode involving Demodokos. In addition to the Horatian *delectare* of simple entertainment, literature can also be highly useful (*prodesse*): it can contribute to forming reputations, projecting them over long distances, and transmitting them down the generations; it can generate fame, posthumous glory, and *kleos*. The general point which Georg Franck[40] made so vividly, holds for ancient Greek society in a very extreme way: 'The attention of other people is the most irresistible of

---

[36] Havelock 1982.
[37] For criticism of this, see in the first instance Finnegan 1988, especially 8, but one should compare the earlier Schott 1968. Under the general aegis of Collaborative Research Centre, 321, 'Transitions and areas of tension between orality and literacy', the working groups lead by Wolfgang Kullmann and myself pursued this aspect of the question with special reference to Greek culture, see Raible 1998, 41–54, 285–99.
[38] *Od.* 8.62–107, 469–586, at a banquet; *Od.* 8.256–369 for performance in a public space, on the *agora* (*Od.* 8.109), at the games (*Od.* 8.108).
[39] Wecowski 2014.
[40] 'The Economy of Attention' in *Merkur* 534/535, September/October 1993; see also his book with the same title, Munich, 1998.

drugs. Access to it pre-empts concern for acquiring anything else. That is why fame stands above power, and wealth is completely overshadowed by prominence.'

It was of particular importance in Greek society to be able to extend one's social reputation beyond death, something explicitly thematised in the case of the great hero of the *Iliad*, Achilles, but also in the scene in the *Odyssey* set in the underworld (11, 488–91), where the same issue is presented in a very different light. This illustrates my point about the ambivalence inherent in poetic discourse and the way in which one account can relativise another.

This desire for a good posthumous reputation meant that the leading figures in the Greek world were oriented toward posterity and felt the need for poets to ensure it. The poets, in turn, proudly aware that this was their most important function, retold the story of the great deeds and achievements that were the basis of their subject's glory[41] with full awareness of the fact that that was also the foundation of their own fame.[42] This orientation to later epochs on the part of the members of this social reference-group is the germ from which the intentional history of the Greeks grew. To get intentional history, one needs simply to reverse the perspective on what we can see here *in statu nascendi*: Whatever was contained in early songs and poems had been produced – at least so one could later imagine – and was then passed on in order to ensure posthumous glory. From there it was but a short step for later readers to think that it must have been created by contemporary eyewitnesses of the events described.[43]

It is possible to understand the Homeric poems in exactly this way, as a later treatment of things that poets were already singing about in the past period in which the events themselves took place, just as Demodokos sings about the deeds of Odysseus while the hero himself is present. He sings of Odysseus' greatest achievement, the construction of the Trojan Horse, and does so fully in the present, as if he were treating contemporary events.

Later people who listen to the story or read it see it as describing the past, as history, as part of a history with which they themselves are connected. The poet shows and stands for both: the contemporary and the past. The parts of the *Odyssey* that are almost meta-literary – the episode with Demodokos that has just been mentioned and the performance of the singer Phemios at the banquet of the suitors (*Od.* 1.154f. 325–44) – specifically raise this issue from the

---

[41] On this see the very important and inspiring treatment in Foxhall 1995.
[42] On this basic idea with special reference to Homer and the reception of his poems, see Bowie 2010, 77f.
[43] For a hypothetical reconstruction of the way this might have worked, see Fränkel 1962, 21 n. 27.

perspective of the narrative present. In the *Iliad*, the perspective is explicitly expanded to encompass the future, in which the narrative present is the past. In this passage, the heroes complain that Zeus has 'imposed on them an evil fate, so that we shall be the objects of song for later men' (*Il.* 6, 357f.). However, behind the 'evil' there lurked also posthumous glory, for the sake of which that fate could be accepted. Thus, too, Pindar could be confident that in composing his victory odes he was ensuring that his new heroes – who themselves had heroic precursors – would overcome the fetters that bound them to their own time.[44]

So, memory, then, is a kind of inverted cultivation of posthumous glory, something that is absolutely essential to keep in mind if one wishes to understand the specific way in which the Greeks thought of the past. A special vital conjunction between past and present, and also future, is the dominant feature of this view of history, because one can always reverse the perspective: as we remember the past, so in the future people will remember 'us', the present generation. This is the way in which Greeks remembered what was for them the past. One saw the past as a present relative to which one's own present was still the future. Everything 'worked' according to this model. One could, however, consider this past, which was actually deeply contemporary, and, at the same time, look back on it as a genuine past. Time did not run simply in one direction here, like an arrow shot in a certain single direction – although it was possible to imagine that that was the case. Rather, temporal relations were reciprocal, and people were aware of that fact. At the latest at this point it becomes clear what it means when the past becomes the object of creative aesthetic or intellectualist treatment and of potential redescription, as it was for the Greeks: everything comes to be far away and also at the same time very near – the one thing that seems impossible is historical distance, although it can be artificially generated, as we shall see, by using certain methods of magnifying and heroising past action.[45]

The *exempla* from the past, which members of a younger generation heard described in a variety of different versions, and then themselves reproduced, could have the effect of spurring them on to emulation of the great deeds of their ancestors. According to the local historian Dosiadas, in the *syssities*, the customary communal dinners held by the citizen-warrior elites of Crete, after the meal there was a service of

---

[44] Grethlein 2010, 13, 34–40; this idea is also dominant in the genre of the epigrams (at least those inscribed on monuments), see p. 34.

[45] On the normative proximity of past and present (despite attempts to distance them), see now also Bichler 2012.

remembrance of outstanding military achievements of the past and of the brave men who accomplished them. The point of this was to incite the younger members to manliness (*andragathia*). This was for a long time a constant in the various forms of the cultivation of the past that one finds among the Greeks; it was associated with the official recognition and transmission of an individual's reputation after death for the purposes of the educational effect which that could have on successive generations, either as a good example to emulate or a warning of what to avoid. The speech given by the influential Athenian politician Lykurgos (c. 385–324 BC) against Leokrates (c. 330 BC) is a good instance of this; here, poets who report past events – Euripides, Homer, and Tyrtaios are cited – have become teachers, and they are said to have their effect not, as the laws do, by threatening the use of force, but by giving accounts that are convincing (98–109).

Conversely, there was, at any rate starting in the classical period, something like the cultivation of negative reputations, which operated according to the same mechanism of appeal to an imagined future. In the speech by Lykurgos just cited, he points out that judges, by punishing a bad man, can create a kind of inverted 'celebrity', in that is they can cover a criminal with shame. Punishment makes him a negative example of what to avoid. Consequently, a legal judgement should also be seen as a message to posterity – an *aeimnēstos krisis* ('a judgement that is always remembered', 7) – and can therefore easily become part of intentional history. This is especially true given the particular orientation of this form of history to that which is exemplary. A condemnation in court can be a (sobering, negative) 'example to those who come after us' (*paradeigma tois epigignomenois*, 9). This is, as it were, the reverse side, of posthumous glory (51, 150).

If one imagines the court case between Lykurgos and Leokrates from the perspective of its present, seen proleptically as a future past, it would look something like this: The accused Leokrates is contrasted in the present with the Athenians of a previous generation, especially with those who fought at Salamis (74). Lykurgos is appealing to an already existing reservoir of *exempla*, which one is to imagine continuing to be topped up and invoked in the future, and he tries to place Leokrates in it, of course, as a negative example. This form of inverted posthumous notoriety can also be combined with the mechanisms of intentional forgetting and can even have a material embodiment: one could, for instance melt down the statue of someone who turns out, after the fact, to have been a traitor and use the metal for *stele* on which to inscribe the names of later traitors, thereby memorialising their shame. Concretely speaking, this is what happened to the statue of Hipparchos, son of Charmos (Archon in Athens 496/95[46]). Once this had been done, it could itself be cited later as a precedent (117f.).

To return, however, to the Archaic Period, given the importance of having a good reputation and a 'name', it was inherently unlikely that the practices of systematically cultivating (or denigrating) reputations would remain restricted to the circle of those who could attend a symposium. Despite the fact that the circle of those included could be expanded – as the case of the Cretan and Spartan *syssities* show – the performance and influence of poetry was not limited to these convivial meetings, but rather it was an object of public conversation. This is shown in works as early as the *Odyssey*. Again, to take the case of Demodokos, after he performs at the banquet in the house of Alkinoos, ruler of Phaeacia, he sings in the agora, in the context of games, that is, on the occasion of an *agon* before a large crowd, and accompanies the young people as they dance a formal dance (*Od.* 8.106–10, 256–65).

To demonstrate the public character of literature and performance of this kind, one need not have recourse to citing Solon's hortatory Salamis Elegy (which in any case would have the disadvantage of requiring a response to queries about its authenticity), it should be enough simply to note the importance of performance at the festivals, which were probably the most significant context for those forms of interaction that were relevant for generating and maintaining feelings of cohesion in the community.[47] Here poetry was an obvious part of the divine service, a 'singing for the gods'.[48] In many festivals, poetic performance was part of the associated programme of competitions, *agones*, or was part of a parallel programme. Think here of Attic drama.

Poetry had its place, in general, at all festive occasions, including public banquets, celebrations of victory, and such; the *epinikia* of Pindar and Bakchylides are an instance of their role in the second of these categories.

Given that there were so many festivals, there were numerous occasions for poetic performance, both in local communities and in the wider context provided by regional, amphictyonic, or even panhellenic events.

---

[46] He was the first victim of ostracism (Aristotle *Ath. Pol.* 22.4) and was convicted of treason *in absentia* (cf. Himmelmann 1994, 65); I shall not discuss the question whether the *stele* in question here is identical to the one mentioned by Thucydides (6.55.1f) with the names of the Peisistratides. This was not an isolated case (see Gehrke 1985, 222).

[47] The basic work is Bowie 1986, further developed in Bowie 2001, and especially 2010 (especially 59, 66, 80, 82–4); on Solon's Salamis Elegy in this context, see Irwin 2006, 40–4. On occasions and contexts of performance in general, see Calame 1996; Kõiv 2003, 28–32; for a vivid description of performance, see Fränkel 1962, 8–19.

[48] This is the title of Barbara Kowalzig's 2007 work on this subject.

This dense network of opportunities to perform in the marketplaces, in sanctuaries, theatres, or other public spaces, which were always provided by city-planners, was further expanded by the habit of intra-polis and intra-regional exchange, for instance by the travels of officially sponsored 'embassies' to various festivals.[49]

This is also the basis for the quasi-international character of Greek poetry, as we could see in the example cited above in which the poet Aristodama of Smyrna was honoured by a *different* polis from her own, or in the example like that of Pindar who had patrons in various different communities. It was not just one of the members of the reference-group of a particular intentional history who was always responsible for providing it. This makes the structure of intentional history/histories even more complex and even more pluralist. Concretely, poets were concerned with the man who was to be honoured and also the established reputation – that is, the historical reputation – of his family and/or of his polis, a reputation that will have been founded on certain achievements. As a general point, though, the references to the past, and that means to the events and ideas that were thought to be part of the content of intentional history, were always embedded in a wider poetic-literary context, and therefore this content never dominated the resulting literary product. For instance, narratives about the gods often constituted a large part of a poem. The boundaries, however, between the various things mentioned in a poem were fluid, and the events related could, as has already been suggested, be taken to be historical. On the other hand, it was essential that they be embedded in a framework that was artistic and poetic.

A further characteristic of this Greek way of cultivating the past was that at the performances the representatives of the various communities and the numerous and varied crowd of guests were not present only as consumers of literature, but often also as active participants. Often, it was not just individual singers or rhapsodes who performed, but groups, primarily choruses, who sang and danced, accommodating text, melody, and rhythm closely to each other; so they had to be spiritually, artistically, and physically engaged and attuned to each other, in ways that were both artistic and communicative. The poetic subjects treated, and thus also the intentional history, were therefore made into parts of a fully integrated and all-encompassing work of art, which was a collective community experience.

---

[49] On the spatial aspect of this question, see especially Hölscher 1998, 37–45, 60–2; on ambassadors to festivals, see Gehrke 2013b. On the general significance of such ceremonial and physical practices, see Connerton 1989, 41–111.

The need for rhythmic co-ordination to conform with the metre of the poem strengthened the communal nature of this experience. As early as in the *Odyssey* in the public performance of Demodokos mentioned above, the formal order of the dance of the young men (*kouroi*), and the need for all of them collectively to keep time, is specially mentioned (*Od.* 8.258–65).

Collective participation, then, was common, and it was also very often the case that in the performance these choruses (or other groups) themselves specifically represented the community or individual subdivisions of the community. They had, that is, an official character and were directly connected to the political system. Here the population was dancing, as it were, as a people that was politically organised, and it sang, among other things, its own story, its own history. For instance, in Athens, the dramatic contests (*agones*) were organised as competitions between the *phylai*, the subdivisions of the population in the new democracy, which had been created by Kleisthenes. The dithyramb contests, in which choruses of fifty men and of fifty boys each per *phylē* competed against each other, were probably even more significant for maintaining the social coherence of these subdivisions, and thus also of the polis itself as a whole. The large size of these choruses meant that each year 500 men and 500 boys in total were active participants.[50] Everyone had his chance here, and it seems clear that, in performing, citizens acquired a certain mnemic and aesthetic formation that stayed with them for life and which also enabled them to follow other comparable performances, for instance, the competitions between tragedians, with a high degree of connoisseurship. They were perhaps comparable to contemporary amateur musicians who are not strictly speaking artists, but who are able to sing the *St Matthew Passion* and have an educated opinion about the *Art of Fugue*.

Performances were, as a rule, instances of 'singing and dancing for the gods', but poets could be carried away along a path marked out by the rules of poetry and aesthetics so that their poems gradually departed further and further from anything that could be classified as 'sacred song' in the narrower sense. One instance of this is the story of the sexual intrigue between Ares and Aphrodite and the revenge of Aphrodite's husband, the cuckolded smith-god Hephaistos, which is inserted into the Demodokos-episode in the *Odyssey* (8.266–366). The story is completely human, and it ends in a completely human peal of 'Homeric' laughter by the gods, a laughter that would have been paralleled by that of the humans who heard the story. What finally emerged from this artistic liberty was a huge

---

[50] Zimmermann 2008, 36–9.

spectrum of possible topics for poetic treatment, a space for raising questions about origins and ancestry, which are precisely the main topics of intentional history.

So, we have every reason to assume that the poets and also the citizens who learned the poems by heart, assimilated them, and practised them had an intimate knowledge of the various stories and objects that were treated in them. They will have been aided in this by the development of specific techniques for memorisation, and also probably by the connection that existed between the text and physical dance-movements they had practised. Thus, it is not an accident that Simonides, a poet who is particularly important for intentional history, is credited with the introduction of a system for training the memory, which was then further developed and professionalised by rhetoricians.[51] Literature, in the context of intentional history, then, means performance with even some amount of participation by a population who was knowledgeable about a wide range of the familiar topics that might come up.

Songs and variants of songs were in general treated in a flexible, relaxed way, but parallel to this certain practices came to be established which ensured that certain texts or certain authors, who were thought to have special authority, particularly authority about the past, were treated appropriately. These texts were performed repeatedly and, finally, even inscribed on monuments, which meant that they were practically canonised.

Walter Burkert[52] has shown how Homer, in particular, in this way became a 'classic'. The poems of Tyrtaios were regularly recited in Sparta in a military context, and it was even claimed that there was a law to that effect (Lykurg. 107). In other places, poems were inscribed on permanent materials, for instance on Paros, the poems of Archilochos, who came from the island and was even in the third century BC honoured with a cult there.[53]

The Seventh Olympian Ode of Pindar, a victory ode to the highly prominent Olympic victor Diagoras (464 BC), the most important boxer of his time and a member of the Rhodian aristocracy, was even inscribed on the wall of the temple of Athena in Lindos in letters of gold.[54] This ode gives a kind of early history of Rhodes, extending from the legendary

---

[51] On memory training among the Pythagoreans, see Vernant 2007, 250; see in general also LeGoff 1988, 127f. and with reference to rhetoric, see Schade 2011.
[52] 1987/2001.
[53] IG XII 5 445 (and XII Suppl. pp. 212–14; FGrH 502); SEG XV 517, see also Archil. fr. 89f. 93–8 IEG; for further discussion, see Andreas Bagordo in Zimmermann 2011, 138f.
[54] Schol. Pind. O. VII.

founder Tlepolemos, a son of Herakles and reputed ancestor of the family to which Diagoras belonged, back into the past to the origin of the island itself, which rose out of the sea and was given as a gift to Helios, who was the main god worshipped in Rhodes (and to whom the famous colossus was dedicated).

A poem by Pindar, which in the large repertoire of Rhodian mythohistory represented only one particular variant, here becomes an official part – and, because of the way it originated, an important part – of Rhodian history.[55] Here one can see intentional history virtually *toute pure*. At any rate, in this case one can see very clearly at work the mechanisms that operate in intentional history.

If one pursues this line of enquiry into the Hellenistic epoch, one will be struck by the increasing importance of rhetoric as the medium through which intentional history/histories were passed on and transformed. Here, too, it is important to note the situations and context in which rhetorical exercises were carried out. These included festive occasions, for instance, in Athens the public funeral speeches for those who fell in war (*epitaphioi logoi*), political debates, but also forensic discussions. One can relatively easily reconstruct an intentional history of Athens from these speeches, especially the funeral orations.[56] In public speeches on festive occasions, speakers operated with historical set pieces. Gradually, they began to be expected not only to follow the aesthetic and intellectual rules which we have already mentioned above, but also to make use of the *rhētorikē technē*. This art of rhetoric became increasingly elaborate in the fifth century BC and by the following century it had taken its classical form and had become a fixed set of intricate techniques for deploying stereotypical elements in varying configurations. Even the first historians, Herodotos and Thucydides, felt the need to react to this development.[57]

There were various ways in which the different genres influenced each other, and these operated in both directions, so that an intellectually structured, but also rhetorically shaped historiography could eventually

---

[55] See here in the first instance Prinz 1979, 78–87 and, for the further elaboration in Hellenism, Wiemer 2001, 207–18; 2013, 304ff. It is also characteristic of this type of intentional history that one seemed to know more about the past, the later one started to study it. This seemed suspicious as early as the time of Ephoros (see p. 114).

[56] Nicole Loraux (1981/1993) went so far as to ascribe to them 'the invention of Athens'. See also the older work by Strasburger 1958/1968, and also Wilke 1996, and more recently Grethlein 2010, 105–25. Steinbock 2013 treats some of these issues in a wider context and relative to a specific set of questions. Finally, for further discussion of rhetoric, see p. 93.

[57] Given that Jonas Grethlein (2005; 2006b) has recently treated this topic with particular clarity and incisiveness, I do not need to enter into it.

The Locus of Intentional History

even enter into the dense web of existing intentional history.[58] In the later tradition, any account that had ever been given, even if it had been produced for a very different purpose, could come to be taken to be history and to count as a historical document. One can see this happening in the 'biographical' readings of the older poets, which begin to be made starting in the fifth century BC. Something similar happened, in a completely different area, when legal decisions began to be used as material for a kind of intentional history that was based on the citation of paradigmatic cases.[59] Even oracles and texts like that of the 'Great Rhetra' of the Spartans could be integrated into this project, and here, too, one finds the characteristic cross links between past and present.[60]

In the Athens of the fourth century BC, speakers did not hesitate to fabricate purportedly ancient documents or documentary texts from an older period, to discuss them repeatedly in public speeches, and to put them up in public places. To that extent, the way in which Lykurgos instrumentalises the past in his speech against Leokrates was paradigmatic. In this speech, Lykurgos cites a passage from the 'Oath of Plataia', which the Greeks are supposed to have sworn before the battle there in 479 BC, and he claims that he can treat this as a 'trace' (*ichnos*) of the bravery of the men who fought in the Persian Wars (80f). And as a monument to the achievements of the ancestors, the Athenian demos posted up a decree – one among many others – which had purportedly been passed by Themistokles before the evacuation of Athens in 480 BC.[61] These activities, too, are part of the 'invention of Athens' and are characteristic for the intentional way of cultivating the past. In this case, this was not done prospectively, but *ex post*, however, the same conceptions are involved.

In Hellenism, these same ways of thinking have an effect that reaches even into the public discussion about decrees honouring individuals; these are cases in which the community itself, the demos, could appear as narrator.[62] This results in what one might call history by popular decree.

---

[58] See Chapter 4.
[59] On the biographies of poets, see Irwin 2006, 40f.; on the use of legal judgements, see p. 25 about Lykurgos.
[60] Nafissi 2010, 90f., 104, 110; Giangiulio 2010b, 124–31, especially 128 on Kypselos.
[61] Already the ancient historians Theopompos and Kallisthenes considered some such texts inauthentic (see especially Meister 1982, 58–63; on the oath of Plataiai and the decree of Themistokles, Meister 1982, 62f). Nevertheless, defenders of the respective authenticity can be found time and again in modern debates. Here Habicht (1961) has already given the decisive arguments in his almost classical study; see now especially Blösel 2004 247–54; van Wees 2006. Recently, Krentz (2007) related the oath of Plataiai to the Battle of Marathon. The debate is evidently ongoing!
[62] Luraghi 2010.

One can see a concrete and typical case of this in official documents like the dossier, with which the citizens of Magnesia on the Meander tried to increase the status of the most important cult of their city, the cult of Artemis Leukophryene. These documents are of inestimable value to us because they are unique, but they were certainly not the only ones of their type to be created. Part of this dossier was an official version of the story of the founding of the polis, a kind of intentional history *kat'exochēn*. This text, together with a large number of other related documents, was chiselled into the stone wall of a special purpose-built hall on the agora of Magnesia.[63] The inscriptions were intended to serve as a monument to the history of the polis, as an *aide-mémoire* to keep alive the memory of those things that were important to the community and which it did not wish to allow to be forgotten.[64] Here intentional history is eternalised in stone. Such stones often also provided the backdrop for performances such as ceremonies for awarding honours, which was an act that looked toward the future, but in which sometimes the past also came to be commemorated.[65]

This then brings us to the general question about the media through which intentional history is constructed and propagated. As has already been mentioned, it is important to keep in mind that an oral culture and literacy co-existed, and also that, in the transmission, many aesthetic forms were combined: word, music, and movement. Furthermore, we have seen that domains where there is a continuing tension between the oral and the written provide particularly extensive space for the play of references and for intertextuality, and this can in turn have a repercussive effect on the narrative structures themselves, which were already extremely complex in Homer. This is because of the enhanced performative capacities and competences of the audiences, many of whom will have on previous occasions themselves been performers of work in the domain and because of the increase in mnemotechnical power that this entails. A further factor is the way in which epic at a very early stage devolved into other genres: elegy and epigram, individual and choral song, dithyramb and tragedy, oratory and history. In all these cases intentional history was thematised either as a principal or a secondary topic.[66]

---

[63] For the story of the foundation of the city chiselled into stone, see IMagn. 17 (FGrH 482 F3; Prinz 1979, testimonium 92, see also Kern 1894; on the whole dossier IMagn. 16–87, see especially Gehrke 2000, 1–9 with further references.
[64] Chaniotis 2014.
[65] On this aspect which has up to now been neglected, see now Bielfeldt 2012.   [66] Bowie 2010.

Nevertheless, in addition to the significant role that orality and performance played in structuring Greek intentional history, there is a third element: the materialisation of forms of memory, that is, the existence of material monuments, '*monuments commémoratifs*'.[67] These monuments came to have great significance for the Greeks not least because of their importance in the cultures that the Greeks themselves took as models: the Orient, where texts were baked on clay tablets to make them durable, and Egypt, where the cultivation of the past through the construction of monuments led to a very specific association of stone with cultural persistence through time.[68] Even in later periods, that which was written down, and consequently also the archive, had a greater significance for these cultures than they had in Greece.

The fundamental criticism that Flavius Josephus directs at Greek historiography in his polemic work '*Against Apion*', which is written from a perspective that is at the same time inside that tradition and outside it, makes this difference clear: because they lacked written documents, the Greek historians were reduced to making conjectures about the past, and thus they gave deeply contradictory versions of what had happened and therefore missed the truth.[69] To be sure, eventually the Greeks did surround themselves with archives and libraries, even in their public spaces, which were constructed with some monumentality. We see this gradually but clearly taking place in Hellenistic times and in the period of the Roman Empire. It was then only natural to find learned historians like Timaios spending their whole time in such places, doing research, although more politically oriented and pragmatic historians like Polybios criticised them for this.[70]

Still, one must keep in mind the structural duality and the tension that existed between the oral and the written in Greek culture. As far as remembrance was concerned, *kleos* was the decisive element in Greek poetry. This 'reputation' – what someone was 'called' (which is what *kleos* actually means) – was something rooted in an oral culture. However, starting in the Archaic Period someone's *kleos* could also be entrusted to an inscription, or an inscribed epigram, which then became its vehicle. Such an inscription was at the same time a sign (*sēma*) and a reminder (*mnēma*) or, as we would say a 'memorial'. Such monuments were always located in a very specific way within the field of tension which

---

[67] LeGoff 1988, 116. [68] Assmann 2003/1991.
[69] Ios. c. Ap. 1.9–22; see also bell. Iud. 1.16, and Cancik 1986; Cohen 1988.
[70] On this issue see Schepens 2007, 52f. who tries to defend historians like Timaios, see also p. 136.

existed between past and present. A monument is oriented in a forward-looking way, to posterity, so one can play the literary game of projecting oneself imaginatively into the future, as Hektor does in the *Iliad* (7.87–91), and addressing those who come after us. The basis of this is the idea that a kind of immortality can be created by memory and by a monument, which is a reminder of the past (*sēma* as *mnēma*).[71] The intersection of past and present can also be seen in the fact that the communication of the monument runs over time: it speaks to those who are, from its point of view, 'later' readers of what it expresses.[72]

The texts inscribed on these monuments often speak pleonastically of 'imperishable, ever-lasting glory' (*kleos aphthiton aiei*). Equally, one used a highly durable material, chiefly stone or bronze in what one might see is a redundant way, for the surfaces on which the text was inscribed, in order to ensure that the memory lasted. This made it possible, of course, for the text to enter into a kind of competition with the material, as Horace's *exegi monumentum aere perennius*[73] itself proudly announces. This should remind us of the continuing predominance of the spoken word in the Greek world, even in the period in which one began to commemorate the past by constructing monuments,[74] and it illustrates once again the special importance of literary narrative in the collective memory of the Greeks. There tended also to be a fusion of the literary and the concrete; very often an inscription took the form of a poem – the very name of the genre 'epigram' has its origin here. However, then it might happen that literary products began to circulate freely or finally were invented as responses to purely fictitious situations. Eventually this practice became so sophisticated that it was no longer possible to distinguish 'real' inscribed epigrams from freely invented literary ones. The Hellenistic epigram played with this ambiguity, and we can find instances of it even in later collections like the *Anthologia Palatina*.[75]

Nonetheless this should not be taken to mean that monuments can be neglected. They also included elements other than an inscribed text, for instance, visual representations in the form of statues and reliefs. These, to be sure, needed further written or oral explanation, but they did also tell

---

[71] See the especially clear discussion by Doris Meyer 2005, 53–9.
[72] See Meyer 2005, 53–9; on epigrams in general, see now the important collection by Baumbach, Petrovic, and Petrovic 2010.
[73] 'I have raised a monument more enduring than bronze' (carm. 3.30.1).
[74] This is particularly clearly argued by Foxhall 1995, 136ff., with special reference to Pindar N 5.1–6.
[75] See in the first instance Bing 2009 and various of the contributions to Baumbach, Petrovic, and Petrovic 2010.

the viewers something about the persons and deeds that were being memorialised, and thus they also contributed to keeping memory alive.

There are sometimes commemorative complexes, which combine words, images, and material in a special way. Particularly in panhellenic sanctuaries, the objects dedicated to the god or goddess also served to remind visitors of what he or she had done.[76] In Delphi, for instance, there were images of mythic figures (with associated poems), who were extremely important for the identity of various political groups (such as the Arcadians or the Phokians) and for the claims these groups thought they could make.[77] One could produce and deploy images and sculptures as vehicles of tradition in a wide variety of ways, employing direct representations of the past or indirect ones that were derived from literature.

Myths were visually illustrated even in the Archaic Period,[78] and later it is even possible to speak of a quasi-genre of 'historical pictures'.[79] The famous, so-called 'Stoa Poikilē', the 'Painted Porch' in Athens, which took its name from the pictures displayed there, is a classic example of this. It stood in a central location in the public state of the city and in it were displayed four pictures, each depicting a battle or war that, in the view of the Athenians themselves, occupied an essential place in Athenian history: the victory over the Amazons; the Athenian participation in the Trojan War; the battle of Marathon; and a victorious battle waged against the Spartans, this last an item of contemporary history. What is represented here is the 'we' of intentional history, which guarantees the stability of the group, continuity in the pursuit of collective goals, and the repetition of past successes. In 455 BC, that is visually displayed for all to see. At the same time, the creation of this monument can be connected with a highly specific political situation that existed at that time and with certain clear political goals.[80]

The sculpture on the Temple of Zeus at Olympus, the two pediments and the reliefs depicting the labours of Herakles, can also be read as presenting an account of mytho-history:[81] The Eleans, who were in charge of organising the Games and who were also famous for their local clans of seers, here presented to a wider panhellenic public the great figures of their

---

[76] Sinn 2004, 62f.
[77] On the dedications by the Arcadians (Pausanias 10.9.5; CEG 2, 824), see also Maaß 1993, 201; Nielsen 1997, 145f; Pretzler 2009, 89; Ruggieri 2009, 51. On the various dedications of the Phokians, see Pausanias 10.1.10. 13.4–7; Daux 1936, 146–48: Jacquemin 1999, Nr 396f, and the work of Elena Franchi (2016) on the intentional history of the Phokians.
[78] Fittschen 1969. [79] Hölscher 1973. [80] Gehrke 2003, 21.
[81] See the recent treatment by Helmut Kyrieleis 2012/2013.

own history, under the guise of myth and in connection with other great figures and with the traditions of other communities and of the Greeks as a whole. In doing so they also laid down the claim that the great hero Pelops, who was an important figure for many, was one of their own. Here, too, one can trace connections between this particular structuring of intentional history and certain contemporary political factors.[82]

The art-historical details cannot be investigated further here, but two points should be noted. First of all, in this domain, too, intentional history fell under the influence of aesthetic rules, which expressed a particular form of interconnectedness between past and present. This interconnection[83] depended on a certain characteristic absence of distance between past and present. The visual language alone did not reveal in what era the depicted action was taking place. However, and this is the second point, precisely this property made these visual representations particularly suited for the functions of intentional history, one of which was to encourage identification with the past. In this way, then, the image of certain figures who were essential for the identity and self-understanding of the group – whether they were contemporary figures or 'atemporal' ones[84] – could be fixed for the future and then for all time, in the full knowledge that they would be accepted later as part of a past that never faded away and thus was imperishable, a past that bound the members of future generations together and was binding on all of them. It is in no way surprising then that these motifs can frequently be found on temples and treasuries, that is, on particularly important and religiously relevant buildings standing in prominent places in the public space. This was a way of connecting the visual (and the oral explanations given of the images) with the sempiternal sameness of the rituals, and, as such, it strengthened in its own way the sense of an interconnection between past, present, and future.

In addition, certain objects could become bearers of memory, too.[85] There was a firm place for this, too in social life, namely the exchange of gifts so as to document and cement social relations. This exchange had the

---

[82] For further examples see Kyrieleis 2012/2013. One should also mention in this context the work of Ralf von den Hoff on the 'Arch-Hero' of Athens, Theseus (see e.g. von den Hoff 2010). Ioakimidou 1997 contains a treasure trove of examples involving groups of statues. See also in general the important overview in Queyrel 2012.

[83] As Luca Giuliani (2010; 2014) has recently shown.

[84] Think of the Parthenon-frieze. Foxhall 1995, 142f; see also Queyrel 2012, 77–81 in general on the Parthenon as a *lieu de mémoire*.

[85] On methodological issues, see Veit 2005, 25–7, 33 (with further references); on these aspect in classical antiquity see especially Alcock 2002, and the encyclopaedic treatment by Hartmann (2010) in his dissertation.

function of literally embodying in a material form a connection, or even a friendship, and it was to serve this function even beyond the lifetimes of the individuals who originally initiated the exchange; it thus placed itself beyond time, at any rate for those affected, primarily for the descendants of the original individuals. Gifts then were vehicles of remembrance: Before they fight, Glaukos and Diomedes (*Iliad* 6, 119–236) discover that they are guest-friends from paternal times, because each knows of the gifts that were reciprocally exchanged by their grandfathers, a purple belt and a golden goblet. Consequently, they reaffirm this tradition by a renewed exchange, this time an exchange of weapons.

In another passage, there is an exchange of a belt and a sword. They are exchanged by Ajax and Hector after their remarkable duel in the Seventh Book of the *Iliad* (303–5) as a sign that they both agreed voluntarily to end the duel. The sword appears again, with a clear reference to a continuity with its former owner, in Sophokles' *Ajax* (1029–35), when the protagonist kills himself with the sword Hektor gave him. Naturally, the reference to a remembered past is a literary conceit here, but it illustrates how closely one paid attention to these objects, even after a significant lapse of time. It is as if things themselves had a life of their own, which could serve the purposes of remembering. Thus, in the *Iliad*, too, archaeologically older objects that are something like heirlooms are mentioned. The best-known example of this is the boars-tusk helmet.[86] From the perspective of the author, these references probably served to suggest high antiquity and thus to give temporal distance to the events being narrated. To operate in this way with such objects implies, however, that their role as a medium of memory was well known.

As mentioned before, these objects were important not just to reaffirm social relations and then also political connections, but also to keep them alive in memory. An especially good example of this was the artificial shoulder blade of Pelops. According to the famous myth, the boy Pelops was cut up by his father Tantalus and set before the gods as food. The gods, however, noticed what was going on, all except Demeter, who accidently ate a piece of the shoulder. Pelops then was reassembled, except for the missing shoulder blade, which was replaced by one made of ivory. When Pelops grew up, he seized power in Elis and Olympia, after defeating the legendary king Oinomaos in a chariot race, a race depicted on the east pediment of the temple in Olympia. After Pelops' death the artificial

---

[86] On this aspect and the poetic development of this motif, see esp. Patzek 1992, 193–202, also Grethlein 2008.

shoulder blade became much sought after because, according to an oracle, only one who possessed it could conquer Troy. However, the ship on which the shoulder blade was being transported back home after the destruction of Troy, sank in the waters around the island of Euboia, and with it the ivory artefact was lost. Only much later was it found by an Eretrian fisherman, Damarmenos. When he consulted the Oracle at Delphi, it explained the situation to him and revealed the true owner. Thereupon the Eleans named Damarmenos and his descendants 'Keepers of the Bone', while the shoulder blade itself returned to Pelops' grave in Olympia. This amazing story, which we have to thank Pausanias for preserving, is too good to be true, but behind it there obviously lies some truth about special relations that existed between the poleis Elis and Eretria.[87]

In general, sanctuaries or other sacred spots were the places where such objects were kept; they were mostly dedicatory offerings or at any rate were later taken to be such. Votive offerings in this way became memorials, and the famous temple chronicle of Lindos[88] is able to group a significant chunk of the history – the intentional history – of Rhodes around a collection of such objects. Intentional history in any case was always connected with the sphere of religion. Sometimes objects like this even attained the status of relics,[89] playing the role that the purported bones of heroes often played in Greek history. One might cite here the translation of the bones of Orestes and his son Teisamenos or that of the Athenian hero Theseus.[90] These events marked particular stations in the history of Sparta and of Athens.

Even animal bones could become famous, for instance, the lower jaw of the Calydonian Boar, which was turned into a memorial of a famous deed in mytho-history. The Hunt of the Calydonian Boar played an important role in the Hellenistic period in the identity politics of the Aitolian League.[91]

There is a close connection here with the specific locations at which a certain kind of remembrance is cultivated. These are *lieux de mémoire* in a very concrete sense, and they existed in ancient Greece, were of particular importance, and also very characteristic of intentional history/histories.

---

[87] Pausanias 5.13.4–6; on the story in general see Hartmann 2010, 80, 160, 430, 540, 555; on the relations between Elis and Eretria, see Gehrke 2013b, 47f note 48.
[88] Higbie 2003; see also Hartmann 2010, 505–10.
[89] Scheer 1996; on the terminology see Hartmann 2010, 47–51; see also now Schnapp 2011, 128–30.
[90] On this general issue, see Hartmann 2010, 246–63; see also Fell 2004 (on Theseus).
[91] Jördens and Becht-Jördens 1994.

The Locus of Intentional History 39

It is not really surprising that we can document the existence of such locations already in the *Iliad*, where they are already the objects of poetic treatment. However, objects with other functions can also serve as material bearers of memories, for instance, walls, in particular, the walls of fortifications. In general, ruins occupy much space in cultural memory.[92] This tendency could be developed further so that eventually it became quite natural to point out the graves of Achilles and Patroklos on the plains of Troy-Ilion, and Alexander the Great could offer sacrifices there together with his friend Hephaistion.[93]

There is certainly a connection between this development and a custom that seems to have begun to emerge at about the same time as the *Iliad* was being composed. This is the custom of instituting cults on older – Mycenaean – graves, venerating the dead who were buried there as heroes, and thus establishing good relations with them, as if they were ancestral representatives or guardians of the community, or at any rate were in some way associated with it.[94] All of this was a late construction projected back on the past, but since this purported relation with the older hero was something in which people 'believed', it was a part of intentional history. Here, too, we can clearly see what function this had in actual contemporary life. In many societies, the cult of the dead, usually located on their graves, plays an important role in memory, both on the individual (family) level and on the collective level and in very elementary forms of representing the past.[95]

These tendencies are intensified when something as vital as the well-being of the community as a whole is in play. The Greeks expressed this in their veneration of heroes (even where there were no stories about a particular hero or when very different stories about him were current). Thus, there is the figure of the *hērōs ktistēs*, the founder-hero of a Greek colony, who usually received a cult on a special place reserved for him on the agora of the polis that he founded or organised. This cult-place could be seen prospectively as a *lieu de mémoire* and later it often fulfilled exactly this function.[96]

---

[92] On this see Patzek 1992, 181–5, 203–10; Hertel 2003, 185–274; Grethlein 2008; Schnapp 2011, 116–30.
[93] Arr. An 1.12.1.
[94] On this see first of all Boehringer 2001, also Patzek 1992, 162–85; Alcock 2002, 146–52; Bowie 2010, 82–4; and Gutzwiller 2010.
[95] The literature on this, especially for pre-history and early history, is much too extensive to be summarised, but graves represent an especially important source of information and the study of them requires special methodological care; on the methodology see, for instance, Veit 2005, 27–31; on the anthropological foundations see especially Kohl 2003.
[96] The excavations of the German Archaeological Institute under the direction of Dieter Mertens have brought to light what seems obviously to be a space of this kind in Selinus.

Here, too, one finds the characteristic interlacing of present and future past, and can see the connection this can have with the 'relics' of heroes which were mentioned above. Imagine the following historical sequence: as forms of remembrance of the hero develop, they become more clearly and explicitly retrospective, which means, etically speaking, that they are constructed memories. This process is accompanied step-by-step by forms of cultic veneration, which also gradually spread. This led to a felt need to exhume and transfer the bones of the heroic figure in question (that is, purportedly to bring them back 'home'). Erwin Rohde[97] saw in these heroes 'major figures, one might say, paradigmatic individuals, whose life was projected into deep pre-history in the legends and stories told about them, forefather of those who came after them'; he even speaks of a 'cult of the ancestors' with reference to them. *Cum grano salis* that might be true of the founder-heroes, but they, too, are no ancestors in the literal sense.

The main property of figures like the ones just discussed is that they could be shifted from one time and place to another and claimed by different groups. As we shall see in the following chapter, they could also be created *ad libitum* where needed. Again, the personalisation of commemoration is connected with a peculiar complexity of Greek intentional history, which we already find in Homeric epic: the past is the preterite form of a future that is already imagined in the present. And from the point of view of this present the Greeks not only imagined their own past, but also constructed it concretely. In this context, we can say that the veneration of heroes gave itself a material embodiment and by so doing also gave material form to a bit of 'constructed' memory.[98]

It is important to repeat what has already been said about the aspect of materiality: the bare object itself, the mere location (for instance, of a hero's grave) is never enough. What was required was also an explanatory discourse which added details to what one could see. What was even more necessary was a constantly repeated cultic ritual, that is, a certain kind of performance, to confirm the memories and keep them definitively alive.[99]

This is true also of cult places, such as the battlefields of Marathon and Plataia, places that became *lieux de mémoire* for more than one polis.[100] The graves here were a material reminder of the events, but the real commemoration were the actions associated with cult of the fallen, who

---

[97] 1899, 154.
[98] Boehringer 2001, 25–33, 44f has clarified this complex relation with special reference to the cult of heroes and the problem of its relation to the cult of the ancestors, and to the role of Homer in this process. On the connection between ritual and literature, see Nagy 1986.
[99] Foxhall 1995. [100] See, in the first instance, Jung 2006; also Alcock 2002, 75–86.

had now been transformed into heroes (and were called 'heroes' in literary treatments), actions that were repeated regularly.

Once again, then, one can see how complicated intentional history was in ancient Greece, that is, how complex were the ways in which the Greeks handled it. Despite the complexity, there continued to be a dominant principle, which was ritual or ritualised repetition, that is, concrete performance in which, in a cultic context, words, music, and dance could be immediately enjoyed. The whole reciprocal relation between past and present, which runs through Greek intentional history as a common thread, finds its adequate expression in this constantly repeated activity of rendering the past present. This shows, once again, that history, of whatever kind, if it is to have substance and continue to exist, must be actively called to mind.

The next chapter will deal with the structure and the form of stories (or histories) that are recalled in this way; in the first instance, we shall be concerned with the Greek case, but then also with forms of history that had their roots in Greece.

CHAPTER 2

Greek Myths As a History of the Greeks
Motifs – Forms – Structures

Armed with the general concept of 'intentional history' – the history of a group which gives it its collective identity, as it appears in the self-understanding of members of the group – we can now turn our attention in this chapter to the contents of such histories, the various forms and structures, motifs, and goals of their representations of the past. The focus will be on the world of Greek myth and its particular narrative features. The term 'myth' is used in so many different ways, in everyday life and also by artists, philosophers, intellectuals of all kinds, and scientists, that it is extremely difficult to reach consensus and get clarity about its proper use.[1]

Nonetheless, for the reconstruction I am proposing here, I do not need to enter into the complexity of the word's various contemporary uses, because for my project I can focus on the basic meaning, the original conception associated with the Greek word *mythos*. '*Mythos*' is simply that which is said or recounted, and so originally it is not at all different from *logos*, despite the fact that later thinkers came to be particularly keen to contrast *logos* and *mythos*. The failure to make a sharp distinction between *mythos* and *logos* can be seen even in a work as late as that of Herodotos.[2] *Mythos* is speech, report, legend, but, in the first instance, it is a tale, the elementary and archetypical form of narrative. Greek myths constitute classic examples of myths in this sense.

So, I would like to show in this chapter that the study of myth is the royal road to an understanding of the history of the Greeks as they understood it themselves. Their myths constitute Hellenic intentional history, in terms of its content, its form, and its structure. I will use the

---

[1] For a first orientation, Graf 1985 is particularly helpful; he also gives an analysis of myth as history which has some similarities with the one advanced here (117–37).
[2] Nickau 1990. The opposition of *mythos* and *logos*, which was highly significant for the history of thought and which continues to be trumpeted, sometimes in a rather crude and unsophisticated way, has been very clearly analysed by Vernant (2007, 577–611), who also, however, relativises and redefines it.

term 'mytho-history' to refer to the complex structure that is object of my research, and I would like to proceed typologically in treating it. My reconstruction will be based on traditional myths but will abstract from the completely unsurveyable plethora of alternative versions that exist. Instead, it will draw out imaginatively and develop some existing tendencies, so as to bring out clearly the typical motifs and structures, and focus on the main narrative lines, which are often lost from view behind the almost infinitely proliferating welter of variants. To put it another way, if one accepts Hans Blumenberg's persuasive characterisation of myth as a matter of 'theme and variations', this treatment is focused on the 'theme'.[3]

It is a commonly accepted view that narratives, including myths and legends, constitute an essential way in which human cultures allow their members to make basic sense of the world and of their lives.[4] As we have seen, humans have a natural tendency – which exists in individuals and in groups – to find out the meaning of 'things'. They are themselves one of these 'things', and one of the ways in which they try to make sense of their identity is through narrative. Recent research on autobiography that tries to straddle the boundary between psychology and narratology[5] has shown that as individuals we are constantly retelling ourselves the story of our lives but doing so in such a way as to try to impose some coherence, despite obvious discontinuities, and also at least to minimise the role of contingency. So, breakdowns, changes of direction, events that were not expected or not even dreamed of are all toned down, or even denied. Sometimes we even try, despite appearance, to give them a positive value; in any case, we take them up into a web of stories and in this way get at least a narrative grip on them. In the final analysis, everything even becomes matter for a story, which we continue to tell and retell, working it over again and again. We continue it, add new events, impressions, experiences to it, all as a way of assimilating it. This is why one can say that if we cannot tell the story of our lives in this way, we have no identity or are suffering from a personality disorder. Clearly, then, our memory is so constituted that we

---

[3] Blumenberg 1990, 40.
[4] Bal 2002, 9 considers narrative to be the 'instrument in our cultural knapsacks, which we use first and which permits us to make some sense of a chaotic world and the incomprehensible events that take place in it' (cited in Rüth 2012, whose work on this topic (esp. 2005), and whose private conversations with me, have been very helpful).
[5] On this, see for instance Lucius-Hoene and Deppermann 2004; on the connection with historical consciousness, see especially Straub 1998b.

take such narratives to be true with no further qualification: these stories are simply the story of our lives, *full stop*.

All of this is true in at least the same measure for collectives, for intentional history and myths, because, after all, as has been shown in Chapter 1, the subject and object of collective memory is a 'we' that is construed as extended indefinitely over various times and places. With Paul Ricœur (1985, 14) one might also say: 'the narrative operation transforms irrational contingency into a rule-governed, meaningful, intelligible contingency'. It is no accident that Ricœur, in his fundamental work *Temps et récit* (especially in the second volume where he treats time and literary narrative) starts from the concept of *mythos* that one finds in Aristotle's *Poetics*.[6] *Mythos* in this work refers primarily to the plot of a tragedy, but its more particular focus is narrative coherence (one aspect of *systasis*). This discussion, in any case, reminds us of how massively the Greek past was imagined and represented in poetic works. That, in turn, means that this past can also be opened up to us by analysing the domain of *mythos* in general, and the various specific myths it contains. On inspection, Greek myth shows itself to be a good instance of Blumenberg's principle of 'theme and variations'.

I cannot pursue the narratological aspects of this enquiry any further here.[7] The main point is that historical narrative, that is, a narrative that refers to past events and states of affairs, is essential for the constitution of meaning and the introduction of coherence into the framework of collective life. Here, too – in parallel to the performative constellation described in Chapter 1 – orientation in our human environment and mythic *narratio* are closely connected. One could once again cite Ricœur,[8] who speaks of 'narrative identity, both of individuals and of historical communities'.

The Greek myths often concern individuals who are taken to be the eponymous representatives of fixed communities: Doros stands for the Dorians, Aiolos for the Aiolians, Ion for the Ionians, etc. The particular interest of these myths is questions of origins and descent, one of the marks of Greek intentional history. The same thing has been observed to be true in general for pre-literate societies by anthropologists who study the legends told there.[9] Intentional history, then, is also primordial history, or even cosmology. Mythic narratives anchor a given community in the very depths of time, at the very beginning of the world. The gradual

---

[6] For a summary, see also Ricœur 2005, 213ff. See also Straub 1998b, 142–52; Rüth 2005, 23; 2012. On this aspect of Aristotle's poetics, see the very enlightening remarks of Sauer, 2011, 13–28.
[7] One can find a convenient discussion of many of them in Grethlein 2006a. [8] Ricœur 2005, 70.
[9] The fundamental work is Müller 1987, 94–106.

emergence of various social units from some primal entities and groups is described, and their course of development through space and time is tracked. So, it makes sense to use mythic conceptions of space and time as the guiding thread of this enquiry.

To start with stories about origins, we find them documented very early in the history of Greek mythology (or mythography); to be more exact, one can find them already fully developed in a very authoritative and effective form in Hesiod, who was obviously influenced in various complex ways by Oriental conceptions:[10] In the beginning the world arose from chaos, and this led to the emergence of the gods, in a succession of generations, first that of Kronos and then that of Zeus. The formation of humans followed, and this was partly construed as a process of splitting off from the gods. In any case, early humans were still very close to the gods. This is expressed in what is in many ways a peculiar myth about the ages of the world, starting with the Golden Race of Men. Already in *Works and Days*, however, Hesiod inserts the Race of Heroes into the chronological schema of the succession of four metal races (gold, silver, bronze, iron), so that this Race of Heroes is distinguished from the present Race of Iron (the one contemporary with him, or, for that matter, contemporary with us) and from the previous Race of Bronze.

This special position attributed to the Race of Heroes is an established feature of Greek conceptions of the past. The drawing of a clear boundary between the Race of Heroes and the present Race of Iron clearly reflects the strict distinction that Homer draws in the *Iliad* between 'contemporary men' ('as mortal men are now' *Il.* 5.304) and the heroes of the time of the Trojan War, who could easily, with one hand, lift up and throw huge stones and other heavy objects. The properties of these heroes are exaggerated into something grandiose and they themselves are also in other respects 'monumentalised'.[11] Hesiod writes (erg. 159–173) of them:

> [T]he godly race of men-heroes, who are called demigods, the generation before our own upon the boundless earth. Evil war and dread battle destroyed these, some under the seven-gated Thebes in the land of Cadmus while they fought for the sake of Oedipus' sheep, others brought in boats over the great gulf of the sea to Troy for the sake of fair-haired Helen. There the end of death shrouded some of them, but upon others

---

[10] Most recent discussion is dependent on West 1997, 279–333 and Burkert 2004, 49–70. Lane Fox 2008, 360–89 brings up some unconventional and interesting speculative points.

[11] *Il.* 5.302–4, 12.378–83, 445–62; van Wees (1992, 21) correctly says they have been 'glamorised'. Bichler 2012, 88 has emphasised that this does not imply any moral distancing from them; this is parallel to the Oriental cases.

Zeus the father, Cronus' son, bestowed life and habitations far from human beings and settled them at the limits of the earth; and these dwell with a spirit free of care on the Islands of the Blessed beside the deep-eddying Ocean – happy heroes, for whom the grain-giving field bears honey-sweet fruit flourishing three times a year. (trans. Most)

On the other hand, these heroes are cut off in a most striking way from the previous Age of Bronze by the Deluge, which marks a new point of departure for history. The 'Catalogues of Women', which are attributed to Hesiod (*Ehoiai*),[12] start at this point, as one can clearly see from a perusal of Apollodoros' handbook, which is based on these catalogues.[13] This period is in fact a turning point in Greek mytho-history. For one thing, the Race of Heroes is the start of its paradigmatic period, which is centred around the Trojan War. For another, the Greek tribes, and consequently also various later Greek groupings, the Aiolians, Dorians, and Ionians all trace themselves back to the only two survivors of the Deluge, Deukalion and Pyrrha.

Both of these points merit further consideration. The Age of Heroes has, as already mentioned, special standing in Greek mythology in that it forms, as can be seen by consulting any work of Greek literature in any genre,[14] the essential horizon of the world that the legendary stories describe. The events recounted in Greek legends all essentially take place within a period of three generations, each of which is carefully[15] set off from the others, but also placed into relation with them. This seems clearly to be a consequence of the great importance attributed to Homer and thus to the Trojan War, which is the turning point raised to a higher power of Greek legend. We have the generation that is dated to 'before' the Trojan War,

---

[12] Here I am primarily concerned with the *gynaikōn katalogos* (the *ēhoiai*), however, one should also mention the *megalai ēhoiai*. Both works were attributed to Hesiod. For a reconstruction of the *Ehoiai*, see in the first instance West 1985, and also the commentary by Hirschberger 2004. See also the collective volume edited by Hunter 2005; Dräger 1997 argues for the authenticity of the attribution. See West 1985, 44f on the relation of the *Ehoiai* to Apollodoros' *Library*.

[13] And Prometheus had a son Deucalion. He, reigning in the regions about Phthia, married Pyrrha, the daughter of Epimetheus and Pandora, the first woman fashioned by the gods. And when Zeus would destroy the men of the Bronze Age, Deucalion by the advice of Prometheus constructed a chest, and having stored it with provisions he embarked in it with Pyrrha. But Zeus by pouring heavy rain from heaven flooded the greater part of Greece, so that all men were destroyed, except a few who fled to the high mountains in the neighborhood (Apollod. 1.7.2, translated by J. G. Frazer).

It is disputed whether the Deluge was already mentioned in the *Ehoiai*. Hirschberger 2004, 84, n. 89 argues in favour (West 1985, 55f against).

[14] Pallantza 2005, see also Bowie 2010.

[15] In the sense that there is a 'chronology of the legends', see Prinz 1979.

the generation of heroes such as Herakles, Theseus, Kastor, Polydeukes, Jason, Telamon, Tydeus, and we have certain important events that take place during that period, such as the voyage of the Argonauts, the expedition of the Seven against Thebes, the various legendary deeds of Herakles (including the 'first' Trojan War), the battle between the Amazons and the Athenians under the leadership of Theseus, and the battle against the Lapiths, under the leadership of Theseus' friend Peirithoos, against the Centaurs.

The Trojan War, then, which is the main subject of the *Iliad*, is the axis of this history;[16] it is *the* Great Event of Greek mytho-history, and thus also of the early history of the Greeks, as they themselves understood it. The Epigones of the Seven against Thebes, who successfully attacked the city in order to avenge their fathers' failure and death, were thought to be contemporaries of the heroes who fought at Troy, although their story was less influential than that told in the *Iliad*. The following history – and this is characteristic – was directly connected to the complex of tales about Troy, in particular with the *nostoi*, the stories of the return of the Greek heroes from the War. As the *Odyssey* tells us, during that period, the next generation, here in the form of Telemachos, came into view. Other figures of this generation could be cited, such as Orestes, who, not accidently, is named right at the start of the *Odyssey*, and there were other important events, such as the return of the Heraclids.

These three generations that are grouped around the Trojan War mark out the essential referential space within which events in Greek mytho-history are located, and they mark it out as a space of memories that are common to all the Greeks and thus are shared by them all. This is the space on which all those who produced the Greek myths focused their telescopes.[17] The heroes who lived during that period were clearly different in their powers and capacities from men of the present – quantitatively speaking, they could quite simply *do* more. Qualitatively, however, that is, in the values and attitudes they had, they were on a par with them. This meant that as literary figures they could be developed in a variety of different directions, as archetypes and idealised models for action. This shows just how important art and poetry were for creating paradigms. The heroes who had been active in this mythical space were omnipresent and could be made out to have acted in multifarious different ways, to represent

---

[16] In the *Ehoiai*, this event is used to mark the boundary between epochs, the end of the age of 'real' demigods (fr. 204, 96–119 Merkelbach-West), which corresponds to what is said in the passage cited above from *Works and Days*.

[17] On 'telescoping' in research on memory see Fried 2004, 50, 214, 216f.

the most diverse moral conceptions, and to have been motivated by a wide variety of different impulses, reasons, and desires. They could be made to stand as 'exemplary' for virtually anything. Attic tragedy shows this with all requisite clarity: one could ring the changes on the stories of Menelaos and Helen, Ajax and Odysseus, Philoktetes and Orestes, or Hecuba and Andromache and thereby express anything at all one wanted to say. In doing so, one would expand the repertoire of variations on basic mythic themes, and one could also, by modifying the stories slightly, make them psychologically more plausible and more effective.

In order to construe their whole past as part of a single story, the Greeks tried to attach and connect their 'present time' – which was a 'historical time' in our view, for instance, the sixth century BC when many of these stories took the form in which we now still read them – to the stories of what took place in the 'classic' heroic era in the past. It is an integral part of their way of conceiving history that the Greeks tried to make this connection, but the specific way in which they did that is also noteworthy. The connection between the heroic era and the 'present time' was made through inserting a time of migrations, namely the wandering of those who survived the Trojan War. Despite the attempt to make the transition as smooth as possible, there remained an awareness that there was a visible seam here, which persisted even in the later historiography: The 'classic' writer of universal history, Ephoros, began his proper, historical account in the time of these mytho-historical migrations,[18] because they were what constituted a bridge between 'Once upon a time' and the present time.

Obviously, the epics that dealt with the return of heroes from Troy and the stories about their descendants had an important place in this project. Just as important was the recourse to genealogical trees of the time after the Deluge. The new beginning represented by the Deluge could become the point of origin of a whole stemma, which could then be amalgamated with stories about the best-known heroes and their deeds. The result was a genealogical tree of Hellen and his descendants, specifying the ancestry of the various different kinship groups. This genealogical account was expounded, as one might have expected, primarily in poems that have been handed down under the name Hesiod, the 'Catalogues of Women' (*Ehoiai*), which have already been mentioned. The point at which these genealogies, which reach down into present times, connect with the 'new start' of humanity after the Deluge lies before the axis constituted by the Trojan War, so that the genealogical lines which one could draw, tracking

---

[18] See p. 51, 115.

very often migrations, from the period just after the Trojan War to the present, actually also ran back to the time before this axial event.

Stories about the return of the Heraclids, which were paradigmatically located in the sphere of legend, were combined with the story of the migration of the Dorians into the Peloponnese. An early fragment of the work of the poet Tyrtaios documents that this connection was made as early as the seventh century BC (see p. 11). These Dorians traced their ancestry back to Doros, son of Hellen, that is, to the generation after that of Deukalion and Pyrrha, namely, the generation after the Deluge and the new beginning for mytho-history. Using this procedure, one could eventually arrive at the present, and that was the thing that was most important: one could build a bridge to the past which arched over the epochs. The genealogical procedure was used everywhere in many different contexts, as demonstrated by the fact that Hekataios used it on himself, tracing his ancestry back to a god in the sixteenth generation.[19] It is an essential element in 'archaic forms of organisation',[20] and ancient Greek authors took it very seriously, so seriously in fact that one can often still today use it as a template to reconstruct otherwise lost versions of these stories.[21]

There is also a particular spatial component to this form of diachronic treatment, as the myth about the return of the Heraclids and the Dorian Migration illustrates. The past is organised in the same universal spatial schema, which also provides the scaffolding for the chronology; the chronology essentially takes the form of a genealogy. This spatial framework is even more important, and more characteristic of Greek mytho-history than the creation and use of genealogies is. Greek poets and bards created a network of stories of wanderings and migrations, which one cannot fail to remark, but which is also so complex as to be virtually unsurveyable, and which expressed 'narrative identities' of a highly peculiar kind.

The Greeks had a penchant for telling stories of wandering, even from the earliest times, and they constituted an essential element in the way in which groups located and oriented themselves securely in space and time. They permitted the creation and elaboration of a unitary, but also internally highly differentiated, space in which to locate the past, and were thus another instance of the dialectic between unity and plurality that recurs as a common trait of much of Greek culture and history. The Homeric epics do not yet exhibit this feature, although they show a clear

---

[19] Hdt. 2.143.1, 4.
[20] For more on this concept (to be sure in a different context), see Will Richter *Gegenständliches Denken, archaisches Ordnen. Untersuchungen zur Anlage von Cato 'de agri cultura'*, Heidelberg, 1978.
[21] As shown in the important work by Friedrich Prinz 1979 on chronology in legends.

awareness of human mobility in various forms, such as that of Phoenician traders or Cretan pirates, and they are even acquainted with a distinctly 'colonialist' perspective, at any rate in the *Odyssey* with its descriptions of the land of the Cyclops (9.105–51) and the city of the Phaeakians (6.255–72, 8.1–18). Nevertheless, the various catalogues, for instance the catalogue of ships or of the Trojan-allied contingents, give very detailed and deliberate listings and descriptions of different peoples and social groups,[22] but contain no references to large-scale movements of populations, things which in texts written in a later period, would regularly have been mentioned. So it is certainly no accident that Thuycdides in his 'archaeology' (1.2.1) asserts that Greece – that is 'what we today call "Hellas"' – was massively shaped by 'displacements of populations' (*metanastaseis*), and that he also particularly emphasises that these began after the Trojan War. The fact that 'migration and the founding of new settlements took place' (*metanistato te kai katōkizeto*)' was what prevented the accumulation of social and political power.

One can see in Herodotos how deeply this motif of migration had impressed itself on the way in which the Greeks themselves understood their own history. He is the first author who exhibits this feature in a way that we can discern. His declared intention, after all, was to preserve the memory of earlier events and people, and prevent them from being forgotten. To this end, he puts them together and even, one might say, systematises them.[23] In his work, it is the Pelasgians who constitute the autochthonous element in the population of the territory called 'Hellas', the population that was not composed of immigrants. The Pelasgians are the 'old' Greeks, but later they become aliens – not-really-Greeks – and they represent a minority and are an exception among the inhabitants of 'Greece' because they are autochthonous. The autochthonous Arcadians and Athenians, and a certain fraction of the Ionians, also belonged to this group of exceptions. And the members of these groups were themselves partly, or even to a considerable extent, immigrants, especially the Ionians.

In contrast to these groups, we can identify the Dorians, who, at any rate in the mind of the Greeks themselves, were most certainly immigrants, as the 'pure' Greeks. In the work of Herodotos, they figure as in one way at least the 'real Hellenes'. Herodotos mentions that Kroisos, the great King of the Lydians, had had research done that discovered that the

---

[22] On this issue see now especially Visser 1997 and Kullmann 2002; see also p. 17.
[23] On this and what follows see Busolt 1893, 163–74, which remains the 'classic' treatment (not only of this topic).

Lakedaimonians (Spartans) and the Athenians were the most pre-eminent among the Greeks, that the former were of Doric descent and the latter of Ionian: 'These two, then, were distinguished, the Athenians from the very beginning a Pelasgian tribe (*ethnos*) and the Lakedaimonians a Hellenic one.'

It is also significant that the (universal) historians of the fourth century BC, especially Ephoros, Kallisthenes, and Theopompos, really begin their histories at exactly this point, the time of migrations after the Trojan War.[24] The time before this was still essentially a time of stories of gods and demigods in close communication with each other, that is, it was a *spatium mythicum* in the narrow sense.[25] Diodoros speaks of 'old mythic stories' (*palaia mythologia*, 4.1.3). This corresponds to Hesiod's view that this was the time of a 'Race of Heroes'. So, the old boundary that we noted in early epic is obviously still being observed. In epic, it was the gap between the Age of Heroes and the age of the Race of Iron, people 'as they now are'; in historiography, that which is all too 'mythical' and full of wonders and miracles is separated from the historical, although the latter category may also well contain material that we would call 'mythohistorical'. So the analogy to 'our' distinction between *spatium mythicum* and *spatium historicum* holds only partially, and one must not put too much weight on it.[26] The migrations, in any case, constituted the bridge that led from the time of the heroes of old toward the present time.

The two seventh-century BC authors who were cited in Chapter 1 as examples for the use of the communicative 'we', Tyrtaios and Mimnermos,[27] also document the centrality of narratives of migration in structuring the way the Greeks thought about the past. The passages that were cited epitomise what I have called 'narrative identity'. They also contain striking references to those movements of peoples which were called, and which we still call, the Dorian and the Ionian Migrations: movements from Central or Northern Greece to the Peloponnese ('the wide island of Pelops' for Tyrtaios) and from the Peloponnese, or at any rate the Greek mainland, to Asia Minor ('charming Asia' for Mimnermos). These versions of the migration narratives, found in the works of the early lyric poets, originated at about the same time at which the authors of the so-called 'catalogue'-literature (especially the *Ehoiai*, which have already been mentioned) were beginning to try to organise the Greek past

---

[24] Diod. 4.1.1–3.   [25] See p. 45–48.
[26] Diodoros invalidates the distinction himself by his euhemerism (4.1.4), which, of course, undermines the idea that there is any absolutely sharp difference between gods, heroes, and humans – but that is a later development. On this, see also Cohen-Skalli 2012, lxxxii–lxxxvii.
[27] See p. 11f.

genealogically, but also, at least to some extent, spatially. The authors of the catalogues tried to do this while linking their genealogies to the old cosmologies and genealogies of the gods (such as those found in Hesiod).[28] One might, therefore, even call the *Ehoiai* a 'map of the Hellenic world in genealogical terms'.[29] The structuring of local history by reference to the migration fits into this order, at any rate in principle it was supposed to. The heroes and eponymous figures who stand *pars pro toto* for individual groups embody both of these two aspects. It is no accident that these two categories, ancestry and spatial location, are generally the central ones in collective identity and thus also in intentional history.

The ways of representing these migratory movements are rather uniform. The displacements of peoples figure in an older corpus of shared and accepted knowledge; it is knowledge shared by both the producers of the stories – primarily artists, especially singers and poets – and their consumers – the communities and festive assemblies. The oldest narrative stratum that forms the basis of these stories of migration is to be found, for us, essentially in Homer and in the older material one can speculatively extract from the *Iliad* and *Odyssey*.[30] This purported kernel used to be called 'the saga of the heroes'. To some extent some of this material is also accessible in Hesiod's *Theogony* insofar as that work constructs bridges to the world of men.[31] These stories, though, were considered by the Greeks to be fundamental and as no longer subject to radical modification. This invariance stood in a reciprocal relation with the authority of these authors: their authority partly rested on the fact that the stories they told – in their wonderful poetic form – were taken to be fundamental. Despite this position of authority, one could always, however, add to the accounts given in Homer and Hesiod, new or newly found, older versions (or older versions that newly popped up) as supplements, and one could even allow some of these to circulate under the names of the two great authoritative poets. Again, it was a question of 'theme and variations'.

As the examples cited from the corpus of Mimnermos and that of Tyrtaios show, the poems written in this period (around the seventh century BC) had as their subjects and their main actors primarily social groups (tribes, poleis, etc., each with individual religious cult) who were

---

[28] A specific textual link is made by repeating the last two verses of the *Theogony* as the first two of the *Ehoiai*.
[29] Hunter 2005, 1.   [30] Kullmann 1960.
[31] That it does this is controversial from the point of view of historical philology, for instance, in the treatment of the figure of Latinos in verse 1013, although he is documented as appearing, at any rate, in the *Ehoiai*. See Hesiod fr. 5 Merkelbach/West.

contemporaries of the authors of these poems. The poets tried to connect stories about these groups with tales about older groups, especially groups that could be considered the ancestors of their contemporaries. The poets adjusted the various different versions of the tales they knew and put them together to form new stories; partly, they relied on material that already existed, which they simply took over, but partly, in fact overwhelmingly, they created new versions of the stories, assimilating them to contemporary events, and, of course, introducing new names. They constantly tried to re-organise the stories into new constellations, so as to maintain consistency among them. These constellations could be multiplied *ad infinitum*, just as the variants of individuals stories on which they were based were infinitely numerous. Poets developed various methods that allowed them not to play one version off against another (in order, for instance, to separate a 'correct' one from an 'incorrect' one), but to let them co-exist peacefully side by side, or even to allow all of them to mesh with one another.[32] This process continued to take place throughout the whole period, which is what allows us now to do a kind of archaeology of mytho-history, distinguishing the older from the newer variants. In favourable circumstances, this even allows us to determine the date at which a certain variant arose and the political and social context in which the integration of new versions took place.[33]

Under such circumstances, it was possible for larger complexes of stories to arise whose plots overlapped to such an extent that they formed a narrative and historical sequence (or at any rate something that was taken to be a historical sequence), so that, for instance, something that might look like a causal chain could emerge.[34] I would like now to illustrate

---

[32] Gregory Nagy (1986) has shown how this could work in his analysis of Pindar's First Olympian. In this poem, we find a substitution: instead of recounting the myth of Pelops' dismemberment, Pindar tells of his abduction by Poseidon. This substitution, he says, 'as represented in *Olympian I* is in fact a poetic expression of a pre-existing fusion of two myths, where the earlier myth is officially subordinated to, but acknowledged by the later myth' (71f.).

[33] West (1985, 133) was able to do this kind of analysis even of the *Ehoiai*, for instance, explaining the claims that Sikyon was a son of the Athenian Erechtheus as resulting from the influence of the pro-Athenian tyrant of Sikyon, Kleisthenes. For further (later) examples, see Mavrogiannis 2003; his examples are drawn from the domain of Roman literature, but it was structured according to the same principles, which just shows how massively Greek conceptions were adopted by the Roman elite. See also Gehrke 2005b on Elis and the Eleans, and also Di Goia 2011, and now especially Franchi 2016 on the Phokians.

[34] The specific account given here follows Prinz 1979, 346f. In general, see Prinz 1979 *passim*, for instance 258, 269, and especially 294 (on Herodotos) and 308–13 (on the Heraclids). Busolt 1893, 203f. has reconstructed the Dorian Migration, following the ancient sources, primarily Herodotos; one can read this as a summary of the way the Greeks imagined this event: the Dorians under Deukalion lived in Phthiotis, as was appropriate, given that they were the authentic Greeks

by examining a few particularly important examples how such complexes of stories connected events and people with each other, how the various versions then took account of and accommodated each other, and how they interacted. We shall first consider the Homeric Achaians, whose name is used in older epic as a collective term for all the Greeks. Originally, that is, in the period of time in which later stories were located (particularly the stories about migrations), the Achaians were described as occupying a correspondingly large territory, including the whole of the Peloponnese.[35] However, in historical times and even in the period in which the stories about the migration arose, the Peloponnese had an overwhelmingly Dorian population.[36] Only in the north were there areas occupied by Achaians, who were by that time considered to be a distinct subgroup of the Greeks, an *ethnos*, which, as we would (etically) see it, had nothing in common with the Homeric Achaians beyond the name, but who for the ancients Greeks themselves (emically) were (or at any rate might be) the very same as their Homeric namesakes.

The Greeks then recognised that something had happened with the population of the Peloponnese, and they looked for a mytho-historic explanation of it, namely through telling stories of huge and complex displacements of populations, resulting from large-scale migration and also the idiosyncratic wanderings of smaller groups and individuals. There are very different variants of the stories they told, although each one was internally consistent. Most of these stories included episodes of violence, especially forcible expulsions, which, in turn, gave rise to further whole sequences of complex events. Simplifying enormously, one could summarise them in this way: The Dorians migrate, as we have seen, into the Peloponnese. Under pressure from them, the Achaians retreat northward and, in so doing, drive out the Ionians who were living there, that is, in the region that then and also later was called Achaia. Then some Ionians, who had lived in Pylos in the Western Peloponnese but were driven out,

---

(see p. 50f); under the leadership of Hellen's son Doros they moved to Hestiaiotis, but were driven from there by the Kadmeians and eventually they reached Mount Pindos, where the name *Makednon ethnos* was applied to them; then they moved to Dryopis and shortly thereafter to Doris; from Doris they finally reached the Peloponnese.

After this, there were also some further migrations. They expelled the Lelegians from the islands of the South Aegean (Busolt 1893, 183, 185) and settled in Crete (Busolt 1893, 326–8) and on the islands of Melos and Thera (Busolt 1893, 352–4); on Rhodes as a special case, see Prinz 1979, 78–97, 217–21.

[35] Prinz 1979, 346. On the similar problem of the relation of a 'historical' population to a 'Homeric' one (to be sure, with a different name), namely, the Eleans and the Epeians, see Gehrke 2005b, 27–41.

[36] On this, see Busolt 1893, 190, 192 n. 2.

joined forces with the Achaians. The whole group of them emigrated to Asia Minor; in some later versions, they did this via a detour to Athens.[37] This is the way the complex patchwork of interconnected effects came about – the final distribution of populations – in a sequence that followed the logic of pushing and being pushed.[38]

Apart from the Trojan War, which remained, as we have mentioned, the central event in Greek mytho-history, two further large-scale events, or complexes of events stood out in mythic versions that, however, were taken, from as early as the seventh century BC, to be history (and thus were part of Greek intentional history). These were the Dorian and the Ionian Migrations.[39] These were essentially processes of settlement and colonisation, usually in conjunction with expulsion of the indigenous inhabitants. They, too, constitute turning points in early Greek history as they themselves viewed it. If one wanted to map the Greek past as it appeared in intentional history, it would appear as a grid with one horizontal axis – the Trojan War – and two vertical axes – one each for the Dorian and the Ionian Migrations. The result would be far from being anything like a Cartesian co-ordinate system, but it would allow a kind of rough-and-ready localisation of events, for instance, 'three generations after the Trojan War', in the historical line that (eventually) passed through the Ionian Migration. As has already been emphasised, these events were used as natural markers even as early as the time of Tyrtaios and Mimnermos.

The mytho-historical stories in their various versions are grafted onto an old stock of legends; often they seem just tacked on without much apparent serious attempt at seamless integration. One can clearly discern a number of different ways in which the connection was made, for instance, by inventing various relations of kinship or ancestry, sometimes of a most ingenious kind.

---

[37] On this, see primarily Prinz 1979, 330, 334 (on Pylos), 338 (on collaboration with the Achaians, in the Attic version of events), 340.

[38] Friedrich Prinz 1979, 206–313 has reconstructed the history in a plausible way, focusing particularly on the example of the Dorian Migration and the later return of the Heraclids to the Peloponnese (as mentioned by Tyrtaios). See also Hall 2002, 80; on the Dorian Migration and the way it was construed, see Malkin 1994, 15–45; Hall 1997, 56–65; Hall 2002, 73–89; Luraghi 2008, 46–61.

[39] On the Dorian Migration, see above n. 38. On the Ionian Migration, see first of all Busolt 1893, 277–317, especially 285, 304–6; Prinz 1979, 314–76 with summary 371–6; here, the *apoikia*-aspect is particularly prominent (see below). On the present state of knowledge about the Ionian Migration, see especially Ragone 1996, 915–21; Hall 1997, 51–6; 2002, 69–73; Kerschner 2006 who makes a definite effort to integrate mythic and archaeological accounts; Cobet 2007, 732–5, and now particularly Crielaard 2009, 46–57.

To take one example,[40] Endymion was the lover of the goddess Selene and as such a prominent figure in Greek legend. His ancestry connected him to the period immediately after the Deluge, because his paternal grandmother was a daughter of Deukalion, but he was also one of the Aiolians because his mother was a daughter of Aiolos, son of Hellen. He also then had a son named Aitolos and thus became the titular progenitor of the historical grouping, the Aitolians. In addition, already in the sixth century BC, we have evidence that he was thought to have connections with Elis, where he had a cult on the site of his purported grave in Olympia. He also, however, had contacts that reached as far as the Latmos-Mountains in Asia Minor, so that, at the end of the third century BC, one could mobilise appeals to this 'kinship relation' in support of the close political alliance between the polis of Herakleia in Asia Minor and the Aitolian League.

In this way, one could construct connections with famous figures, who were then presented as ancestors, or friends and partners of ancestors. So, the Dorians claimed a connection via the Heraclids with the great hero of legends, Herakles himself, who eventually even became a god, and the Ionians could affirm their link with the famous Neleus, father of the aged Nestor, who was very well known from the *Iliad*. In this way, one could try to increase one's prestige and the venerability of one's ancestry.

It was even possible to construe events that came later in the chronology of legend in the same way. These events could be articulated internally into a number of distinct processes, and at least some of these could partly be connected with things that happened in one or another of the migration narratives. At the same time, it was also possible to combine different groups and communities. One good example of this is the story of the settlement of Asia Minor, which was connected with the Ionian Migration, but was then said to have been accomplished by Pylians, Ionians, and Athenians, with a further admixture later of Aiolian and Dorian elements. Finally, a number of highly varied structures arose, which existed side by side with sequences of events that could be univocally located relative to one of the three major landmarks, and which I will now simply list. There was an Aiolian Migration,[41] a Boiotian Migration,[42] a Thessalian Migration,[43] and also

---

[40] On this example, see Gehrke 2005b, 30–3; further, see also p. 63 n. 72.
[41] Busolt 1893, 133–5, 273–5. This is also called an *apoikia* (see passages cited by Busolt, 1893, 277 n. 1). On the state of recent research, see Hall 2002, 67–73; Hertel 2008, 187–93 (with emphasis on the archaeological record); Rose 2008.
[42] Busolt 1893, 171f, 249f, 255–9. For the state of recent research, see Kühr 2006, 264–9.
[43] Busolt 1893, 243–9; on early Thessaly in general see Helly 1995 and Calce 2011, 113–5.

migrations of other groups. With these events, one could explain the distribution of populations in the northern part of Asia Minor and in North and Central Greece, and there was the added advantage of connecting the population map with the older legends. Just as in the case of the Achaians, here, too, differences between the various groups and the areas of their settlement that existed between the various layers of the myths and legends could be explained by reference to the facts about migration and the conquest of land.[44]

The special case of the Argonauts[45] merits attention, as do the stories about the return home of the heroes from Troy, the *nostoi*. The tales about these adventures arose very early, but the events they describe stood at the end of the period when the chronology implicit in the legends was worked out, a chronology that itself became more and more complex and highly structured as time went on. These narratives about Greek migrations were finally even applied to and used to classify non-Greek populations. Thus, Herakles in the west or Odysseus and Diomedes in Italy were said to have had liaisons with various native women, and to have had several Italian tribes and peoples as their offspring; in this way, the existence and ancestry of those groups could be explained by being incorporated into the Greek narrative.[46] Since they thereby found a place in the imaginary space of the Greek past, they were not in principle radical 'Others'. In the same way, for instance in the *Ehoiai*, other 'barbarian' peoples were anchored genealogically in the world of Greek heroes, as names like Aigyptos, Arabos, and Phoinix attest.[47]

The same thing was true of groups that were considered to have constituted the aboriginal population or an older layer of settlers, such as the above mentioned Pelasgians or the even more mysterious Lelegians. An essential and even more consequential link was also made between the Pelasgians and the Thyrsenians, that is the Etruscans. The two people were even to some extent identified, which led to tales about their migration that were exceedingly complex and difficult to follow.[48] Something similar is the case with the Lelegians and the Karians, and about the internal

---

[44] On this issue, see in general Ulf 1996b, 250–71; on Asia Minor, see the survey in Marek 2010, 160–1 with further references. Marek also relates the stories of migration and the foundation of settlements with the archaeological evidence.
[45] Busolt 1893, 186f; Zahrnt 2012 with further references gives the current state of research.
[46] The fundamental works are Malkin 1998 and Giangiulio 2010a, but see also Biraschi 1996; Maddoli 2000/2013, and Erskine 2004.
[47] Fr. 127, 137–40 Merkelbach-West. On moveable heroes, who to that extent function as figures who cross boundaries, see Gehrke 2005c.
[48] Busolt 1893, 172–85, for newer research see, for instance, Drews 1992.

relations different Karian subgroups had with each other.[49] The Phoenicians are also particularly important here, who, as is well known, had been integrated directly into Greek mytho-history by virtue of their role in the central founding myth of the city of Thebes.[50]

In the second part of this chapter, I would like to discuss how significant constructive transformation and literary reshaping were for Greek mytho-history. What did it mean for the structuring of the content of the various narratives that they were the work of artists? How did the professional aesthetic training and orientation of those who produced these narratives influence the resulting stories? To what extent were these poets able to express what were widely shared experiences and views? The easiest way to get an answer to these questions is by looking at the patterns and stereotypical motifs that the poets used to ornament, colour, and make plausible their tales. The first thing that is striking is the recurrence of certain narrative structures, primarily concerning the motives of the agents involved in the story but also concerning the way in which events unfold.

Let us take again the two examples of the Dorian Migration (with the return of the Heraclids) and the Ionian colonisation of Asia Minor. As supplements to this, I'll also cite the stories of the settlement of Thera and Kyrene, which are preserved in Herodotos (4.145–67). These stories eventually lead us, in their later segments, into periods of time that we can see as historical and to which we have a certain independent access, and this allows us to supplement Herodotos' account and provides a certain 'external control' on those stories that are, for us, 'pure' myth.[51]

To start, then, with what seem to have been current ideas among the poets on what would constitute plausible motivation for human action, the motives are usually very elementary ones that would arise in the course of normal human interaction: kinship relations, friendship, and potentially conflicting loyalties. One characteristic feature of these is that they are thought to be transmitted from one generation to the next. This is true both of positive relations – such as kinship relations and the solidarity that arises out of friendship – and of negative ones – inveterate enmities and a desire for revenge that could pass down the generations. Both of these could be 'inherited'. Thus, the Heraclids fled from Eurystheus, the mortal enemy of their father, leaving the Peloponnese and taking refuge in Trachis in Central Greece, where a friend of Herakles was ruler, and the descendant

---

[49] Busolt 1893, 183, 185. See also the collective work edited by Rumscheid 2009 and also Hose 2002, 137f.
[50] Busolt 1893, 250, 263–71; for the current state of research, see Kühr 2006, 83–133.
[51] On the analysis, see first of all Vannicelli 1993, 123–48; Bernstein 2004, 171–222.

of Herakles, Tlepolemos, the legendary founder of Rhodes, also took flight because he was afraid of vengeance.[52]

The essential elements in the stories about the foundation/settlement of Thera and of Kyrene also depend on the action of very basic motives that derive from sexuality, kinship relations, and ancestry. The Spartans accepted the Minyans as kin, a relationship that was 'supported' genealogically and was supposedly founded in the common enterprise that their ancestors ('fathers') had undertaken, the expedition of the Argonauts. The two parties confirmed this relationship by marriages, that is, the establishment of new, artificial (but no less powerful) relations of kinship.[53] Here, in this early example, one can already see that the narrative patterns used appeal to modes of behaviour and forms of motivation, which are summed up to be completely plausible and to operate reliably in a wide spectrum of cases. It was hard to find a substitute for this kind of thing because poets did not have enough information about the past that would have allowed them to give any other explanation of what had occurred, and so had to make something up.

There was, sometimes, to be sure, appeal to forms of motivation and concatenations of events that were less elemental. In these cases, the behaviour of the main figures in the story is less motivationally transparent.

Despite this, the narratives about the migrations imagine and represent these actions, too, in exactly the same way – as if the behaviour in question were something that was to be expected or an obvious reaction to the situation. This is a point that is for us historically of great importance because most of the important events associated with the migrations are imagined to a very considerable degree either as acts of direct violence or at least as accompanied by a significant amount of coercion. The migration narratives are about taking possession of land, from which the previous occupants are forcibly ejected. These previous occupants then themselves moved and displaced others, so that a kind of chain reaction could be set off that eventually resulted in the final complex pattern of settlement in the region.

One special feature of the migration narratives is that the occupation of the land is often represented as a return home of the migrants to what was really their original homeland, from which, however, they had been driven out. The return of the Heraclids is a classic example of this, but by no means the only one. The use of this *topos* can not only give a better

---

[52] For details see Prinz 1979, 81f. 217–21, 225.   [53] Herodotos 4.145.3–5.

explanation of events, but it also gives a better justification for the presence of the new arrivals.[54]

Of course, the story of migration and the occupation of new lands was not exclusively one of direct violence, but rather of a wide variety of different phenomena that were in one way or another connected with the use of force, including a wide range of types of blackmail or extortion and the threat of the use of violence.[55] And even resistance to this kind of extortion leads to war.[56] Conflicts also originate when persons or communities offer asylum to those who approach them in the attitude of suppliants (as *hiketai*) when driven out of their homes,[57] a motif that also occurred frequently. It had plausibility because the ritual plea for protection imposed obligations on those to whom it was made. That migrants were often forced to leave their homes is clear in the stories of Thera and Kyrene, which make a point of mentioning that the action of going to found a new settlement was not voluntary.[58]

These instances of direct violence and of the structural use of force show what expectations the Greeks had about what, as a matter of the logic of power, would 'automatically' happen: Someone forcibly exiles other people because he is afraid of their potential power, even if they do not, at the moment, actually have any power. It is simply assumed as uncontrovertibly given that if they did have power, they would use it against him. So Eurystheus follows the principle *principiis obsta* ('Nip things in the bud'); he takes proleptic action against the offspring of his enemy Herakles, whom he takes to be quite literally his hereditary enemies, even when they are children and pose no threat to him.[59] Other cases involve wars that result from upholding the obligations of an alliance that has been forged.[60] If an ally actually comes to one's aid in time of need, this can create ties of loyalty that last over generations.[61]

---

[54] On the Heraclids, see Prinz 1979, 222f; Gehrke 2005a, 33 contains a further example; on the grounds that can serve as justifications, see Gehrke 1994, 240 n. 4.

[55] This is what Eurystheus does to Keyx of Trachis, the old friend of Herakles who has given shelter to Herakles' children. See Prinz 1979, 207, 222.

[56] This explains the war of the Athenians, who supported the Heraclids, against Eurystheus (see Prinz 1979, 233–40).

[57] For instance the Heraclids and the Ionians in Athens, Prinz 1979, 338; on the significance of this motif in tragedy, see Grethlein 2003 and Steinbock 2013, 173–86.

[58] Herodotos 4.150.3, 152.1, 156.3.   [59] Prinz 1979, 207.

[60] This is why the Peloponnesians fight against Hyllos, son of Herakles; Prinz suspects that anachronistically the Peloponnesian League is being invoked in the background, as something which gives plausibility to this mytho-historical detail.

[61] One example of this is the expedition of the Heraclids into the Central Greek region of Doris; Herakles had given aid to the ruler there, Aigimios, who was in fact a son of Doros (Prinz 1979, 209f).

In addition to war, *stasis* (civil unrest/civil war) was a sufficiently frequent and well-known phenomenon[62] that one could count on it being immediately understood as a motivation for action. It is particularly important in the stories about Thera and Kyrene,[63] which contain references to *stasis* in all its various aspects and examples of the various different ways in which it can play itself out. The motives involved are the striving for power and the *hybris* which accompanies it, which are treated as nothing surprising. Nor is it thought to be at all surprising that others show themselves unwilling to accept being subject to their opponents' power and that they prefer to escape this by emigrating.[64] Accounts of the means used to prevail in a *stasis* and of the various actions that can be involved include such well-known things as the use of deception and trickery,[65] cases of taking prisoners, forcible expulsion, and fleeing for one's life,[66] and, finally, *stasis* even can explain why fugitives settle in an unfertile or otherwise marginal area.[67] So, emigration, too is a way of escaping *stasis*,[68] and consequently any new *apoikia* can be taken to be the result of an antecedent *stasis*.[69]

The conclusion then seems warranted that the mechanisms and the 'logic' of power were so widely established and well known that they could be deployed strategically in the narrative to give it enhanced plausibility. This means, too, though, that they reflected the background expectations that contemporary readers would have had on the basis of their own experience.

Narratives are as a rule connected to empirical reality; it is just that they are not necessarily directly reflecting some one given particular concrete case. Rather, they are plausible because of their relation to a constellation – to the kind of thing that people think is, in general, given their experience, likely to happen. In that sense what the story tells belongs to lived experience.

Similar things could be said about accounts of the general course of events during a migration or the process of settling in a certain region: for migration, too, certain structural features recur and dominate the narrated sequence of events. In this case, it is the founding or organising of a colony that is the model. This is expressed even in the choice of the technical word used to describe what happened during migrations: one speaks of *apoikia* or even simply of *polis*. It is especially noteworthy that the concept

---

[62] Compare this account with Gehrke 1985, 214–20, 224–35, 238–40, 332–9.
[63] As Frank Bernstein 2004, 171–222 shows. [64] Herodotos 4.146.1, 147.4.
[65] Herodotos 4.146.3f. [66] Herodotos 4.162f. [67] Herodotos 4.146.4. [68] Herodotos 4.148.2.
[69] Herodotos 4.160.1.

of *mētropolis* ('mother city') is used here even when no city in the strict sense is involved. The region in Central Greece that was just mentioned and which plays such an important role in the Dorian Migration, Doris, is described by Herodotos (8.31) as the 'mother city of the Dorians', although in the same breath it is called, not a *polis*, but a *chorē* or a *gē*, which means 'region' or 'territory' (and which is in fact the more correct designation of it).[70] In these colonial contexts, the figure of the 'founder' (*ktistēs*, *oikistēs*) has a particularly important, in fact essential, place.

Here, one could try to orient oneself on the solid and, in our sense, 'historically documented' facts. There were ways of proceeding in founding colonies, and we know about them: Colonies (*apoikiai*) had as a rule *realiter* an individual founder, the leader of the expedition that set out to settle the place and the first organiser of its social and political life. There was even, as we saw in Chapter 1, a material and ritual form of remembrance of him, because he was usually venerated in a religious cult as the 'founding hero' (*hērōs ktistēs*) of the place in question. Such a figure is present, as a type, as early as the *Odyssey* (6.4–10) in the form of Nausithoos 'a man like the gods'. This hero led the Phaiakians away from the unsociable proximity of the uncivilised, but powerful Cyclops and had brought them to Scheria: 'far away from men who eat bread, [he had driven] a wall about the city, and built houses, and made the temples of the gods and allotted holding' (trans.Lattimore). This is what an *oikistēs* would traditionally do.

The figure of the *oikistēs* results from the kind of individualisation that is a well-known phenomenon in other parts of myth, too, and which has already been mentioned: the hero, especially when he is eponymous and gives the group its name, stands for the group as a whole. So Aiolos, Doros, Ion, Aitolos, etc. stand respectively for the Aiolians, the Dorians, the Ionians, the Aitolians, etc. As a rule, this makes it possible to connect the founders and the groups that take their names from them genealogically, and this can be a way of symbolising, as in the case of the Ionians, the fact of common ancestry but also other kinds of proximity, such as the existence of a network of mutual obligations arising from wider kinship links or simply from relations of friendship.[71] This also permits inferences to be made about older strata in the legends and about which figures had special authority.[72] Greater age, of course, conferred greater prestige. The Greek

---

[70] See also Thucydides 1.107.2.   [71] Prinz 1979, 356–64.
[72] See p. 56; for testimonia about Neleus as the *oikistēs* of Ionia, see Busolt 1893, 305 n. 2 (discussion primarily of Herodotos). Hellanikos provides a good example of the attempt to bring *ktistai* into

settlements in Italy tried to give themselves a 'pre-colonial' history, by claiming a connection with the heroes who returned from the Trojan War.[73] In some cases, renowned lawgivers can appear in the record, as independent figures in addition to the founders of the settlement. They too had a function in the life of the community like that of the founders in that they, too, gave it order.[74] These lawgivers also recur in widely different contexts and the results of their activity were visible in the everyday experiences of members of the groups, so when these lawgivers make an appearance in a specific narrative they increase its plausibility.

One should not overlook the fact that these various figures are not, and are not even imagined to be, genuine tribal ancestors in the biological sense, even when they appear and function as such. Such genuine ancestors existed, of course, as one would expect, given the logic of genealogical organisation, but frequently the eponymous heroes were actually merely the leaders of expeditions, whether these expeditions were motivated by the need to flee from some danger or by a simple desire for conquest.

Then, after the new territory was occupied, they were the 'founders' of the colony. So the 'founder' figures, who were inserted into genealogies retrospectively by poets and singers, could be understood in the same way. Not all these heroes, then, were 'genuine' forefathers, who stood in as cover for real ancestors (in a biological sense), or, for that matter, behind whom one will even find proper cults of ancestors. They rather represent the groups and communities in question themselves, as it were *pars pro toto*. However, here, this trope is construed concretely, as embodied in a real actor. The conflation of literal and figurative usages involved here is difficult for us fully to comprehend, but it is also completely characteristic of these narratives.

---

genealogical order in order to connect them with the 'major events' in history, according to Prinz 1979, 328f. Hellanikos can connect 'Neleus' with the prominent family of the Neleids because two 'Neleus' share the same name. This was a common practice used to make connections and pull together variants in the narrative tradition. See Di Gioia 2011 on Phokos, the eponymous ancestor of the Phokians. In Herodotus (4.147.1) a name for the founder of the colony on the island of Thera is clearly derived from the name of the island (as Studnicka 1890, 61–5 and Busolt, 1893, 353 already noticed). Herodotos then gives him a complete family tree, which provides him with roots in one of the older strata of Theban mytho-history, with Polyneikes, Oidipous, Laios, Labdakos, and, finally, the Phoenician Kadmos as ancestors.

[73] See p. 57; see also especially Maddoli 2000/2013, 67.

[74] Consider, for instance, Aigimios, mentioned earlier as lawgiver of the Dorians. He was the model for Dorian order in general, as is clear from his prominence in the story of Hieron of Syracuse and the foundation of Aitna; see Pindar's 1st Pythian, 61–6; see also Prinz 1979, 255f; Dougherty 1993, 83–102. On the interpretation, see also Fränkel 1962, 516–27. On traditional narratives about lawgivers (using Lykurgos as example), see Nafissi 2010, 89–93 (with further references).

This indicates, too, that these heroic figures had not been venerated in the form in which we know them from time immemorial, but rather were essentially constructed *ex post*, and that it is the new communities – that is, the poets and singers in living contact with these new communities – who took the initiative here.[75] In addition, these communities, even if they are partly held together by bounds of loyalty arising from kinship and common ancestry, should not be conceived as being mere groupings of families, nor as derived from any such groupings. This remains true even in cases in which the community in question was thought to be of great antiquity. *Mutatis mutandis* one can apply to all of these groups what Alfred Heuß said[76] about Greek tribes:

> Tribes in this sense do not retain their characteristic form and identity by virtue of the fact that they cling stubbornly to a common stock of old traditions, but rather they are nourished by the living use of common imaginative patterns to interpret the present, and also by the strength of the self-confidence with which the states that formed the tribe identify with it, and the strong confidence with which the representatives of these states identified with the 'tribe'.

The actors in these early narratives – who had a status which mutated easily from that of ancestor, to that of founder, and to that of eponymous hero – were an extremely varied group. There were the old legendary heroes who could be found in the traditional sources, but these could be supplemented artificially by invented figures *in infinitum*. One could create and elaborate them in a completely perspicuous way, by starting with the particular groups, cities, or institutions with which they were to be associated and projecting from there. The central figures in the narrative then could function almost indifferently as ancestors, name-givers, eponymous heroes, lawgivers, and founders, or rulers and informal leaders. The most common case, which, precisely because of its frequency, gave rise of a particularly sharply defined type, was one in which the eponymous hero was the leader of a warlike expedition that set out to found a colony.

The religious aspects, which play such an important role in these myths, indicate how massively the model of colonisation determined their

---

[75] The role of the community is clearly visible in the stories about Thera and Kyrene, especially with regards to the way the Spartans treated the Minyans (Herodotos 4.145.3–5), and in the inter-communal relations between the old and the new settlers in Thera (Herodotos 4.148.1). It is characteristic that the kinship relation between Spartans and Minyans is not enough and that the Spartans must 'make a formal decree' that the Minyans are part of their community and then further cement this with marriages (Herodotos 4.145.5).

[76] Heuß 1946, 33.

narrative structure. The stories showed how close was the relation between colonisation, force, and violence. Concretely, this meant murder, manslaughter, and grievous bodily harm – usually the shedding of blood. Bloodshed, however, was religiously problematic because it constituted a case of pollution (*miasma*). If no purgation took place, the consequence would, according to the then current conceptions, be punishment by the gods, which would take the form of natural catastrophes, failed harvests, and some similar otherwise inexplicable phenomena. To free oneself from these there would have to be a formal purification from the *miasma*, which otherwise could, as an unexpiated outrage (*agos*), have an effect for generations to come, as is shown to happen in the story of the foundation of Thera.[77]

Against this background, it was tempting to construe emigration or mounting an expedition to found a colony, or even the whole process of the Dorian or Ionian Migration, as an attempt on the part of the figure who was the leader of the enterprise to purge blood-guilt or as an attempt to avoid the punishment that could be expected for some misdeed.[78] In general, there is a strong cultic-religious component in the storylines and in the topos-based set-pieces that recur again and again in these narratives.[79] Blood-guilt introduces the themes of *miasma* and thus also of possible purification into the narrative, which means, in turn, that oracles come to be relevant; before all others, of course, the Oracle at Delphi. This is very clear in the stories that clustered around the foundation of Kyrene.[80]

In any case, one cannot overestimate the significance of oracles in these stories about migration. They were particularly important in prescribing what rules had to be followed, when someone was planning a migration or an expedition to settle a new region, or, indeed how one had to act, if one was forced to undertake one of these. To discover what had to be done, one asked the oracle. The primary questions were the choice of the leaders of the expedition (*ktistai*) and what place would be appropriate for settlement. The replies, as was not at all unusual, and thus almost to be expected, usually comprised mysteriously formulated injunctions, which, predictably enough, were often misunderstood. Such misunderstandings were then fertile breeding grounds for further complications and conflicts. Since an incorrect interpretation meant that in the end the divine

---

[77] Herodotos 4.149.1f.
[78] For instance, the blood-guilt of Tlepolemos, see the version in Prinz 1979, 208–10.
[79] On this, see Dougherty's (1993, 15–82) schemata; see also Bernstein 2004 with instructive examples, especially on flaws and purification, and the place both of these had in everyday life.
[80] Herodotos 4.150.3, 155.2; see also Bernstein 2004, 178.

injunctions were not followed, this meant that a new layer of religious transgression was added to the mix, a transgression which, of course, itself needed, in turn to be expiated.[81] This was a point at which motifs and forms derived from fairy tales might enter into the story.[82] These motifs are present in other places, too – in the case of Kyrene there is even a wicked step-mother[83] – and this only strengthens the impression one gets that these narratives often operated with *topoi*. In particular, the figures of founders like Battos of Kyrene, came to be utterly overgrown with a thick layer of legend.[84]

We cannot give any kind of clear account of the groups or socio-political communities who were involved in the migrations for whom the various founder-figures stand, because we have no information about their internal structure. Their names, though (Thessalians, Achaians, Aitolians, Phokians, etc.) frequently converge with those given to groups that we have reason to believe were originally ethnically organised; that is, they were tribes and segments of tribes, in the Greek sense of the word 'tribe' (*ethnos*). We can then assume that those who produced and consumed these narratives thought of them in this way too. However, as already indicated, we cannot connect these actors in mytho-history with concrete historical units, that is, with tribes in the real sense. Frequently, to be sure, there are clear points of contact between these mytho-historical groupings and later historical groups, as we have seen in the identificatory use of 'we' by the Spartan Tyrtaios (which has been mentioned already more than once) and by the Kolophonian Mimnermos. So, we must construe the group-agents of intentional

---

[81] One example is the misunderstanding on the part of the Heraclids about the three generations or the riddle of the three-eyed Oxylos (on the story see Prinz 1979, 208–12); see also, in general, Dougherty 1993, 45–60, and also Prinz 1979, 256, 299–309.

[82] See Käppel 1999, 648; also Hölscher 1989, 27–34 on the *Odyssey*, both of them with references to further literature.

[83] Herodotos 4.154.2–5.

[84] Battos (Herodotos 4.154f.) combines elements of the fairy tale and of legend, see Bernstein 2004, 204. The same is true for the Tyrant of Korinth Kypselos (see Giangiulio 2010b, 128–31). Kypselos is turned into a hero by embellishing the stories, particularly of his birth, with all kinds of motifs from fairy tales. Some of them are derived from oriental sources, and some are things that are ascribed to him *ex eventu* which are then projected back into the past in the guise of oracles. The story of Kypselos is also part of the intentional history of the tyranny in Korinth, in the context of the history of the polis. This whole historical sequence is interwoven with the history of Delphi, which was something that gave the tyrant a higher religious sanction. This makes it obvious that one cannot simply classify this narrative as 'fairy tale' despite the presence in it of motifs that really belong in fable. Giangiulio (2010b, 128) makes this clear when he writes: 'The birth story of Kypselos is not mere folklore but an oral tradition which granted a new statute to its protagonist in the cultural context of the times.'

history primarily from the point of view of the time that was the present for those who wrote about them.

It is, however, also a striking property of these narratives that a tribal, ethnic form of organisation was by no means an essential defining feature of the actors, because exactly the same kinds of statements are made about members of tribes and inhabitants of poleis – especially the Athenians and the poleis in Asia Minor – without any distinction being made between them. Just as Doris is sometimes called 'mother city' and sometimes a 'region', so, too, there is no distinction made between polis and tribe; mytho-history does not recognise a difference at all. Poleis act like tribes, or like parts of tribes, and they might show an internal structure that followed that of the overarching large-scale tribal groupings, such as the Dorians or the Ionians. To put it differently, the groups that appear here represent virtually any point on the broad spectrum of forms of political organisation that existed in Greece. This spectrum could, to be sure, also, more or less, be construed as being organised according to criteria of kinship, but kinship was never an exclusive organisational category, or indeed one that was uncontroversial. This is shown by the strong internal conflicts that existed within the Dorian tribe, especially, for instance, in the war of the Spartans against the Messenians, conflicts that were inscribed in the very heart of Greek mytho-history.

The references to well-known practices and contemporary experiences, to things that were commonplace and familiar, reveal another aspect of the interlacing of past and present, which we noted in Chapter 1 as a particular characteristic of Greek intentional history. This tight connection made it easier for poets to treat the space of the past in a literary way that could, however, also, one might almost say, be highly routinised, and it also gave their various stories and variants on stories, no matter how free their particular individual form, greater plausibility. One might even speak of a 'logic' here that governed the construction of narratives. This becomes particularly noticeable in cases in which poets simply and visibly projected the present back onto the past, onto the *status nascendi* of some contemporary state of affairs or institution.

Obviously, important sanctuaries, which were often trans-regional in their appeal, played a significant part in this process. This was especially true in the case of the Panionion with the cult of Poseidon Helikonios in Mykale.

As we have seen, the early Greeks used elementary genealogical and kinship categories as their framework of thought about the structure of the world.

Starting from this point, it was also natural for them to think that the common cult that was practised there by all Ionians was based on their common origin, that is the common ancestry of the Ionians. They constituted a community united by a common fate: they had all had to migrate to Asia Minor.[85] The divine *epiklēsis*, Helikonios, was of great use here because it permitted a link to be made with another place of a similar name; Helike in Achaia. This was sufficient to claim a relationship and then to pour that into the mould of a story of migration: the Ionians came from Helike.[86] This shows a second method, in addition to backward projection, for creatively producing mytho-history: performing operations on names, and especially with similar names, but in such a way that no permutation or combination was in principle excluded.

Derivation of the name of a hero or a founder from the name of the group that was acting, as a rule a group that continued to be well known later, or derivation from the name of a locality (Aitolos from the Aitolians, Phokos from the Phokians, Perinthos from Perinthos, Theras from Thera) were particularly easy to do and thus widespread. This is a case of individualising retrojection, where, from our point of view, the chronological sequence was reversed: the hero who gave his name to the tribe, or of some other group of actors, and was considered to be its leader, is invented on the basis of the name of the group, and this person is then thought to stand for that group *pars pro toto*. In this way, one could extrapolate to the community that Tyrtaios thought existed between the Heraclids and the Dorians, whose founding heroes were Hyllos, Pamphylos, and Dymas, on the basis of a backward projection of the Dorian socio-political units that existed later, the *phylai* of Hyllians, Pamphylians, and Dymans.

However, one must not misunderstand this obvious and easily visible willingness of the Greeks to 'construct' their own intentional history/histories.

One must try to understand it relative to the place and the time in which it originated, and that means to think of it as an expression of the conceptions about the past that gave structure to their various identities. In other words, we are thrown back on what was said in Chapter 1 about the social, cultural, and (importantly) communicative context of these narratives. Those remarks reveal what lies behind the constructions and retrojections. Because of the general socio-cultural framework within

---

[85] Prinz 1979, 331; on the current state of research about the Panionion (with special emphasis on the archaeology) see Lohmann 2005, and (differently) Herda 2006.

[86] Prinz 1979, 344; Lohmann 2005, 67f argues that the *epiklēsis* Helikonios does not really have anything to do with Helike.

which these narratives were produced and consumed, the constructive techniques they used reflected very sensitively the ideas that members of the various groups had when they communicated with each other, and they did this on a number of different levels. This resulted, particularly in the sphere of religious cults, in a situation in which different groups and subgroups held and asserted a bewildering variety of different views about who was 'close' to them and who 'far' from them, who 'belonged' and who was 'alien'.

If it is the case that such ideas of what was 'close to us' and what was 'alien' emerge in the tales and myths so clearly that, even now, we can see how they influenced these narratives, then the stories must contain observations and experiences that anyone at the time would (or, at least, might) have made in real life. These similarities and differences were the subject of the continual verbal exchanges, sometimes in the form of poems or stories, which were part of almost any encounter. These would include, for instance, conversations within a circle of friends at a symposium or at a festival, or in the context of a religious cult.[87] A variety of different networks arose in this way from these very different forms of communication and exchange, and they constituted the imaginary, but also the real, space, within which the picture of history that has just been sketched was constructed, using the available materials: everyday experiences, observations, and forms of explanation. The construction took place in a lively interaction between producers and consumers of narrative, singers, active participants, and listeners. Intentional history drew a continuing stream of nourishment from the observations people made in this kind of encounter and it needed to remain plausible to them in that context. So, the connection the Ionians made between Poseidon Helikonios and Helike may seem to us invented and far-fetched, however, it expressed a fact. This fact was the real sense of communality and community that the people who took part in the cult registered, a sense of community that participation in the cult practices only strengthened. In this sense, intentional history does not operate in a vacuum; its songs and narratives were not *l'art pour l'art*.

The fact that intentional history was firmly anchored in real life had further consequences for it, which were and continue to be important, even for modern interpretations of it. Since the myths that are most relevant for Greek intentional history, and particularly the narratives about migration and settlement, all deal with the seizure and occupation of land, with the control of it, and with political dominance, they clearly, in addition to

---

[87] For more extensive discussion of this point (with further references), see Gehrke 2013b.

their stated intention to explain the present by reference to the past, also have another function: to give a deep legitimation of current arrangements. This is shown by the way in which narratives of migration come to be overlain with stories that emphasise that the new immigrants are 'coming home'. 'Coming home', of course, gives a stronger claim to legitimate ownership of the land than simple migration does.

The most important aspect of these narratives, however, was that they created and maintained a collective identity for the diverse groups involved in the migration, by assigning them a firm position in space and a self-image that also gave them a confidence in themselves rooted in the past, or – as we might say, a self-confidence 'derived from history'. This complicated operation could succeed, even if – we would add 'paradoxically' – the 'real' or 'genuine' story about the past was completely unknown or exceedingly obscure. In fact, in that case it could be an even greater success. And, in principle, the stories that were told did not deviate from this model, even when one did know something about what actually happened, as one did (at least partially) about the foundation of Kyrene. This is just what makes these stories part of an intentional history. Here, too, we encounter a circularity in the process of identification because, in extreme cases, the history that was relevant for the identity in question had been created at the same time as and in conjunction with the real processes that placed the members of the group in the very same situation, the situation of being, for instance, all Ionian migrants; yet, the story about the past had made itself, to some extent, independent of that context of origin, and, in the course of transmission, the migrants encountered it as something objective – as 'their history'.

If these narratives actually served their function of explaining and legitimising and of creating an identity, then there was one decisive reason for that, and it lies in the constructive architecture and the internal detail of the stories: it is precisely the commonplace nature of the stories, their extensive use of *topoi* and clichés, and even the not infrequent admixture of elements from fairy tales,[88] which gave them their inner plausibility for people of the time, and thus allowed them to act as explanations and justifications. These stories were – if one looked at them from the point of view of the actors in their own Greek world, with its present and its past – deeply aetiological.

They explained something that existed, such as the origin of and reason for (*aition*) a cult, and did so by reference to the past. In this sense, they

---

[88] On this issue, see p. 66 and, in general, also Dougherty 1993 and Kõiv 2003.

stood on a par with aetiological myths, which in fact also appeared again and again in the stories.[89]

In general, then, one used motifs and patterns of behaviour that were widely recognised in the existing system of values and of valid reasons for action. This applied also to political actions and especially the act of migrating: forcible expulsions and involuntary ejections, violent conflict, murder, and manslaughter almost irresistibly presented themselves as obvious motivations for migration, and then, too, came the established models for migration that applied the schema of colonisation or *apoikia*. This all seemed plausible and even commonsensical, which permits one to conclude, if one accepts the view about the context of narrative that is being defended here, that there was an experiential *fundamentum in re* for this kind of story at the time that was most productive of migration myths, the eighth to sixth centuries BC. People at that time knew that the sort of thing being described actually happened, and thus, in case of doubt or uncertainty when one had no other information, one could slot in a story like the well-known ones, just as one could give specific contour to a fairy tale by adding traditional motifs.

Although I cannot pursue this topic any further here, it should be clear that if the above account is at all correct, this would have very wide-reaching consequences for the reconstruction of early Greek history. There is no point in proceeding as many historians still do and looking for traces of concrete historical memories in the narratives about the wanderings of heroes or about migrations. Or, at any rate, that should not be the primary way of approaching this material. Rather, one should recognise that these tales belong in the first instance to the realm of the imagination and were produced to have their place there. One should read each primarily as a construct, not, to be sure, a completely arbitrary invention, but one which the Greeks explicitly and determinedly used as an instrument to interpret their world in cultural and cultic terms. If one understands the stories in this way, and takes them on their own terms, then one can also see that these imaginative narratives do refer to a particular complex of experiences, but the way in which they refer to it is not concretely historical, but structurally historical.[90] The easy familiarity with which they deploy set-pieces suggests the same conclusion. If one does proceed in the way I am suggesting, what one discovers as the background for these stories is a culture very prone to violence with a high degree of

---

[89] The *aition* for a cult of the Erinyes is given in the story about Thera which Herodotos tells (4.149.1f).
[90] See Kõiv 2003, 30.

mobility, much of it resulting from internal political and social conflicts, and, finally, with a certain clear experience of colonising other places. We have plenty of other sources that confirm this picture, including sources from other cultures.[91]

The fact that the Greeks consciously shaped the space of their past in this way suggests that we can learn something from their narratives *realiter*, regardless of the actual details of the individual events purportedly described. They took these experiences, and the ways of looking at the world and interpreting it that resulted from them, and they repeated and varied them endlessly in different communicative situations, in the most multifariously diverse forms and rituals. This became part of the common stock of their culture, something they took absolutely for granted. What is more, it contributed to making them feel that they constituted a unity, a nation with a distinctive culture and set of religious rites.[92]

---

[91] The Greeks (or, more exactly, the groups mentioned in the ancient sources whom we can identify as 'Greeks', see Rollinger 2011) seemed to the Assyrians to be aggressive seafarers, against whose depredations one had to take protective precautions (a view documented for Tiglat-Pilesar III (744–727); Sargon II (721–705); Sanherib (704–681); and Asarhaddon (680–679)).

See also Haider 1996, 79–95. In Ezekiel (27:13–19) (see also Joel 3:6) they are traders, dealing in bronze wares and slaves, and are mentioned together with Tubal (North Cilicia) and Meshech (Phrygia). (According to Haider 1996, 71, Ezekiel was composed following a Phoenician original about 590; n. 74 gives documentation; see also Crielaard 2009, 42 n. 32 with further references.) In general, they frequently appear as mercenaries (often together with Karians, as in Abu Simbel). See Haider 1996, 91–113 and in general Luraghi 2006. A limited picture emerges, but one which gains depth if one also considers the *Odyssey* and the role which seafaring, piracy, and violence played there, particularly in Odysseus' lying tales.

[92] In this sense Heuß 1946, especially 30–8 (1995 vol. I, 6–14) was path-breaking. See also Walter 2010 on the contemporary context of Heuß' work and Gehrke 2011 for the relation of it to contemporary research (with further references).

CHAPTER 3

Greek Historiography between Past and Present

Up to now, my reflections on Greek conceptions of the past have basically ignored that genre which one would generally think was *the* point of reference for treating this topic, and which is treated as such in scholarly works, namely historiography. I would like, in this chapter, to turn to a discussion of this topic against the background of my remarks in Chapters 1 and 2. In particular, I would like to call to mind one important feature of early Greek intentional history: the context in which these mytho-historical narratives arose and were transmitted was one of public performance by bards, and one important consequence of this was that the artistic and literary dimension of the construction of intentional history was and remained extremely important. The Muses were thought to guarantee not only the elegance and aesthetic properties of the songs that singers and poets created, but also the claim they made to the truth of their narratives.[1] However, there was a fundamental problem that quickly arose in this context, which was already thematised by the poets from the very beginning: there was rarely a single, universally accepted version of any tale. On the contrary, the usual state was one in which many alternative, and potentially rival, versions of any given story were in circulation. This meant that connoisseurs at any rate knew that what the Muse announced was not always unambiguous. The story she inspired could be called into question, in fact, the song, seen from a poetological point of view, could itself raise questions about the account it contained. The Greeks assumed that the gods in general, all of them, could lie and deceive (or at any rate mislead), and this was true of the Muses, too. So, humans could not really rely on what they said.[2]

Recently François Hartog[3] has drawn special attention to this aspect of Greek conceptions about art and truth, illustrating it with an analysis of the

---

[1] Primavesi 2009, especially 106–11.   [2] On this issue, see especially Deichgräber 1952/1984.
[3] Hartog 2003/2012, 77–83.

Demodokos episode in the *Odyssey*. Odysseus, according to Hartog, sees the Muses or Apollo as the 'informants' of the *aoidos*, but says to the bard that he has sung 'too perfectly' (*liēn kata kosmon*), that is, he has sung as if he had been present at the events he described (*hōs pareōn*), or as if he had heard it from another (eyewitness) (*akousas*).[4] Odysseus, who is listening, however, is able (in his capacity, as it were, as consumer) to accept this almost preternatural accuracy by (*gar*) ascribing it to the Muses or Apollo, who inspired the poet, although this would normally be a sign that the narrator was an eyewitness. This is a point that Hartog does not discuss at length.

Even if the audience is pacified by this, the poets themselves now began to focus on the issue. They even very pointedly raised the question of truth and explored it in a literary and poetic way in all its dimensions, even going so far as to give explicit examples of characters telling untruths. The deception speeches of Odysseus flicker between invention (or lies, or, at any rate, camouflage) and truth, so that Uvo Hölscher could write that the poet of the *Odyssey* 'has bizarrely inverted the qualities of truth and mendacity: the lies are what seem to be the truth, whereas the truth seems utter fantasy'.[5] When speaking to his faithful wife, Odysseus 'said much that is deceptive but like the truth' (*pseudea etymoisin homoia*).[6]

One might be able to turn a blind eye to the behaviour of a hero who was so notoriously wily. The problem was that the Muses themselves behaved in exactly the same way. They say as much themselves when they contemptuously greet the shepherd Hesiod, using exactly the same words the duplicitous Odysseus did: 'We know how to speak much that is deceptive, but like the truth (*pseudea etymoisin homoia*), but we also know how to say true things (*alēthea*) if we want to.'[7] 'If we want to': that's a nice guarantee of truth. And poets knew very well about the enchanting and seductive power of what they did and about the game they played on the borderlands between deception and truth: what lovely guarantors of posthumous fame they were.

If one wanted to, one could fall into deep pondering about this. The Greeks, at least some of them, luxuriated in doing exactly that. This is

---

[4] *Od.* 8.487–91. The following account owes much to a lecture by Bernhard Zimmermann in the winter semester of 2012/2013 given as part of a collective lecture series at the Freiburg Graduate Collegium on 'Factual and Fictional Narration'. See now Zimmermann 2015.

[5] Hölscher 1989, 213, see Rengakos in Rengakos and Zimmermann 2011, 129, who cites this passage.

[6] *Od.* 19.203.

[7] Hesiod *Theogonia* 27f. See Kannicht 1980; Pratt 1993 (following references in Figal 2000, 301 n. 3); see Bruner 1998, 61–3 on this kind of ambivalence from the point of view of the history of literature.

what I wish to treat in this section. First of all, though, this deep reflection led to an essential change, in fact, an expansion of the Greek conception of the past and of the way it needed to be articulated. This is the development that will be in the focus of attention in what follows. What eventually emerges into clarity is nothing more, but also nothing less, than a new genre, history-writing as a distinct activity with its own traditions. Even today, we sometimes see ourselves as standing in this tradition.

It goes almost without saying for us that such history-writing must have been *the* medium, or, at least, a central element in the cultivation of the past, the collective memory of the Greeks, but in fact it was rather, in the ancient world, something exceptional. Anthropologists have isolated, studied, and described a multiplicity of forms of collective memory, and their results strongly suggest it is by no means a foregone conclusion that history-writing would even exist in Greece, much less that it would be of fundamental importance. Given the ways in which, as we have seen, Greek mytho-history was created and propagated, even the existence of historiography is a phenomenon that requires explanation.

The proper point of departure for this investigation is clear: the Greeks had a real treasure trove of stories, through which they had knowledge of and came to terms with their past, and these stories had some standing for them – they were not mere idle and arbitrary fantasies – but they also had an open structure so that they could be re-written and also extended if necessary. These stories contained elements from the past and the present, fictional material and true reports, false and correct accounts, all of them complexly and almost inextricably intertwined in multifarious ways. We must simply accept it as a fact that this bothered only a very few individuals, although the ones who were upset by it were irritated in a lasting way. At the time when history-writing originated, the Greeks already had a history of their own (or an open set of histories of their own) which had found expression in numerous variants in a variety of literary and other forms. The stories they told were well composed, rhetorically polished, and aesthetically attractive, and, as an ensemble, they were well known to everyone, precisely because they were very carefully cultivated and presented. The Greeks were not waiting with bated breath for historiography to arrive in order to have it give them the gift of a past, and, in fact, once it did arrive upon the scene, it was widely ignored. It was probably ignored to the same degree to which the normal population in most countries even today simply fails to take any cognisance of debates within the ranks of historians or of the results that historical science has reached.

As far as its origins are concerned, the writing of history certainly does belong with the above-mentioned modes and genres of memory. To see this, it is sufficient to note how massively these forms of memory, with their deliberate orientation to passing down inherited lore and thus also the cultivation of posthumous glory, actually influenced incipient history-writing. This influence was especially marked in areas like the forms of linguistic expression that early historians used, the verbal artistry with which their accounts were presented, and the narrative structures they deployed.[8] It even became possible to express important components of these 'memories' in prose.[9] These included genealogies, and also, in particular, complex networks of interlocking stories about the foundations of new settlements, heroes – both heroes directly involved in the foundation and older figures who could be appropriated – groups, and institutions and events in the present.[10] We can follow the lead of Felix Jacoby and call some of these prose writers mythographers and genealogists, and we can sometimes trace their history back to the sixth century BC, although the great majority of them belong to the fifth century BC and later. In this way, the traditions recorded in mytho-history became one of the topics treated by the newly emerging prose literature that was developing very rapidly in this period, and with that mytho-history entered the purview of the increasingly professional discipline of rhetoric. At the same time, these traditions continued to be dealt with as an integral part of the various subdivisions of poetry; one can draw a clear line illustrating the way in which historical narrative developed through the various genres, starting from epic, moving through the gradual opening up of other forms, and ending eventually with dithyramb and tragedy. The special and continuing importance of performance is visible in the prominent place that dithyramb, tragedy, and also, the previously mentioned discipline of rhetoric, occupied in ancient society, and precisely because they were able to have such broad effect on the citizens, the significance of such performances was greatly enhanced and its audience became much larger than it might otherwise have been.[11]

---

[8] On this, Boedeker 1996 and Rengakos 2006 are especially instructive, but they stand in the place of many others who could also have been mentioned. On Herodotos see Pohlenz 1937, and see p. 84 n. 37, 92 n. 61.

[9] Felix Jacoby 1949, 202 already pointed out that the panhellenic epic, that is, the main representative of this mytho-history was the 'main source' for the early history of the Greeks.

[10] Strabo (1.2.6) mentions that the oldest relevant prose authors (he specifically names the completely legendary Kadmos, but also Pherekydes and, interestingly enough, Hekataios) had really done nothing but 'free themselves from the demands of metre', and otherwise had proceeded exactly the way the poets always had done.

[11] The observations and reflections of Grethlein 2010 point in this direction; also Chapter 4.

A new, in fact, totally new, element entered upon the scene, however, as a result of developments in Ionia. There, philosophy and *historiē*, two enterprises that initially had nothing to do with memory or history, arose and began to flourish in the sixth century BC.[12] These projects originally were concerned with asking about and looking for the *archai* of nature, with measuring and counting, with constructing and harmonising, and with forms of critical judgement that applied rules of rationality and were reflectively acceptable to human subjectivity. The fragments of Xenophanes of Kolophon (c. 565–470 BC),[13] among others, show to what extent questions about the gods and dissatisfaction with the way in which they had been portrayed up to that time, and also problems about how to distinguish truth and certainty from appearance and mere opinion, played a role in the development both of philosophy and of *historiē*. In this milieu, a further question arose, and this concerned the deceptive aspects of poetry – the rip that runs through the fabric of mytho-history from as far back as our knowledge of it reaches. The new Ionian thinkers were no longer satisfied just to listen to the stories of the bards; rather, they took it upon themselves to tread a new path, the path of *historiē*, on which 'in the course of their seeing, asking questions about what they had seen, and reasoning about it, they found themselves pushed forward to ever new discoveries'.[14] The intellectual who engages in mental gymnastics while asking and trying to answer questions that do not have any immediate practical point is not just a literary invention of later times – think of the story about the Thracian slave girl who laughed at Thales. Rather, such types existed and distinguished themselves from the mass of the population who were less gifted at this kind of speculation and also had no interest in it. The type was decidedly elitist.

The first man who is known to have undertaken the study of geography and history, and thus to have entered the domain of memory, while also being motivated by all the concerns mentioned above and attempting to follow all the rules just sketched, is Hekataios of Miletos. In the first sentence of his work, he expresses the new Ionian attitude very clearly when he writes: 'Hekataios of Miletus says following

---

[12] Von Fritz 1967, a work that now is undeservedly almost forgotten, traces the history of these related developments. One might find in Polybios (9.1.4) a foreshadowing of some of von Fritz's views. Polybios distinguishes in this passage between older historiography (genealogies and *ktiseis*) and the writing of political history.
[13] Especially 21 B 11–16.18.23–26.34–36 Diels and Kranz 1952. These concern the criticism that the Homeric gods are deceivers (B 11f).
[14] Deichgräber 1958, 655.

(*hōde mytheitai*): I write what seems to me to be true, for the stories (*logoi*) of the Greeks are many and ridiculous (*polloi kai geloioi*).'[15] Here, he announces that in his work there is no place for the traditional forms, and he pointedly turns his back on the received ways of cultivating remembrance and on Greek intentional history. Rather, he promises something better, particularly with respect to truth, which singers of old, as we have seen, thought was guaranteed by the Muses, not by the dictates of their own individual judgement.[16] The struggle to attain truth, and a truth that was defined by its distance from mere opinions, superficial views, appearances, and mere surface phenomena, was very clearly in the absolute centre of attention of the theoretical debates that were being carried out at that time.[17]

In the strictly philosophical debate, this had very far-reaching consequences and led to a series of important conceptual changes; even today, one has excellent opportunities to fight about truth and the concept of 'truth' on various levels. Here, however, with the focus on history and what was asserted in various narratives, the question reduced itself to two versions of the same, very simple query: Did what was narrated correspond with the facts? Did what was reported really take place as it was reported to have done, and in the manner reported? A reference to these questions is implicit in Sextus Empiricus' definition[18] that *historia* is 'the presentation of something that is true and that took place'.[19] The analogous case here is the determination of the facts as they really occurred in a court, where the truth of a statement depends on whether or not what is asserted actually took place as asserted.[20] To put it differently, truth here refers not to coherence or soundness of argumentation, or to any form of higher insight, but to the correspondence between an assertion and an empirical state of

---

[15] Hekataios FGrH 1 F 1 (see p. 18); see also the very vivid account in Corcella 2006, 40–2 of the intellectual background and the methods used (with references to Herakleitos). For Hekataios' significance at the beginning of this new direction, see Bertelli 2001, and the more sceptical treatment in Nicolai 1997; 2007, 17. On the role of Xanthos (especially in relation to Herodotos), see the important comments by Schepens 2007, 46 and also von Fritz 1967, vol. II, 348–77.

[16] For the persistence of this methodological approach in Greek discussions of historiography, see Plutarch, *Theseus* 1.5, and also Chapter 4.

[17] On this, see the references in Gehrke 1993, 11f.   [18] *Adversus mathematicos* 1.263.

[19] The example that Sextus immediately uses for 'something that is true', namely the murder of Alexander the Great by poisoning, shows how difficult it is to discover the truth in the sense of finding out 'what really happened' in detail; but Thucydides already knew that (Gehrke 1993, 9–12). On this aspect of the relation between truth and history, see Walbank 1960/1985/2011, 401, with citation of further passages from the literature of rhetoric.

[20] *Dissoi logoi* (90 Diels and Kranz 1952) 4.2: 'Whenever a speech (*logos*) is spoken, if things turn out just as the speech has asserted, the speech is true, whereas if they do not turn out like that, the same speech is false' (Trans.: Laks and Most (Loeb)). See also 4.7.

affairs. To that extent, too, eventually there came to be a difference between philosophy, especially logic and metaphysics, and history or historiography. *In statu nascendi*, though, the two belong closely together, united by the common emphasis on striving for the truth.

Part of the elitist ethos that was shared by these early thinkers was also the competitive struggle against other – a few other – similarly placed and similarly minded grandees. In this struggle, each individual, as is the habit among aristocrats, tried to push the others into proximity with 'the many fools' and so make them look ridiculous. Because the ostensible goal was the truth, the main form of *agon* was the debate, something that was linguistically and conceptually close to a judicial proceeding. Each side tried to subject the opposing position to rational scrutiny (*elenchos*), and in the ideal case, to comprehensive refutation. Parmenides, one of the most radical thinkers of the time, put the following advice in the mouth of a goddess who appears in his poem: '[Let someone try] by argument (*logos*) [to] decide (*krinein*) the much-disputed refutation (*elenchos*).'[21] '*Krinein*', of course, is a word commonly used in legal contexts. It is then also perfectly consistent that the law of contradiction comes into its own here in a way in which it does not, for instance, in poetry. Someone said of Parmenides' pupil Zeno that 'he practiced an attitude of a refutative kind and locked [*sc.* his interlocutor] into an aporia by means of antilogy (*antilogiai*)'.[22]

This way of proceeding did not remain limited to the immediate context of active discussions, that is, to actual live 'performances' of disputation. The medium of writing, which was important in poetry, although it continued to take a back seat to live performance, acquired a new specific function in philosophical (or, in general, in theoretical) debates: what was correct and true was something one argued out, but no longer did the argument have to be oral. Rather, now it was possible to communicate one's views to a wider audience through writing books. The debates between sages came in this way to have a diachronic dimension. Since that time, the virtual community that arose then did not ever entirely disappear and exists even to the present day. One result was that there were

---

[21] 28 B 7.5f. Diels and Kranz 1952. I take *elenchos* here not to mean 'test, examination', as Hermann Diels believes, but to refer to a refutation that has already taken place, that is, I take it as Fränkel 1962, 405 did. Plato *Phaidros* 266e-267a is a confirmation of the view that *elenchos* evokes the context of a court case. On *elenchos* in philosophy, see Figal 2000, 314. Finally, the range of the concept is extended (as is clear in the case of its use by Sokrates) to apply to any structured examination of features of the world or of affirmations.

[22] Plut. Perikles 4.5 = 29 A 4 Diels and Kranz 1952 (Trans.: Laks and Most (Loeb)).

long sequences of arguments, which raged back and forth, and which, depending on what exactly one wished most to emphasise, could be read as a history of progress or, at any rate, of progressive development. How exactly that came about is something one can study by looking at the first book of Aristotle's *Metaphysics*, in which the philosopher gives his own particular twist to the story he tells about his predecessors, by sketching their views on principles and topics of interest to him in sequence, and thereby doing what one must admit is a kind of history of philosophy.[23]

Similar things could be shown about other areas of research and other genres, not least about historiography. Here, too, argumentative and polemical disagreements were endemic. The same topics were taken up again and again, topics that had been treated by predecessors, but which each successive individual tried to show himself to be better able to deal with than they had been. This process took place over very long periods of time – and in some sense it is still taking place today. This is what Jan Assmann had in mind when he spoke of 'hypolepsis'.[24] The whole spirit of competitiveness of Greek intellectuals, including historians, was focused on this aspect of *elenchos*, the continuing critical examination, and, if required – and it is not infrequently required – refutation of given positions, and it was this that permitted such competition to flourish occasionally in a thoroughly ruthless way. *Elenchos* in this sense, then, is central for historians, too.

In the beginning, much of this remained merely implicit, but it was distinct enough, for instance, in Herodotos' remarks comparing Hekataios' attempt to do genealogies with the enormous chronological achievements of the Egyptians, and when Herodotos makes fun of the authors of his time who engaged in cartography – of *gēs periodoi* – he probably had Hekataios in mind because he had produced just such a work. To some extent, Herodotos tries to assign Hekataios' work a place among exactly those *logoi* that Hekataios had found so problematic.[25] A much later representative of the genre is also typical of

---

[23] Aristot. metaph. 1.3.983b7-1.10.993a27. Flashar 2013, 213 shows clearly in what way this is not really a history of philosophy in the proper sense, but rather simply a discussion of topics and problems that interested Aristotle, with citation of the historical views of some other thinkers.

[24] Assmann 1992, 280–5, see also p. 19. In Isokrates or. 11.30 the word *hypolepsis* is used for the process of taking something over from another, but with the intention to criticise it. See Corcella 2006, 53 for an account of the way in which, through this kind of *hypolepsis*, something like progress through the attempt innovatively to surpass one's predecessors can come about (as could already be seen among the poets). See Marincola 1999, 321, in general, for the relation between convention and innovation. Nevertheless, all of this is still far removed from our idea of scientific progress; see p. 125.

[25] 2.143 (on the use of genealogies); where Hekataios appears as a political adviser (5.35. 125f), the impression he makes is more positive, because the advice he gives is based on thorough knowledge of

it, Arrian of Nikomedia (c. 85/90–150 AD). Arrian encourages his readers to consult the works of his predecessors, but he also equates his achievements for Greek literature with what Alexander the Great accomplished for world history.[26]

In the ancient world, each historian kept the work of others under competitive scrutiny, and it is precisely in this respect that ancient historiography comes closest to the intellectual professionalism that is such a mark of modern intersubjective-critical history. The use of modern historical methods results in an increased plurality of accounts (Le Goff 1988, 193, 197f.), but, at the same time, modern historiography uses a particular criterion of 'objectivity' – only that is acceptable which can be intersubjectively imagined and understood (Le Goff 1988, 196). The application of this criterion can lead to a process of successive 'rectification' of claims.[27] This closeness between ancient and modern history has often been cited, and it is perfectly right that it be, even if it is also true that it has not been, the object of much sustained reflection. However, one should not overstress it, for reasons that I shall now try to explain.

The great leap forward in the emergence of historiography arose precisely from the logic of competition which was rooted in those philosophical debates. For a long time before this period, in various of the older and more recent genres that were concerned with the cultivation of memory, practitioners of these genres had learned to draw long continuous lines tracking sequences of events back into the past, and they had also learned how to argue historically by connecting these lines with the present. So, when there were conflicts or competing claims, legal disputes or wars, they could trace the history of the different claims and of the accusations each side made against the other. They knew who had been right and who had started the conflict, who had collaborated with whom, how the densely textured fabric of aggressions and vengeful reactions had been woven. Nonetheless, given the plurality of historical accounts, which we have just mentioned, all

---

the world, and this at the same time gives Herodotos the opportunity to display his own knowledge (5.35); on the *periodoi* see 4.36: on *logoi*, see p. 85 n. 38. That Herodotos calls Hekataios *logopoios* (2.143.1, 5.36, 125) should probably be explained in the same way, given that he also uses this term of Aesop (2.134.3). Thucydides' method seems rather to give his predecessors the silent treatment; he criticises Hellanikos only for a detail (1.97.2) and does not mention Herodotos at all. Comments in the chapter in which he discusses method, which are often taken to be an implicit criticism of Herodotos, should, then, probably be taken differently; see Grethlein 2010, 207–9; on the actual proximity that exists between Herodotos and Thucydides, see also Rogkotis 2006. Generally, on 'the truly polemical spirit' see Schepens 2007, 49.

[26] Arr. Praef. 1.12.5.
[27] Following Paul Ricœur (*Histoire et vérité*, 1955), as cited in Le Goff 1988, 199 and Adam Schaff (*Histoire et vérité*, 1971) Le Goff 1988, 199f.

of this would always have been controversial, because all of those involved could bring forward and draw attention to some other aspect of the historical situation.

Even today, we can recognise and monitor the deployment of these methods, and Herodotos was just as familiar with them as we are. He even speaks about them at the start of his history when he broaches the question of whether or not the great existential war between the Hellenes and the barbarians was really caused by the abduction of some women – and in treating this question he ridicules this way of treating it.[28] In another passage, in the course of a debate he has himself constructed between the Athenians and the Tegeans about which position each of them should occupy in the order of battle at Plataia, he contrasts the methods of historical argumentation we have just seen with a completely different way of arguing.[29] In both of these cases, the present, or at any rate the recent and easily accessible past – we might even say 'contemporary history' – is made directly relevant to the discussion. However, the beginning of Herodotos' history also makes it clear that the need to appeal to the present, to what is close to us in time, arises from a basic heuristic, that is, methodological problem. This problem is inherent in the logic of the way of proceeding to which Herodotos is committed. This procedure is based on individual ratiocination, and the problem is then one about the way in which purported knowledge claims can be justified, given that such knowledge always depends on a subjective factor that is rooted in personal experience. Knowledge rests on immediate acquaintance, the model for which is direct perception (*opsis*), and also on personal judgement and the individual historian's own abilities to discriminate and make a definitive choice among conflicting arguments (*gnōmē*). This last-mentioned faculty is the one that comes to expression in Hekataios' well-known use of the expression *hōs emoi dokei*.[30]

When it comes then to the presentation of the results of research (*historiē*), it is always a question of testimony in a very basic sense: of eyewitnesses or of people who 'heard what was said with their own ears'. Testimony, especially that of an eyewitness, is the guarantor of truth. As early as the *Odyssey* this is true; for instance, Odysseus' comment on

---

[28] Herodotos 1.1.1–1.5.3; on Herodotos' Prooimion in general, see Węcowski 2004.
[29] Herodotos 9.26f.; for further discussion of this passage, see Grethlein 2010, 173–86 and, on Herodotos generally, see Giangiulio 2005, which has a special treatment of the narratological aspects of his work.
[30] Herodotos 1.5.3. See Timpe 1993, 19 who argues that this new approach applies 'in the first instance' to contemporary history.

Demodokos' performance indicates as much.³¹ It was precisely in the intellectual-critical movement in Greek thought, which we have just described (and of which the new historiography was a part), that the importance of the testimony of eyewitnesses came to the fore. When Xenophanes speaks of knowledge, it is 'based on direct observation',³² and Herakleitos remarks in a lapidary way that the eyes are better witnesses than the ears. Characteristically, this quotation is preserved in Polybios' criticism of the 'bookish scholar' Timaios.³³

This very pointed emphasis in epistemology on seeing for oneself with one's own eyes, or at any rate on hearing directly from eyewitnesses (Herodotos I.20) has very significant consequences both for historical knowledge and for historical judgement. For one thing, it restricts the view one can have on the past, concentrating it on the three, or, at most, four generations who are consulted in *oral history*, those who are bearers of 'communicative memory'.³⁴ Consistently with this position and following the criterion articulated in it, then, Herodotos pursues his research into the past as far back as he can go, and ends up with Croesus. History in this sense, that is, which obeys the rules of philosophy and *historië*, of thinking and certainty, must of necessity be contemporary history, or at best history of the immediate past. The genre 'historiography' that was inaugurated in this way, therefore, did not need to engage in complex and indirect processes of trying to imagine and visualise the past, because the past it treated was still very close to – and still in touch with – the present. History, after all, could only be undertaken – the past could only be opened up and understood – on the basis of the living present. If history wanted to be and to remain true to its own best aspirations and pretentions, then it had to remain, even at the deepest level, committed to basing itself on what it could see from the point of view of the present. One might even

---

[31] See p. 74, and see also Hartog 2003/2012, 78f; Schepens 2007, 40; Marincola 1997, 63f gives further examples from epic.

[32] Fränkel 1962, 382 on 21 B 34 Diels and Kranz 1952 (n. 20 for parallels); in general see Fränkel 1960, 342–9.

[33] Herakleitos 22 B 101a Diels and Kranz 1952; Walbank associates this with the gnomic remark which Kandaules makes to Gyges in Herodotos 1.8.2 to the effect that humans trusted their eyes more than their ears. This is why Kandaules has Gyges see his wife naked, which has disastrous consequences for the former, just as Herodotos had announced immediately before telling the story. One might also cite the great emphasis put on seeing as a means of knowing at the beginning of Aristotle's metaphysics (1.1.980a21-27).

On the importance of *autopsia* see Reichel 2005, 58 (with citations in n. 53) and also the fundamental article of Schepens 2007.

[34] Vansina 1985; Assmann 1992, 48–52; Foxhall 1995, 133–5. On the historical dimensions of Herodotos, see especially Vannicelli 1993, 13–6, also Corcella 2006, 45f. On the role of grandparents in traditional societies in this connection, see Connerton 1989, 39 (with further references).

wonder, then, whether Herodotos could himself at all be called a historian. And, given this background, it was not at all implausible to deny that he was.

That, to be sure, upon closer inspection, would be a completely unjustified step to take. Herodotos is fully committed to the new method[35] and he knows perfectly clearly that he is, but this does not lead him to throw the past overboard, in fact, quite the reverse. The way in which he immediately turns to Croesus, after discussing the various claims about the historical abduction of women at the very beginning of his work, does not represent a complete repudiation of the *spatium mythicum*.[36] He carries forward the older forms of memory with him, and, despite the new approach he adopts, he does not restrict himself to discussing the new and that which he can directly investigate. Or perhaps one might say that he extends the concept of that which he can immediately investigate to include the dimension of what people can *tell* him, their *logoi*. We have every reason to add that it is fortunate that he did so. The reason for his decision is that his primary interest in any case was not research for its own sake, but preservation of the past, or, perhaps more exactly, saving it from oblivion (*mē exitēla genētai*).

With that, in any case, he reveals himself very clearly to be a historian, and at the same time takes up a position very close to the project pursued in the epic (and then later in other forms of literature), namely the cultivation of posthumous glory. He says as much *expressis verbis* when he announces that he writes so that the great achievements of men might 'not be without glory' (*akleā*). Therefore, part of the subject of his research is that which people in the past used to say and what they recounted about what lay in the deeper and deeper past. The *logoi* of the Hellenes (and of other groups) are not (generally) rejected, as Hekataios announced his intention of doing. If one wants to put it that way, in Herodotos one finds a compromise between the old intentional history and the modern, critical, research-based kind of history.[37]

---

[35] Rosalind Thomas 2000 has described in great detail how far that commitment reached.
[36] As Klaus Nickau 1990, 91–7 has shown. Vannicelli 2001 has described how this large historical space was organised; see also now Bichler 2013.
[37] For lines of argument similar to the one presented here, albeit with slightly different accentuation, see Candau Morón, González Ponce, and Chávez Reino 2004; Stadter 2004; Calame 2006; Rutherford 2012 (who includes a treatment of Thucydides); Wesselmann 2011 puts particular emphasis to the pre-given structures of narrative with which Herodotos would have been confronted. The collective volume Giangiulio 2005 gives numerous individual examples; see also Biraschi 1989 for further discussion.

It seems to me that Herodotos was fully aware of this and even expressed it rather clearly: as a reporter, and thus a narrator of his own *historiē*, he writes down the opinions that are now current about the past, the *logoi*, too, that go back to earlier periods. He, however, does not guarantee the correctness of any of these, as can be seen in the example of his discussion of the reasons why Argos did not take part in the struggle against Xerxes, a discussion which focused on the mytho-historic kinship relations that were supposed to have existed between the Argives and the Persians. These kinship relations were established using a thoroughly traditional form of argumentation.[38] Herodotos did, however, take a position on the further reaches of the past when it was a question of something that fit into his central subject matter, the relation between Hellenes and barbarians.[39] In addition, he undertakes to give interpretations of the past from the point of view of the present, and brings it about that the past sheds light on the present, so he offers his readers his own version of the interlacing of past and present.[40] In any case, he is of the opinion that historical events must be over and closed for them to develop their full didactic effect.[41] So, he took what was in effect a middle position. He did not oppose the traditional and intentional view and find it completely alien to his project. Rather, he attempted to integrate it, just as he tried to appropriate its linguistic and narrative forms.[42] This is by no means the least of the reasons for the attractiveness of his work.

To be sure, the critical-rationalist method constitutes the epistemic foundation of his work, too. He is following it when he tries to give as precise as possible a specification of the basic chronology of events, at least of those that took place within his chosen time frame. Here, the work of Hermann Strasburger remains the starting point for further research, as recent treatments continue to confirm.[43] Herodotos also makes use of the new approach in his critical examination of very old narratives, especially when he demonstrates that they cannot be correct because what they recount is chronologically impossible.[44] The same thing is true for the spatial dimension. Herodotos was well acquainted with the new way of viewing the world to be found in Ionian geography, and he tries to include

---

[38] Herodotos 7.152. He equally keeps his distance when the discussion turns to Hekataios' account of one mytho-historical event, the expulsion of the Pelasgians from Attica. Herodotos' predecessor, then himself moves over to a position very close to that of the *logoi* that he finds problematic, see p. 18, 77f.
[39] Nickau 1990, 91–7.   [40] Raaflaub 2002, 21.   [41] Grethlein 2009, 215.
[42] See the references above p. 76 n. 8, 86 n. 37, and in general also Proietti 2012b.
[43] Strasburger 1956/1965/1982; see also Vannicelli 1993, 13–6; Bichler 2013, 23–6.
[44] A nice example: 2.134.1 (*ouk orthōs legontes*).

it in his *elenchos*.⁴⁵ Beyond all this, with his researches into the past, he also wanted, and especially, to influence current politics and contribute to increasing his readers' ability to understand and judge it – he wanted to shift attitudes in the direction of greater rationality and greater reflectiveness.

In general, one can see Herodotos using very particular argumentative structures (in addition to the ones from chronology mentioned above) when he is investigating older events that cannot be studied through *opsis* but are accessible through narratives, but only through narrative – through *logoi*, that is *akoē*.⁴⁶ There had been intensive discussion of a famous event in late archaic history, the destruction of Sybaris, whose prosperity was legendary, by Kroton, and of the circumstances surrounding this event. The arguments, made by some who had been actual participants in what happened and by some of their descendants, were conducted within a general framework that Herodotos shared with the members of these two groups. That is, they argued by appealing to visible monuments that were still standing and cult traditions that were still alive (in that they were still practised) and they used these as evidence. Relicts of the past in the widest sense, which still existed in the present, in this case, residual traces of the city that were still visible on the site, played a significant role in these arguments, as in fact they did in intentional history in general.

In addition, it is important for the historian to engage in hypothetical speculation about other possible paths down which events could have run, which, in the end, would have forced a different conclusion and led to a situation that would have been very different from the one which actually eventuated. This implies a kind of counterfactual reasoning: if things had gone as agents X, Y, and Z assert they did, then the world would have to look thus-and-so, that is, the present situation would have to be A/B/C. In following this procedure, one assumes hypothetically that a certain present state (A/B/C) would necessarily have been the result of some past event (for instance, the one which X, Y, and Z claim took place), and then one observes that A/B/C is not the case. So, the non-existence of A/B/C demonstrates that what X, Y, and Z said happened, is impossible and must not be true. Just as in the case of chronological arguments, it is the law of contradiction that has the final word here.

---

⁴⁵ Gehrke 1998, 185–8 (with further references), see also Bichler 2013, 26–8.
⁴⁶ Herodotos 5.45. I have Elisabetta Lupi to thank for the following observations. See now Lupi 2019, especially 47–72.

These cases, too, show how past and present are intertwined in a special way. In the first case, past things still protrude into the present. Herodotos then employs the phrase *es eme eti* ('right up until my time') and also uses the imperfect, which designates a continuing process.[47] So, there is still something visible there, which can stand in a direct relation to that most valuable organ of cognition, the eyes. In the second case, certain past events are connected with a present situation in a thought experiment. Here, too, there is a thought experiment: the present *would have to be different* from what it *visibly is*, if some past event really had occurred as claimed. The only difference between the two cases is that in the second reflection and the ability to make complex judgements based on hypotheticals – *gnōmē* – is essential.

The standards of reasoning described here are ones which Herodotos himself would have found already in existence and widely accepted when he started his research. The observations and arguments discussed in the previous paragraph were obviously things that were clearly formulated and presented by the representatives of the various poleis who participated in the discussion, although in one case the polis itself had been physically destroyed. These representatives will have been politicians and/or various other persons who were, as it were, responsible for the history of the polis in question. There was not necessarily an official or fixed and written traditional account, but there will have been something like a 'living tradition'.[48] The structural similarity between this type of argumentation and forensic argument is too obvious to be overlooked.[49] In forensic contexts, too, it was a question of investigating and discovering the truth about some event that was often accessible only through the testimony of witnesses (that is, via *akoē*), or of presenting such a truth argumentatively in speeches. Herodotos, as a representative of critical, research-based historiography, also accepted these principles and refined them theoretically. The decisive features of his project were clear. As Nino Luraghi (2001b, 143) put it: 'personal experience and reasoning are stronger arguments than "what people say"'.

Herodotos' commitment to these principles was no isolated or exceptional case, and the reason for that is not just that he was so influential, but also that he had a competitor, who sought to surpass him, but also imitated him, just as he had tried himself to do to Hekataios before. This is a case of

---

[47] Herodotos 5.45.2. [48] Giangiulio 1989, 192.
[49] Recall the remarks about *elenchos*; see p. 79. See also the comments by Nagy 1988 about the connection between the operations of *historiē* and the procedures used in arbitration.

what we have already learned to call 'hypolepsis'.[50] This competitor struck out energetically on the path Herodotos had already marked, and he proceeded with particular rigorous consistency, but precisely by doing this his work constitutes both a continuation of Herodotos' project and a transcendence of it.[51] He strengthened the component of critical examination of the evidence and of theory-driven *elenchos* in the pursuit of accuracy and truth, as he saw it, and combined this with a particular scepticism vis-à-vis the tradition and the ways in which it was cultivated. This scepticism of his reached its acme, however, when traditional views were presented draped in the garments of rhetoric.[52] He took the principles of the new historiographic approach to their very limits by subjecting the history of long-past eras to scrutiny following the strict rules of logic – an anthropological logic of power. Having decided to proceed in this way he had virtually no choice but to treat autopsy and contemporary history as his starting points. Contemporary history (in the form of the Peloponnesian War) was in any case not only his main object of interest, but it also provided him with the principles from which he could deduce how to go about reconstructing the history of older periods.[53]

In doing this, Thucydides made himself an authoritative model, and we can see how influential that model was by observing how several other historians directly linked their work to his by simply taking up the task of recounting the sequence of events at the point at which the text of his treatment of the Peloponnesian War peters out. As is well known, one of these continuators was Xenophon. If one adds to this the fact that Thucydides himself, in his account of the Pentekontaetia[54] – despite the fact that it is thematically oriented – starts at just the point at which Herodotos leaves off, then what one can see emerging here is a continuous history of 'Greek matters' (*ta hellēnika*) in which one author takes over smoothly from those who went before, and a whole historical period is covered without gaps. All of this, this whole production, took place within the temporal confines set out by the biological lifespans of the authors involved and of the generations of immediate actors whom they could consult and in such a way that every historical work in the sequence

---

[50] See p. 80.
[51] See particularly Corcella 2006, 51, Rogkotis 2006 ('creative continuation, development, and refinement', 86) and Schepens 2007, 47. On similarities between the two historians see Foster and Lateiner 2012, 1–9.
[52] As Jonas Grethlein 2005; 2010, 220–40 has shown.
[53] On Thucydides' 'archaeology' in this sense, see Gehrke 1993; see also Tsakmakis 1995, 25–63 and Nicolai 2001.
[54] On its narrative structure, see Gehrke 2013c.

treated events that were 'contemporary' to its period. This is true despite the fact that the ability to engage in critical scrutiny of the evidence varied, of course, from one author to the next, and there were other striking variations in the quality of the accounts they produced.

Historiography, as it emerged and came to develop in the first three generations from Herodotos, through Thucydides, to Xenophon and others, did not need any empathetic immersion in a past world, because it was at core presentist. In fact, within Greek historiography as a whole, one could draw a single continuous line from these three figures to late Byzantine times, passing through a continuous sequence of authors, each one of whom began where the previous one stopped. The authors in this sequence did not fail to criticise their predecessors, but they did contribute to the continuous writing and re-writing of Greek history as a whole, each starting from the perspective of what he had himself experienced within his own lifetime.[55]

But how was one to deal with the distant past, if one did not follow the example of Xenophon, who simply did not treat it, apart from the *Cyropaedeia*, which is a special separate case? How could one fail to try to come to terms with stories of the past that were overwhelming in their variety and the various forms they took, and which surrounded everyone continually at festivals and during religious cult ceremonies, in the assemblies of the people and even in court, and which flooded any potential historian with images and stories derived from epic, from poems, from speeches, from works of visual art? Herodotos wanted to hold fast and fix the things he saw, even in cases in which he did not fully comprehend them theoretically, and he had a tendency to suspend judgement about what one could and should learn from history, until he could place it in the largest historical context, against the longest possible historical background.

In contrast, Thucydides, as we have indicated, extended the use of rational methods and procedures of critical evaluation even further to encompass the distant past, although he well knew, as the example of the tyrannicides shows, that work on the very early past was even more difficult than research among one's own contemporaries. At the same time, Thucydides himself documents *in praxi*, in his excursus about the tyrannicides, the method by which one can get proper access even to older material, to that which belongs to the genuine past. The way to proceed

[55] On this, see especially Canfora 1971/1999/2011 and Fornara 1983, 46; however one might decide to categorise the genre in question (see Tuplin 2007), there was obviously a need to report about what happened close to one's own time and also to make the connection with predecessors (or at any rate to historical caesuras that were temporally close to their time).

is essentially through research and *elenchos*: one must inspect all the documents and remaining artefacts from the period in question, and consult reliable sources, but one must also use ratiocination – including common-sense forms of argumentation – inferential procedures and the refutation of such things as false assumptions. An example is his discussion of tyranny as a form of monopolisation of political power and his inferences about the age of the various tyrants. This method of operating is very like that of Herodotos – just think of the example given above of his analysis of the conquest of Sybaris by Kroton[56] – but it is also very close to forensic procedures.

Thucydides applied this way of looking at the past in order to subject not only the old traditions but even an authority like Homer to critical scrutiny, but he also developed a theoretical and logical toolkit that was derived from observations and reflections on political events, which in the main he himself experienced and thought about, and which permitted him to reconstruct even the past that lies much further back. This reconstruction is contained primarily in the chapter at the beginning of his book that is called the 'archaeology'.[57] This chapter has an especially strongly marked argumentative character, because it is not concerned simply with older history in general, but is supposed to show that 'Thucydides' war' is the biggest there ever was. Nevertheless, earlier times are reviewed in the chapter, and Thucydides shows how he deals with them and that he does so following certain rules. These rules were of particular importance to him, as he indicates when he speaks of a *ktēma es aiei* (1.22.4), because he thinks he has isolated regularities that result from essentially invariant features of human nature.

This specific attitude toward the past can be seen as a way of trying to visualise it concretely on the basis of present experiences and analyses of current affairs. The final vision that resulted, to be sure, was one that also bore the deep imprint of a certain number of philosophical reflections on human nature, which Thucydides derived from older sources – from the 'wisdom' and insight of older authors, including some poets. This becomes evident if one looks at Thucydides' relation to contemporary tragedy, in particular at some of the striking parallels between accounts in his work and passages in Euripides. To the extent to which that is true, one must then qualify the well-known distinction that Aristotle draws in his *Poetics*.[58]

---

[56] Another example is the common-sense argumentation that Herodotos employs when discussing Helen (2.120).
[57] Thucydides 1.1.2–1.21.2; see nn. 53 and 59.
[58] See Erler 1997, 93 on 'generalisations' in Thucydides.

The past, then, becomes not only an object for study by a conscientious historian who is pursuing his enquiries in a self-consciously 'critical' way, but it can also be subject to analysis as part of a study of human behaviour in general. A crucial part of this analysis is engaging in a process of philosophical and historical reflection on human nature – one which is itself also constantly being refined in the light of contemporary experience. This is an amazingly bold theoretical project, which amounts to no less than an attempt to constitute a new kind of history, one which can lay claim both to truth in a general anthropological sense and to accuracy in its description of contemporary events. As far as I can see, Thucydides had no real successor in this. He, too, starts from the present, but this present is not simply retrojected wholesale into the past; rather, it is regularised according to rules that are thought to hold atemporally (because they are rooted in human nature) and then used as a kind of template for subjecting the past to logical analysis and for re-writing it. The past thus becomes comprehensible and easy to visualise for reflective contemporary readers, and to that extent it becomes familiar and virtually present. History is not simply being passed on, but it is being created, in the light of the present. Not, to be sure, in the form of simple aetiological stories or edifying narratives, but according to a logic of events that construes them through using a schema which focuses on their historically invariant features.

What happens to what the Greeks themselves took to be the 'real' older history, though, the old stories of what was said to have happened in the deep past? Thucydides only took up and treated what he needed for his own argumentative purposes. This means particularly what was necessary to understand *auxēsis* (growth in general but especially growth of power), as he says at the start of the work,[59] or what is required when he discusses the size and importance of Sicily in the Sixth Book, or polemicises against the incorrect ideas the Athenians have about their own history. But how are these older histories and narratives presented in other parts of Greek historiography? Here, too, one can find some examples in Herodotos: the way to treat this history is in the traditional way – in the narrative mode – to be more precise through narrative accounts made even more vivid by the insertion of speeches.[60] The tales are told again and again in ever new ways and ever different variants; the very variety of different versions and of different kinds of performance keeps the old material alive.

---

[59] Maddoli 1994, see also Luraghi 2000.
[60] On the interlinking of past and present in the speeches, see Marincola 2007b, 130. On speeches in ancient historiography in general, see the overview presented in Achilli 2012.

This is as true for the increasing number of different written histories, which themselves all compete with each other in their own way, as it is for works of literature and of the visual arts, all of which teem with their own variants of the old stories.[61] Despite all the polemic directed by more theoretically inclined historiographers against what we might call 'popular' history, as it appears in art and rhetoric, there was greater and greater interaction between the two.

This was true not only of the treatment of the present and contemporary history, but also of the long lines that could be drawn back to the past, always connecting it to the present. So, the traditional modes of allowing history to come to life again – in monuments and in festivals – were retained. And rhetoric, which in any case became more and more *the* medium that was the model for language and style, was also able increasingly to propagate its own images of the past, as it pursued the ideals of epideictic panegyric, that is, as it deployed and developed ways of praising that were specifically honed to be effective in living performance in the present.

All of these modes of treating the past continued to contain references to the social groups and communities that were the bearers of the history in question, and they were all ways in which these groups could structure and develop their own intentional history. Two examples of this from Athens are the tragedies and the official speeches given in conjunction with the Panathenaic festival or on the occasion of state funerals. Both of these were widely understood to be media in which intentional history was to be cultivated.[62] Nicole Loraux even spoke of the 'invention of Athens' as something that took place on these occasions, and an important part of this invention was the production of a historical image that Athenians were to adopt of themselves. They were to see their past and their present as standing in a single line of development, and themselves as the protectors of the weak and the vanguard of Hellenic freedom against barbarian invaders. They revealed their nature in the distant, mytho-historical past when they fought against the Amazons and the Thracians of Eumolpos, fought for the Argives after the expedition of the Seven against Thebes, and fought in defence of the children of Herakles; and in the very recent

---

[61] Certain parts of the literature on narratology have become increasingly influential in recent research on antiquity, see, for example, the contributions in Grethlein and Rengakos 2009 and Forster and Lateiner 2012.

[62] Gorgias B 11.9 Diels and Kranz 1952; see also the case study by Grethlein 2010.

past they showed the same mettle in the wars against the Persians. And this is the way they would continue to be in the future.[63]

In general, the victorious march forward of rhetoric in the fifth century BC had lasting effects not only on the intentional history of the Greeks, but also on the new form of theoretical, elenchic historiography. The consequences of this quickly became clear in the fourth century BC. However, even c. 400 BC, in a rhetorical-philosophical tract called the *dissoi logoi* (*Pairs of Arguments*) we find a treatment of widespread conceptions about how events in the past took place, as part of an intentional history of the Greeks, and, in fact, of the world. Here, in the context of a fundamental moral debate about the good and the bad – no less – (*agathon* and *kakon*), a historical argument is deployed (1.8–10). Just like the lines the Athenians could trace back to their mytho-historical past, the author of this tract constructs a line that he can follow back from the present almost to the very beginnings of history: from the Peloponnesian War to the Persian Wars, the Trojan War, the War of the Seven against Thebes, the conflict between the Lapiths and the Centaurs, right back to the Gigantomachy. This argumentative use of history shows just how current and widespread such conceptions were, and gives good insight into the way the Greeks saw it in crude outline. It is a kind of knowledge about the past that was widely shared, and which connected and interwove it with the present; and the connections ran in *both* directions. But what about truth, the element that was absolutely central to the new approach that the theoretically oriented historiography was supposed to instantiate? Here, the victory of rhetoric was fatal, one might even say it was a pyrrhic victory. Because what was now the guarantee of truth? In the first instance, it was intellectual debate and the struggle of each side to refute the other. The question of truth was an essential topic for the sophists – in fact, especially for the sophists – and thus it was one in the discipline of rhetoric too, which established itself as an art that could be taught and learned.[64]

One of the great masters of this art, Gorgias of Leontini, even literally attempted to orient epideictic speech toward the truth, that which could survive critical examination and hence could be supported. However, there is another side to rhetoric, which the great master himself revealed in his specially composed showpiece, which was his model of what rhetoric could do, the panegyric of Helen. Gorgias states that speakers, in fact, also

---

[63] Loraux 1981/1993; Gehrke 2003, 20–3; on the intentional history of the Athenians with a focus on their relation to the Thebans, see Steinbock 2013.
[64] For further on this issue, see Gehrke 1993, 14.

authors in general, including, therefore, those who write history, can, if they wish to adopt an attitude like that of the poets and strive to charm and enchant their readers, 'fabricate false discourse' (*pseudē logon plasantes*) and can thus 'please and persuade' readers by using artistic skills that are not oriented toward the truth at all.[65] The fact that the speaker then at the end calls everything he has just conjured up, 'an amusement' (*paignion*) (B 11.21), does not exactly make things any better. 'The deceptive which is like what is true' – here, again, Hesiod's formula recurs in modern guise, as rhetoric. Here, too, one could begin again to ask very difficult questions. The struggle for truth was not, then, successfully concluded, at least not yet. The continuation of this struggle in the field of Greek historiography, as it tried to deal with the tension between past and present, and what we might be able to learn from this, will form the topic of the next and concluding chapter.

---

[65] Gorgias 82 B 11.1f. 10f. 13, Diels and Kranz 1952.

CHAPTER 4

Greek Historiography between Fiction and Truth

In the first three chapters of this book, I have discussed some important aspects of the way in which the Greeks represented the past. I developed, as an ideal type, the idea of an 'intentional history' – one that was in general anchored in social life and was integral to the way in which various historical collectives, including the Greeks, constituted their own identity and imposed coherence on the members of the group. For the Greeks, in particular, this took the form of a mytho-history that originally – as far as we can tell – crystallised in epic, and then eventually took a more and more clearly fixed form in the literary genres that developed later. Once it attained a stable form, it was ritually repeated, performed again and again, and passed on to the next generation. I have also tried to distinguish from this, as a further ideal type, a particular kind of 'critical' historiography that is sensitive to issues arising from philosophical questions and procedures, and which attempted to base its assertions on personal research and individual assessment of evidence. This kind of history began to be developed in the sixth century BC and reached its culmination very quickly in the work of Herodotos and Thucydides.

Each of these two ways of dealing with the past stood in a highly complicated relation of tension with the other. In fact, there are two force fields that have to be mapped, and only by locating the changing relation between mytho-history and 'critical' historiography in the intersection of both of these two fields can one come to a proper understanding of either of the two forms of 'history'. First, there is the divergence between past and present, and the relation between these two is historically highly variable and took a variety of different forms. Second, the opposition between truth and illusion was thematised from the time of the very earliest documents to which we still have access. The domain defined by the difference between past and present is in principle separate from that which is defined by the contrast between truth and illusion, but, in fact, each is variously connected with the other so that the influence between them is mutual. The same is true of mytho-history and 'critical' historiography. Ideal types are artificial constructs and they never actually occur in their pure state in history or in empirical reality, so it is no surprise that various diverse amalgamations of literary and critical-philosophical history can be found in the images of the past given in Greek media; the same is true of various transitional forms between these two pure types. Rhetoric, which became increasingly professionalised, especially in the second half of the fifth century BC, came, as I have shown at the end of the previous chapter, to be the central genre in which history was treated and to occupy a privileged position that allowed it to dictate how the past was to be interpreted. This took place despite the reservations both Herodotos and Thucydides had about rhetoric, whose power, however, not even they could completely escape.

For theoretically sophisticated *historiē*, the old question of truth had seemed to be settled in favour of the appeal to autopsy and independent judgement (*opsis* and *gnome*) as the criteria, but suddenly this question was reopened, and 'truth' became once again a problem that had to be dealt with. I have already mentioned this in connection with Gorgias, who took truth to be the 'delightful ornament and form of organisation' (*kosmos*) of speech, but who also knew that speeches could mislead and deceive in significant ways. The founder of rhetoric as a scientifically and systematically developed discipline took it to be the universal 'art' (*technē*) of linguistic and literary expression. Let us see, then, what it means for historiography to become a mere province of a rhetoric in his sense. This will allow us to come to a better understanding of the historiography of the fourth century BC, which has traditionally been seen as especially rhetorical or even completely restructured under the influence of formal rhetoric, and it will permit us to see how fourth-century BC history was nevertheless a further development of the historiography that went before.

Gorgias' 'Encomium of Helen', which has already been mentioned, is a programmatic statement intended for *epideixis*, and was, as such, a kind of advertisement for Gorgias' type of rhetoric. Although, at the end, the speaker refers to the speech as 'an amusement' (*paignion* 21),[1] in fact it deals with a perfectly serious matter, namely with the question of what is appropriate when one is censuring and when one is honouring a particular person or group. In this concrete case, the issue is one of 'honouring through praise' (*epainōi tīmān*,1). This is very close to the

---

[1] This is an element of Gorgias' self-dramatisation, which was said already by his contemporaries to be part of the *epideixis* (Plat. Gorg. 447c, Hipp. Mai. 282b).

concern about the opinion of posterity and posthumous fame (*kleos*), which was an essential element and motivation both in early poetic forms of mytho-history and also in the Herodotean tradition. Helen, to the Greek way of thinking about the past, was a historical figure, and it can hardly be an accident that the choice of words used in section 5 of the speech – which raises the question of the 'reasons' (*aitiai*) for the military expedition against Troy – recall the Prooimion to Herodotos' *Histories*, where he discusses the 'reason' (*aitiē*) why the Greeks and barbarians went to war with each other, and in which Helen herself appears among the associated stories of women who were abducted.

The epideictic and rhetorical intention of the speech in no way excluded the possibility that it might lay claim to truth, if only because, as we have seen, truth is the 'delightful ornament and the organising principle' of a speech. After all, the claim to the truth of what is asserted is the only adequate foundation for the praise that the speech contains, and the acceptance by the audience of that praise as well-founded is the intended epideictic effect. So, the honorific praise of a historical figure in Gorgias is associated with a very clear claim to rationality and logic, as theoretically oriented historiography understood and practised them. The author announces that the speech (as an epideictic showpiece) will proceed by presenting a *logismos*, that is, it will instantiate a 'logic', which, as this very choice of words indicates, is supposed to be located in a domain close to that of mathematics.[2] This particular 'logic' is also linked to a claim to truth, because it is to demonstrate the 'falsity' of those who censure Helen, that is, the falsehood of their claims. In this demonstration, 'truth is revealed', as Gorgias puts it in one of his masterly antitheses: *pseudomenous epideixai – deixai t'alēthes*, 2. As Gorgias says, here all depends on critical examination of the evidence, *elenxai*.[3]

The logic in question here manifests itself in the way in which the possible (or even conceivable) reasons for Helen's behaviour are canvassed and scrutinised, and the argument is forensic in its thoroughness. In the end, she is acquitted on all counts, and that is the real object of the speech.[4]

---

[2] Buchheim's interpretation (2012, 161f.) of *logismos* ('an interpretation of a given legend which changes the evaluation of it') seems to me both too thin and also too far-fetched. See the passages cited in Diels and Kranz 1952, vol. III, 257.

[3] Gorgias could even appeal to Parmenides in discussing *elenchos* and truth (B 7/8. 5f), who in B 2.10 makes a direct connection between *peithō* and *alētheia*.

[4] To this extent, the criticism of Isokrates (or. 10.14f.) hits the nail on the head, although he acts himself in a similar way in parallel circumstances.

Both forensics and epideictics are oriented to truth and this is fundamental for both of them: both of them have their intended effect only if the listener or the judge takes the content of their speeches to be true.

Truth here, then, means simply that the things mentioned in the speech, particularly those appealed to in the section devoted to the forensic 'proof', actually are the case.[5] That is why, as a supplement to basic logical argumentation, these speeches constantly cite what is 'probable' (*eikos*)[6] and the 'signs' or 'indicators' – what we might call 'circumstantial evidence' (*tekmēria, sēmeia*). Any critical historian, even Thucydides, could have approved of this way of proceeding. A simple inspection of the developed rhetoric of the fourth century BC will confirm this.[7]

For speeches, however, there still remains the problem of deception through aesthetic enchantment, *thelxis* (10f.). Gorgias' *thelxis* is reminiscent of the aesthetic effect of epic song, as evoked, for instance, at the beginning of the *Odyssey* when the bard Phemios performs (1.337). Gorgias, too is aware of the fact that he strives for a similar effect, *terpein*[8] (5). There is, however, another side to this coin:

> For incantations divinely inspired by means of speeches (*logoi*) are bringers of pleasure (*hēdonē*) and removers of pain. For the power of an incantation, when it is conjoined with the opinion (*doxa*) of the soul, beguiles it, persuades it, and transforms it by sorcery. For two arts have been discovered, those of sorcery and magic, which are errors (*hamartēmata*) of the soul and deceptions (*apatēmata*) of opinion. (10[9])

What is being discussed here are magic spells, which, like speeches, have their effect through the power of the words and the techniques they use. This leads to the generalisation: speeches can act like magic spells on the soul; they can seduce it to various forms of misbehaviour and can deceive it, perverting its 'view of things', even in the perceptual sense. If one wished to put it in a rhetorical and pointed way, one could say that the authors of speeches are (or could be) people who have 'fabricated a false discourse' (*pseudē logon plasantes*, 11).[10] In a later summary of this period in the history of rhetoric, Isokrates would say that Gorgias and other intellectuals (*sophistai*) showed that it was very easy 'to contrive a deceptive speech'.[11]

This, of course, is the exact opposite of the truth we discussed above. But both of these aspects exist and must be taken into account when one is

---

[5] This can be seen with particular clarity in *dissoi logoi* 4.
[6] B 11.5, see the use of *eikotos* in 7 and B 11a.9; see also in general Plat. Phaidr. 270a–e. The comments by Maier 2012a, 77–91 (chiefly referring to Polybios) are important and suggestive.
[7] See p. 106 n. 43.
[8] See also Homer *Od.* 1.347. On the role of *terpsis* in Gorgias and rhetoric in general, see the references in Buchheim 2012, 169.
[9] Translated by Laks and Most (Loeb). As are all further translations of Gorgias.
[10] See Meister 2010, 157 with important bibliographical references to this aspect of the topic 289, n. 24.
[11] *pseudē mēchanēsasthai logon*, Isokr. or. 10.4.

dealing with rhetoric and poetry, which contain both truth and deception. In this connection, Gorgias calls poetry (*poiēsis*) 'speech that possesses meter' (*logos metron echōn*, 9). In the *dissoi logoi* (3.10), which were written at about the same time, we read that in tragedy and painting that artist is the best who is most deceptive (*exapatē*), in that he produces something that is 'like the truth' (*homoia tois alēthinois*). Here, we are back with the wily Odysseus of Homer and the misleading Muses of Hesiod. And, according to Gorgias, all of these considerations can be extended to apply to any speech aimed at truth. In this case, then, there would seem to be only subjective modes of access to truth, no more 'truth' in the singular that can be grasped by anyone, but only truths in the plural.[12]

Gorgias does not wish there to be the slightest doubt that everything in what we say and in the speeches we give is deeply ambivalent: are they true or are they misleading? He rams home the point repeatedly: this ambivalence exists in all serious intellectual activities that have in any way to do with *logos*, that is, in any that are at all dependent on linguistic formulation. The same thing is true, not only in rhetoric, but even in astronomy (in discussions among *meteōrologoi*) and in philosophy (or, as we would probably say 'science'). All of these activities owe their psychological effect to the operation of *peithō*, to a 'persuasion' that is something further added to the *logos* itself (13). In the domain of rhetoric, in the competitions (*agones*) that take place between rival speakers with different speeches, the 'delight' (*terpsis*) that results from the skill (*technē*) displayed by the speaker is distinct from truth. But it is the *terpsis* that causes the effect on the soul (*psychē*) and which means that here the ambivalence is massive (14).

The difficulty concerning truth and its distortion, which existed from the very first, and is documented in the oldest accessible stratum of what the Greeks considered to be their own history, was that truth and forms of illusion or fiction[13] that looked very much like truth seemed to be immediately juxtaposed without it being obvious which was which. It could even be the case that each of the two seemed to dissolve into the other. Nothing in Gorgias' discussion would tend to make this difficulty easier to deal with. Rather, the contrast becomes even more pointed, and the situation

---

[12] Thus, for instance, Palamedes, in Gorgias' speech defending him (B 11a.2.35), thinks he cannot persuade the judges by an appeal to truth, so he changes the subject, emphasising how much shame (including posthumous shame) the judges will incur if they condemn him. See Buchheim 2012, 175f. about the 'private truth' of Palamedes.

[13] At this point, in particular, one must be exceptionally careful not to import later anachronistic conceptions into the ancient discussion. The discussion about 'fiction' in literary studies is in any case completely unsurveyable (see for instance Iser 1993; Zipfel 2001; Kablitz 2003).

seems even more intractable in view of the fact that truth itself now seems to have become relative and plural. This is true not only for poetry and the visual arts, but also for the prose genres, including rhetoric, although these prose genres appeared on the scene claiming loudly that they would point out the right way to reach the truth. Now they seem to have become bogged down in a swamp of mere competing subjective opinions; in fact, they might even seem to have made things significantly worse, in that they have given a deceptive speaker extra power to persuade, by providing him with additional powerful subjective arguments.

Both Gorgias and the *dissoi logoi* (in the relevant passage 3.10) have painting in mind in their discussions, because they take the optical effect of a painting to be the same as the rhetorical effect of a speech. This parallelism has a particular poignancy given the prominence of visual perception, autopsy, *opsis*, in the methodology of critical historiography. In contrast to this, Gorgias emphasises the deceptive aspect and the dangerous unreliability of *opsis*, especially if one considers its effect on the soul. When what we see is transformed into an image, this changes an impression, which is in itself a mere reflex of what is seen, into a real lasting imprint on the soul. In the specific case Gorgias has in mind, that of a person seeing warlike preparations, the effect is negative in that the soul is genuinely terrified (16). This means that the viewer can easily misconstrue the present, the real situation in which he finds oneself, and instead live completely in an imagined future. The 'power of images' that succeed in impressing themselves on the soul is thus like that of speeches (17). Painting is attractive (*terpsis*, 18) and ambivalent, and it can have positive or negative effects. It can, illusorily through the use of images, generate the impression of reality, for instance instilling (*energazesthai*,18) 'love and desire' in a concrete form.

Nevertheless, what painting and rhetoric create remains in the final analysis an illusion, and that seems also to be unavoidable. What in poetry or the visual arts would be legitimate, and in fact perhaps even a sign of high quality – the shimmering play on the border between truth and appearance – would be something that any historiography simply had to accept as part of the deal, if it wanted to adopt the best literary and stylistic practices. This remains true despite the fact that 'critical' history had announced itself committed to truth and the absence of ambiguity. To put it differently, under the new regime, the new set of rules for art, the problem of truth and of clarity, was still not resolved. To the extent to which rhetoric became the dominant intellectual force, and poetry and the visual arts remained important media through which intentional history was transmitted, the search for truth remained an open task to which no obvious solution was in sight. In view of the power and persistence of these media, the need to find a way forward was all the more pressing.[14]

We do have a guiding thread that can lead us through our further analysis of the history of historiography in Greece. To be sure, we could follow up our familiar theme of the relation between past and present, but there is an even more important guide and that is the fact that representatives of 'critical' history were well aware of the problem of truth, and one might even say that it determined the way they operated. Telling the story in a comprehensive and detailed way is made especially difficult by the fragmentary state of the tradition after Thucydides (if one excepts Xenophon). Strasburger (1977, 14f.) estimated that we have only 2–3 per cent of the texts that were written during that period, and recent studies have served to underline the complications that implies.[15] The fragmentary nature of the evidence is a particular problem for the two authors who are considered to be particularly representative of rhetorical history, Ephoros and Theopompos.

Both of these historians were considered in antiquity – whether correctly or not is something I don't propose to examine here – to be pupils of the great orator and teacher of rhetoric, Isokrates. Given the fragmentary state of the evidence available about their work, I shall start with Isokrates, because the stylistic and literary similarities between him and the two historians seemed self-evident to other ancient authors who knew their works. Even if the claim that Isokrates had been their teacher was completely fabricated to account for the perceived similarities in their style and approach, this is that much the more reason to think that such similarities existed.[16] If this is an invention, then it would be a case of 'transforming a more or less correct stylistic judgment into a biographical fact'.[17] In discussing history in Isokrates, I shall consider not just what we count as 'history' according to our categories, but what the Greeks would have taken as part of their intentional history, that is, I shall include at least some mythic material, or, at any rate, some material that was part of their mythohistory.

It makes sense to start with Isokrates not merely because so much of his work is preserved, but also because he was a theoretician and a practitioner of rhetoric who had also reflected seriously about how to treat history. There is a further reason to treat him as an important link in the historical

---

[14] On the history of these genres, see Grethlein 2010.   [15] See, for instance, Humphreys 1997.
[16] See in the first place Cicero orat. 172; de orat. 2.57, 3.35f.; Brutus 204; Quint. Inst. 2.8.11, 10.1.74; Phot. Bibl. 176 (p. 121 a 23ff.).
[17] Schwartz 1959, 4 (= RE s.v. Ephoros, 1).

chain in that he was most probably a pupil of Gorgias. We shall soon see how strong this chain is. I shall try to show, using the cases of Ephoros and Theopompos as my examples, what concrete effect the use of rhetorical techniques had on historiography. Finally, I shall try to show how in the early Hellenistic period – most likely under the influence of the far-reaching events set off by Alexander's military expedition to the East – a further trend in history-writing asserted itself. This trend was one that completely re-configured the tensions between truth and fiction, by emphasising the poetic elements as a way of allowing reality to be adequately and truly expressed.

We firmly identify Isokrates as a representative of 'rhetoric', and that is not incorrect, but if it is not to be misleading, we must add to this that Isokrates understood himself as a *philosophos*. So, the 'rhetoric' he taught and practised must be construed very broadly and seen as an essential component in 'culture' in the most general sense,[18] and as something that takes as its domain all forms of linguistic and literary expression, including poetry. In this sense, historiography is part of its domain, too. Isokrates did not himself write histories, but he thought that it was a highly praiseworthy undertaking.[19] We shall now look at the way in which Isokrates dealt in his works with topics and figures that were in the Greek sense 'historical' (that is, what we would call 'mytho-historical').

In Isokrates' last speech, the *Panathenaikos*, he proposes and sketches[20] an ideal of linguistic and mental 'culture' that is based on dialogue and on the careful study of existing written works.[21] It is rather easy to see how this model could be applied to any form of literary expression, including to the writing of history. This is particularly clear with regard to truth and interpretative correctness. The way of proceeding that Isokrates proposes is, he thinks, extraordinarily important because cultural education based on rhetoric (that is, 'philosophy' in his sense) creates decent human beings and good citizens (or. 15, 270–309). It is the key to making people 'better and more estimable' (*beltious* and *pleionos axioi*), arousing in them an ambition to speak and a love (*erāsthai*) of trying to persuade others. People are, in short, to acquire the 'capacity to convince'

---

[18] On this, see, for instance, Roth 2003b, 148; Eucken 2003, 35f. The treatment of Isokrates in Christoph Eucken's (1983) dissertation has helped at any rate German-speaking scholars to a new appreciation of his work. This positive re-evaluation has been reinforced by important publications by Orth 2003; Nicolai 2004; Classen 2010 and commentaries, especially Zajonz 2002 and Roth 2003a.

[19] See or. 12.2 with the discussion of *palaiai praxeis* and the 'wars of the Greeks'.   [20] See p. 109.

[21] Usener 1994, 91–7.

(*peithein dynasthai*, 275). *Peithein* – a key word in rhetoric already for Gorgias – does not in the first instance mean to use some clever verbal trick to induce belief. Rather, it designates a process of generating a deeper kind of credibility, which is based on one's 'reputation for decency' among one's fellow-citizens, a reputation that, if it is seen to be maintained, in fact increases one's credibility and persuasiveness (277–9).[22]

To be sure, in actual fact, rhetoric, precisely to the extent to which it presents itself as an art (*technē*), does provide its practitioners with techniques (which one might, if so inclined, call 'tricks') for persuasion that might well seem questionable, if one's main concern was conformity with the criteria for attaining truth. Thus, beginning rhetoricians are enjoined to present something new and surprising in their speeches, and to give the original priority over that which is reliable.[23] In fact, there is even a principle for giving one's speech a sharp edge that enjoins one to 'say the new in an old way and the old in a new way' and also to make that which is small appear to be great and that which is great to appear to be small.[24] As a consequence, the rhetorician has great licence to exaggerate, particularly when engaged in panegyric – *eulogein*[25] – the showpiece of the epideictic genre. The same is true for the genre 'defence speech'.[26] One particularly problematic procedure was the deployment of sharply chiselled antitheses, a practice, to which Isokrates remained deeply committed even at an advanced age.[27]

One can see how in practice this commitment eventually led Isokrates to construct very vivid oppositions that are the exact mirror images of each other and to use them to paint monochrome pictures in blindingly bright whites and Cimmerian blacks. He does this particularly frequently when he is speaking of the past, in his confrontation of the styles of politics and the constitutional arrangements among the Athenians and among the

---

[22] For a definition of the person who has 'culture' in this sense, see especially or. 12.30–3.
[23] Or. 12.237; or. 13.12f.
[24] Technē fr. 2: *ergon rhētorikēs ta men smikra megalōs eipein, ta de megala smikrōs kai ta men kaina palaiōs, ta d'au palaia kainōs*. Isokrates says the same thing or. 4.8; Plato's criticism in Phaidros (270ab) confirms this and thus emphasises the importance of these principles. See also Marincola 1997, 276f; Masaracchia 2003, 165; Nicolai 2004, 75f, 129–31.
[25] 'For although everyone knows that those who wish to praise a person must attribute to him a larger number of good qualities than he really possesses, and accusers must do the contrary' (or. 11.4; translation by George Norlin).
[26] In or. 11.9. 44 eulogy (*epainos*) and speech for the defence (*apologia*) are treated side by side, something which actually would have to be seen to qualify the criticism Isokrates makes of Gorgias' 'Encomium of Helen', namely that it is not actually a eulogy, but a defence, or. 10.14.
[27] On *antithesis* and *parisōsis*, see or. 12.2; also Roth 2003a, 78.

Spartans,[28] in his strict distinction between two different kinds of Athenian ancestors,[29] and, even more than in other cases, in the massive discrepancy he takes to exist between past and present. Isokrates does this particularly in the *Areopagitikos* (or. 7), that is, he constructs a set of opposites that are the mirror images of each other: on the one hand, the present time and, on the other, the construed past that can count as 'history'.[30] This is a characteristic variant of the circularity in identification, which we described above and which here is given a normative twist.

For us, this is the exact opposite of history, namely it is a utopia projected into the past, with a cast list of 'ancestors' who have been designed on a drawing board in order to serve as models for emulation. But even if the 'history' cited by a speaker is not based on a set of completely calcified antitheses, it has, Isokrates claims, a perfectly legitimate role in that, precisely because it is exaggerated, it can serve as a useful foil for comparisons that can increase the rhetoric effect.[31] What Isokrates says about rhetoric and its ambiguity in *Panegyrikos* (or. 4, esp. 8), holds true of history, and that remains a danger for the whole genre, because it would always be tempting to have recourse to rhetorical techniques, especially given the competitive nature of intellectuals and the situationally generated rivalry that existed between them.

This all might lead a historian to shake his or her head and turn away in disgust and horror – and many have done exactly that. That would be an understandable reaction, but it would be rash and premature. One should not try to make things too easy for oneself; rather, it is important to observe carefully and read the available texts closely, and then reflect again and again on that which one has seen and read. In fact, one can learn how to do this from Isokrates himself. The claim to truth plays an essential role for

---

[28] This is one topic in the *Panathenaikos* (or. 12).

[29] The contrast is between the Athenians at the time of the Persian Wars and those at the time of the Dekeleian War (or. 8.37, one is presented as the mirror image of the other: 41–8); similarly, politicians then and later (75f. 121–6), with a comparative retrospective glance at Spartan history (95–100). These accounts are all compatible with the truth, which stands in the centre of interest (38).

[30] Or. 7.17, 20, 24f, 29f., 31–4, 49, 51–5 (and also or. 4.76–81, 85). To this, there corresponds in this speech an inversion of the democratic ideal (21, 23, 26), which has the effect of allowing Sparta to be classed as a democracy (61). So, the early Athenian state is now one based on 'coercion' (26) in the sense that it exercised strict control over the morals of its citizens, but not because the laws were coercive – which is a form of coercion we still know today at least to some extent, and which would have been completely familiar to Isokrates. Rather, in the utopian 'ancient constitution', which Isokrates imaginatively recreates as the direct inversion of his present, citizens had such well-ordered inner attitudes that external coercion could be dispensed with. This, however, is no real story of the past uncovered by research, but a normatively guided rhetorically reconstructed 'history'.

[31] Particularly or. 4.83, 181, 186; or. 9.63.

Isokrates as it did for Gorgias, and not only in the sense that the rhetorician must create the mere appearance of truth. Precisely because the essential goal of rhetoric is to persuade and convince, the speaker must *realiter* bow to the demands of the pursuit of truth, particularly in forensic and epideictic contexts. In speeches of praise or blame, in accusations or speeches for the defence, what is said must hit home – that is, it must be correct, or at any rate plausible[32] – with members of the audience who have a critical attitude, some of whom will even be opponents, and there will always be enough of those present. This is why the speaker strives for truth,[33] or at any rate for plausibility,[34] and this is not a mere formal commitment. The same is true for historical subjects, for instance, when certain legal claims are at issue that are thought to have their basis in the past.[35]

So, the rhetorician makes use of diverse methods for determining the truth or at any rate the balance of probability, which are not in fact that far removed from those we see in Herodotos and Thucydides. Surveying and critically examining the evidence and arguments play a crucial role; *elenchos* and *exetazein* are the key concepts, and the speaker should apply them to his own speech, too.[36] A significant portion of Isokrates' last speech, the *Panathenaikos* (or. 12), which he completed at the age of 97, is devoted to a critical examination of his own speech to see if it is true (*ei pseūdos*, 199–272).[37] The rhetorician is also importantly involved in rebutting criticisms that may have been raised, and he must do this by giving refutations of them that will stand up to the demands imposed by the search for truth;[38] he must even defend mytho-historical figures against criticism, just as Gorgias did in the case of Helen in his speech in praise of her.

Poetic exaggerations – which are clearly part of 'the deceptive side' of the literary arts – are not the least of the things that can come in for criticism, and the arguments here must be based in reason. One particularly important kind of argument is that from chronological impossibility. This is one that we ourselves *mutatis mutandis* would consider to be methodologically sound in the critical study of ancient sources.[39] It is also the case that one

---

[32] Especially or. 15.15, 275–9. Despite the use of rhetorical techniques, what is decisive is *pista* (not *kaina* or. 4.30).

[33] Or. 11.8, 33, 36f; or. 8.38; or. 13.1, 9; or. 12.271.   [34] Or. 11.34f.   [35] Or. 14.10.   [36] Or. 11.34.

[37] The examination takes place not merely in the small circle of one's own pupils, but also in the presence of others who are invited because one expects them to take a radically opposed position (or. 12.200), and the same thing is repeated at 233–72; see also especially Roth 2003b.

[38] Or. 11.38.

[39] Or. 12.203–7 and especially or. 11.37–40 with references to the consensus of 'authors' (*logopoioi*, 37, cf. 34); on *Busiris* (or. 11) see especially Eucken 1983, 195–207; on Herodotos see p. 87. The criticism

can find in the rhetoricians a generalised scepticism about *mythōdes*[40] which is comparable to that of Thucydides. This scepticism is aimed in particular at anything that is simply too monstrous or miraculous, and anything that is simply too misleading (*terateiai, pseudologiai*) in narratives, whether in verse or prose. These are to be treated with suspicion despite the fact that they please the masses of auditors, give them pleasure and enchant them, and thus are effective.[41]

Calculations of probability are what is most important here, and that, in the realm of mytho-history, means performing operations with that which is *eikos*.[42] Just as in forensic argumentation, what counts are indicators and pieces of circumstantial evidence (*tekmēria* and *sēmeia*).[43] Here, too, the proximity of this kind of investigation to Thucydides, both verbally and in matters of substance, is striking. In this context – think of the importance of *doxa* for Gorgias – one should note that Isokrates uses the term *doxasai* which means something like 'have reason to suppose'.[44] This is a central

---

that Isokrates formulates here against the *blasphēmiai poiētōn* (or. 11.37) takes his place in a whole line of intellectuals who criticise the poets for 'criminalising the gods' (see, for instance, Xenophanes; also Masaracchia 2003, 166). This is a tradition to which critical historiography also belongs. So, 'blasphemy' would belong in the same category as the *mythōdes*). However, one might introduce elements like the ones being discussed here into one's speech in certain cases, depending on the intended goal (or. 12.119–23, with a view to praising the ancestors). To be sure, a description of monstrous acts like the ones in question would rather be appropriate for the theatre. This already anticipates the theatrical historiography that would come later, and it shows (as Walbank 1960/1985/ 2011) had already indicated in a slightly different context) that the instruments for this further development have already been prepared in the older rhetoric and needed only to be brought to the fore or made into a part of a programme.

[40] What is being referred to here concretely are stories about the gods (Demeter, in or. 4.28). *To mythōdes* is problematic, but it can be used, like anything else as a means to produce particular effects (or. 12.246). Of course, what is at issue here is not myth *simpliciter*, because 'myth' just means story (in or. 4.158 the Trojan War appears as a historical event in parallel to the Persian Wars). What the rhetorician really objects to is just the same thing that Thucydides opposed (see Graf 1985, 119): things that are simply over the top and thus utterly implausible or miraculous. The polemic Demosthenes directs at Aischines in *On the Crown* (or. 18.149) shows that making this kind of distinction was absolute routine even in 'practical' rhetoric.

[41] Or 12.1. Masaracchia 2003, 166f emphasises the fact that the intended targets are poets and prose authors. This interpretation is preferable to that of Roth 2003a, 75f, who claims to find here an attack on eleatic, sophistic, and socratic-platonic forms of debate. What speaks against this construal is the reference to the popularity with the masses of auditors and primarily the choice of words. We will encounter these words again in contexts that suggest that they refer to a strand of literature, and here, too, we should take them as a criticism of the use of the poetic and theatrical mode in historiography, that is, as a criticism of (excessively) theatrical history-writing *avant la lettre* (if one takes such history-writing to be specific to a later era). See p. 127–130.

[42] Or. 11.35.

[43] Simply some examples among many: or. 4, 30f., 101, 107; or. 7.17, 38, 68; or. 8.95. On the meaning of *eikos* and *sēmeia* see Eisenhuth 1974, 34 (with references to Aristotle *Rhetorica* 1.2.1357a14ff.); on the significance of demonstration in rhetoric in general see Ginzburg 2001, 47–9 (with further references), on Thucydides in this context. Ginzburg 2001, 53f.

[44] Or. 11.35; or. 12.9; or. 13.16f; see Eucken 2003, 32–5 (on *doxa* in general).

category for him, in view of the keen sense he had of the impossibility of certain knowledge about correct speaking and acting.⁴⁵ Therefore, according to Isokrates, all those should be counted as 'wise' (*sophoi*) who come as close as possible to that which was probably true about the good (*tais doxais*), and *philosophoi* were those who work at attaining such a state of reasonableness (*phronēsis*).⁴⁶ Correspondingly, then, the good speaker is not only someone who has a manly and courageous soul (*andrikē*), but also someone who is reliable in what he takes himself to have reason to suppose (*doxastikē*).⁴⁷ This is exactly what Isokrates claims for himself; compared to those who merely claim to have knowledge, he at least comes closer to the truth by basing the suppositions he makes on an evaluation of reasons.⁴⁸ Exactly in this context, common sense – that which 'everyone knows' – and therefore also the common consensus of experts, acquires its special importance.⁴⁹

The tension between the goal of rhetoric and its orientation toward that which is true or at least plausible cannot be resolved. One can see this if one focuses on the historical turning points and the long lines of development that formed the concrete basis of Isokrates' historical ideas, and which he expounds repeatedly in his speeches. In these passages in his speeches, the essential components of his historical orientation become clearly visible. What we have here called 'mytho-history' occupies a very large space in his conception, and the same is true of the very early period in which that generation of heroes lived, who were taken to be the children of gods. This is a time before Agamemnon, thus also before the Trojan War.⁵⁰ The Trojan War, to be sure, was, just as for everyone else, the major event, the great axis around which history turned, and it retained this status of a turning point even relative to the generation of heroes who lived before it.⁵¹ In addition to the Trojan War, the Dorian⁵² and the Ionian⁵³ Migrations serve in the traditional way as the markers relative to which the narrative is structured.

---

⁴⁵ See the polemic against the false promises of those who claim to 'know' (the Socratics): or. 13.21; or. 15.274.
⁴⁶ Or. 15.271, 275ff.   ⁴⁷ Or. 13.16f.   ⁴⁸ *Doxasai men peri hekastou tēn alētheian*, or. 4.9.
⁴⁹ Or. 11.34, 37; in general see Walter 1996.   ⁵⁰ Or. 11.37; or. 12.119ff.
⁵¹ See especially or. 9.12–20; or. 10.18–38 (with a long excursus about the poster boy of virtue in politics, Theseus). See Masaracchia 2003, 163f. On the general structuring of the space of the past here, see ch. 2.
⁵² See especially or. 12.42, 45–7, 177; or. 6.17–23 (in connection with stories about Troy and a discussion about rights, or. 6.24).
⁵³ See chiefly or. 4.34–6; or. 12.43f, 190. The primary topic in these is naturally the role of Athens as the mother city of the Ionians.

In Isokrates' speeches one can also trace long historical lines that connect the past and present in the way intentional history does, and therefore reveal something about the normative orientation of the groups involved.

Centre stage are the Athenians with their traditional concern for protecting the weak and persecuted, and their commitment to the cause of Hellenic liberty, rounded off by reference to various religious and cultural achievements (esp. *Panegyrikos* or. 4).[54] In contrast to this, Isokrates connects the Spartans with a tradition of repression of the helots.[55] In these speeches, we also find various other of the usual elements of intentional history, stories that were obviously very widely current in the Greek world about the past.[56]

Among the historical sequences mentioned, the Persian Wars, too, have their place, often directly attached to mytho-history. Thus, in the *Panathenaikos* (194f) the Battle of Marathon follows directly after a discussion of Herakles' arch-enemy Eurystheus.[57] Then, in immediate succession, come accounts of the period of the First Delian League[58] and the events down to the time of Isokrates himself, although naturally particular attention is devoted to contemporary history, that is, to what happened in the time after the Peloponnesian War. For reconstructing the history of this later period, concrete human memory is a decisive factor, and Isokrates can even draw an explicit contrast in this regard with what is true for earlier times.[59]

In general, one must say that Isokrates is not very original in the accounts he gives of history, but what peeks out from behind his prose is a huge expanse of intentional history, as it was given form again and again in a plethora of poems and dramas, history books and speeches. One can

---

[54] Or. 4.68–70; or. 6.42; or. 12.193–5: Amazons, Thracians, Heraclids, Persian Wars (the same list as that of 'old agons' in or. 7.75). See Heraclids and Argives in connection with Theseus (or. 10.31; on the Argives see also or. 14.53). Or. 7 *passim*: or. 12.123, 130, 151–74: achievement of the ancestors in the domain of domestic cultural politics. See Masaracchia 2003, 162–6 on old Athenian myths about these topics.

[55] Or. 12.177–188. From a different point of view, though, the achievements of these ancestors can also be evaluated positively (or. 6.99–101), see also following note.

[56] The genealogy of the Teukrids in Cyprus (or. 9.19–21); Argos as the original home of the Macedonian royal family of Argeads, via a genealogy tracing them back to the Heraclids (or. 5.32, 111, 114); the Thebans as traitors to Hellas (or. 14.27, 30), and contrasted with the loyal Plataians (or. 14.57–62).

[57] On the Persian Wars, see especially in addition or. 6.42, 101; or. 12.49–52, 189, 195.

[58] See primarily or. 12.53–8, 62–72, 89–101.

[59] Or. 7.64, 66; on the details see especially or. 6.53 (Peloponnesian War); or. 12.53–8 (Spartan supremacy after 404 BC); focus on contemporary history is understandably very strong in *Philippos* (or. 5.30–67) and in *Archidamos* (or. 6.44–7; Dionysios I, Amyntas, Thebes); all of these speeches are ones that have a deliberative political character.

just discern here something like a fourth-century BC panhellenic (to be sure atheno-centric) picture of history, which is evoked by Isokrates in many different passages, but is in itself actually relatively unitary. What stands out are the formal emphasis on the turning points, which we have already mentioned, and the resulting general lines of orientation that they provide, but substantively it is striking that the conceptualisation of history is panhellenic and presented against the background of the sharp antithesis drawn as a matter of principle between Hellenes and barbarians. This is a rhetorically schematised, but entirely coherent position, and further examples of reflections of methodology like the ones discussed here can be found in much of the literature produced by the rhetoricians.

Nevertheless, very significant contradictions do exist, especially if one begins to look at the corpus as a whole and does not focus just on a single speech. These can be found even in the course of the development of arguments that are cited as exemplary instances of an investigation to determine the truth: in *Busiris* (or. 11) essential parts of mytho-history are 'disposed of' as completely non-credible and undecorous horror stories, as part of an attempt to exculpate Busiris from the accusation that he murdered guests and strangers, whereas in the *Panathenaikos* (or. 12), similar horrors are treated as historical facts, and arguments for giving special praise to the ancestors of the Athenians (119–23). To be sure, later in the same speech, the purported great deeds of the ancestors are also called the objects of stale and 'mythically exaggerated' (*mythōdes*) stories (237).

What is truth or even historical truth, if there are obviously so many different truths, or, at best a history that is highly relative, relative to given purposes? The fact that such a relative history is the best available to us has the effect of generating general uncertainty about the past and increasing the sense that any reading of it is merely subjective, leaving us in a situation in which we are confronted with a plurality of truths. The tension between, to adopt as a description the title of Goethe's famous autobiography, 'fiction' and 'truth', which we find in Greek representations of the past, remains, despite our best efforts to resolve it. It quite obviously exists not only in the old mytho-historical genres, but also in the new forms of history-writing, which had established themselves by the time of Isokrates, and all of which continue to be marked with ambiguity. One might call this a genuine dilemma, but it is still remarkable, and slightly unsettling that Isokrates seems so keen to rub our noses in it. The contradiction I pointed out above which occurs within the same speech is something Isokrates constructs entirely deliberately. In this speech, the *Panathenaikos*, a special eulogy of Athens on the occasion of its most important religious festival, the Master, who was at the time almost 100 years old, seemed to go out of his way to emphasise the ambivalence of all speech in a way that made it unmistakeable and incontrovertible. He sets up a fictitious situation of comparative evaluation and puts his own prima facie utterly convincing speech in the balance on one side; he then adds a speech defending the opposing point of view in the pan on the other side. Finally, he puts an interpretation of his original speech into the mouth of a representative of the opposing position. This speech is greeted with general applause, but the author of the first speech (Isokrates himself, of course) remains benevolently silent about the correctness of what his opponent says.[60]

The conclusion to be drawn seems to be: even if history is not artificially constructed from the point of view of the present using antitheses or reconstructed in hindsight, even if there is a basic substantial stock of historical 'fact' that does not change, still, each presentation and each interpretation of history will be different. In fact, over large areas, different accounts will be contradictory, and this is the case even where and when all parties are trying to attain the truth (271). In the interpretation given by the imaginary opponent, Isokrates' original speech seems at the same time excessively weighted down with seriousness and also flighty and deceptive. Isokrates calls this duplicity *amphibolos*;[61] he underlines it and even calls it 'appropriate' (*kalon* and *philosophon*) in discussions that concern 'the nature of men and deeds' (240), that is, *res gestae* – history in the ancient sense. But the speaker who is called upon to interpret what someone else says does not know whether he should 'believe it or not' (*apistein* or *pisteuein*). So, precisely credibility, the persuasive power that is based on truth or at least rational estimation of what one can suppose, goes by the boards. Credibility, however, was something Isokrates particularly valued. Speeches are and remain by their very nature interpretable in a variety of different ways.[62] We may extrapolate from this that the same is true of a historiography that is practised according to the methods of rhetoric.

How should we interpret these last words of Isokrates? As an expression of despair in the face of a massive aporia? It is difficult to say. I think, though, that we should draw another conclusion, at least for ourselves. Isokrates, who was a great teacher and educator, most probably tried to present the problematic aspects of the situation in which any speaker (or listener) finds himself with the greatest possible clarity, primarily to encourage his listeners and readers to think along with him, to continue

---

[60] 265 with Roth 2003b, 142–6, especially 144.   [61] 240, see Roth 2003a, 246.   [62] See or. 4.8.

to investigate and scrutinise what was presented to them, and to warn them against being prematurely satisfied with any given result. Truth, including historical truth, remains hidden, but one can circle around it, by dint of constant active examination and assessment of one's own positions and those of others, following definite rules and principles. One of these is that reading the available documents (and thus having a high degree of skill in literacy) is essential. This, then, is not very different from what Thucydides said.[63] Following these principles provides an opportunity partially to reduce the problematic, Janus-faced aspects of rhetoric, while retaining the forensic orientation to the truth of what really occurred by using the methods of inference from evidence and from statements of those who were directly involved. It is not possible to grasp the truth directly in this way, but operating in this mode permits one to keep it in view.

These are not the final words to be said, though, about Isokrates' students and their relation to history. There needs to be further discussion of who the 'right kind of' historian would be. Any aspiring historian who wished to follow Isokrates' teachings – whatever 'follow his teachings' might exactly mean in this context – would have to be a writer of history who had fully internalised the use of all the techniques of rhetoric. On the other hand, such a person would also have to be thoroughly familiar with theoretical-critical historiography, and finally also with all the varied possible ways of writing so as to continue the existing stories and also with the ways of re-writing history, especially intentional history. Finally, such a historian would have at least to claim to be oriented toward truth; in this respect (as in all the others points) he would be constantly subject to agonal criticism from his competitors and (presumptive) successors. Anyone who did engage in such criticism would thereby further develop the traditional and by no means completely rigid rules of a genre that is now no longer so terribly new.[64] He would at the same time also strengthen and confirm those rules diachronically. Let us look first at Ephoros, then at Theopompos, and examine these general postulates. This will allow us to see, at least in the case of these examples, how a historiography that was fundamentally shaped by rhetoric (in this particular case, by the rhetoric of Isokrates) would look *in concreto*.

---

[63] See especially Usener 2003; on the similarity of Isokrates and Thucydides, see Nouhaud 1982, 115ff; Masaracchia 2003, 166f. The audience (including readers) can then be the judge (Usener 2003, 31), so this is also like a forensic case.
[64] For the fundamental treatment of this issue, see Marincola 2007c.

Ephoros' (FGrH70)[65] proximity to rhetoric is immediately striking. He concerned himself actively with general stylistic and literary questions (*peri lexeōs*) and in particular wrote on the conceptual relation between epideictic and history-writing. In doing that, he obviously pointed out some differences between the two enterprises, without, however, trying to separate them in too extreme a way. Rather, as a historian he placed great value of rhetorical structuring of his work, and in fact had considerable and very powerful influence on others.[66] Consistently with this, Cicero names him together with other historians in his discussion of *genus demonstrativum* and he places him on a level with Isokrates.[67] He therefore clearly belonged, even rhetorically, to the first Eleven. Later writers praise the literary quality of his history, especially the disposition of the material,[68] and he obviously used the opportunity provided by digressions (*epilogoi*)[69] to give assessments of historical personages, no doubt following the rhetorical rules of praise and blame.

This is probably also the context in which one should place his strong penchant for moral instruction and his interest in the moral education of citizens who were aware of their need to act politically.[70] This political and didactic orientation is linked with some of the basic features of *epideixis*. Rhetoric, then, is here construed as part of politics, but also as an element in the education of citizens who thereby are prepared to engage and participate effectively in 'good' politics. 'Good' here is naturally relative to the values accepted at the time.[71] Polybios recognised and approved of this aspect of Ephoros' work, the connection it made between historiography and practical, political action. This was something to which Polybios himself was committed.[72] Ephoros also had, in the legislation of the Greek states, an interest that is clearly documented in the fragments. He had an associated interest in questions of political morality and of social norms, as

---

[65] On Ephoros, see 'the classic' of Barber 1935 and now first of all Schepens 1977; Breglia 1996; Pownall 2004, 111–42 and Parmeggiani 2011; see also the apt and informative surveys in Meister 1990, 85–90 and Marincola 2007c, 172–4.

[66] Polybios 12.28.10f = FGrH 70 F 111.   [67] De orat. 2.57; orat. 172.   [68] Diod. 5.1.4.

[69] Schwartz 1959, 15; on Ephoros' moral orientation see Walbank 1957/1967/1979, volume two, 411; Breglia 1996, 71–3; Cohen-Skali 2012, 266f (with special reference to Diodoros). This tendency of Ephoros' was perfectly consistent with the line Isokrates took (or. 4.9).

[70] See Polybios 12.28.10 (FGrH 70 T 23) on the *gnōmologiai*.

[71] Schwartz 1959, 12f underlines this, although he also evaluates it quite negatively (12–5) This, to be sure, is to measure Ephoros by a standard that is completely different from any that it is appropriate to use for him.

[72] See Polybios 12.28.10f = F 111. The positive remarks of Polybios about the autopsy of Ephoros (12.27.1–3) should also be seen in the context of this 'pragmatic' orientation (12.27.7, 27a). On Polybios' orientation, see in the first instance Maier 2012a *passim*; 2012b.

can be seen in his discussion of individual lawgivers and tyrants, such as Zaleukos, Lykurgos, and Periander of Korinth.[73] However, Ephoros discusses not only the political morality of individuals, but also the ethical dimension of the social, legal, and political behaviour of large collectives, especially poleis.[74] In these discussions, Ephoros' treatment is very close to the sort of thing one finds in Isokrates, or at any rate he exhibits a close familiarity with contemporary trends in rhetoric. There is repeated discussion of the importance of freedom, and the central issue is harmony among the Greeks, according to the then prevailing ideas about panhellenism, which put particular emphasis on the difference between Hellenes and Persians/barbarians in the interest of furthering an inner-Greek concord that was seen to be precarious.[75]

Contrary to the verdicts of Eduard Schwartz[76] and Felix Jacoby,[77] Ephoros shows a genuine and perfectly well developed political sense, as is clearly indicated in his analysis of the outbreak of the Peloponnesian War, which Diodoros obviously followed.[78] In contrast to Thucydides, Ephoros focused attention on the personal and political motives of Perikles, and appealed to the testimony of fifth-century BC comedy with its grotesque exaggerations; this is what Eduard Schwartz meant by 'gossip'. In Ephoros' account, the Megarean Decree, which is mentioned only in passing as part of the background by Thucydides, is given great

---

[73] See F 139 (discussing Zaleukos and social norms); 147–9 (laws and social norms on Crete); 207 (the legal order and Lysander's planned putsch).

[74] F 149 (Cretan customs and norms). F 183 (the luxurious life of the inhabitants of Miletos).

[75] On these aspects of freedom, harmony (*harmonia*) and panhellenism, see chiefly F 149 (about Crete). F 186 (Gelon's victory at the Battle of Himera 480 BC as an act of liberation of Sicily in the cause of Hellenism). F 211 (correspondingly negative judgement on Dionysios II).

[76] 1959, 12f:

> The political thinking in this period had no sense of the large issues, and when the individuals involved do not themselves live a life of adventure, as Xenophon and Theopompos did, so that this can give the narrative some colour, there remains as residue only bourgeois morality for them to base their judgments on. The sapping of the vital energy that animated older forms of social and political morality had been one of the effects of the Peloponnesian War and the rationalist enlightenment. In Ephoros' historical narratives stories of virtue and vice, benefaction and gratitude, cruelty and humanity abound, just as they do in the pamphlets of Isokrates and the rhetoricians.

> 1959, 16: 'Even if Ephoros has low standing as a historian, and enjoys the dubious reputation of having catapulted hellenic historiography down from the unique heights it reached in the work of the two *ktistai* ....'; 1959, 23: 'Ephoros thought he was proceeding critically when actually he was merely playing off the gossip of theoreticians who had no positive knowledge of the past against Thucydides' defence of Perikles.'

[77] Jacoby sees Ephoros merely as a 'large-scale compiler' who, 'judging historical events in a strained and philistine way' 'poured' large amounts of 'moral sauce' over them (FGrH II C [Commentary] 30).

[78] F 196, see Diod. 12.38–41.

prominence. Here, I shall not attempt to clarify the question of the responsibility for the outbreak of the first Greek World War. Anyone who is not sure as a matter of principle of the reliability of Thucydides' version of events can easily find any number of inconsistencies in it, and may well then, like Ephoros, look for some alternative to it. However that might be, Ephoros certainly engages in a series of political reflections that are internally plausible, noting, for instance, that politicians not infrequently try to escape from domestic political problems by taking refuge in foreign affairs, and, by exploiting tensions with other states, they sometimes attempt to divert attention from domestic affairs and thus neutralise the opposition. One cannot simply dismiss this, and it is a hypothesis that has been used repeatedly in modern attempts to reconstruct the outbreak of the war.[79]

On the other hand, with his critical attitude and concern for exact determination of the facts, Ephoros belongs with Herodotos and Thucydides, as indeed he does with his preference for the study of that which is temporally close to him. In the Prooimion of his large work on history, he says as much explicitly and in a way that makes it easy for us to identify with his attitude: 'With respect to events of our time, we think that those who speak most exactly are the most worthy of belief (*pistotatoi*), but when discussing older times, we think such people are the least reliable (*apithanōtatoi*) because we assume that it is not likely (*eikos*) that someone could retain all these deeds and speeches so precisely in memory.'[80]

So, it would follow that in contemporary history the greatest possible precision should be valued, but in accounts of older epochs such precision, especially if one is committed to the criterion of credibility and reliability (*pistis, pithanōs*), must always be suspect because its epistemic basis is problematic. Just as the 'classic' historians did, Ephoros ascribed special significance to autopsy and to the physical present of the historian at the events on which he was reporting.[81] Consistently then with this general

---

[79] One can find the suggestion already in Aristophanes (Pax 605ff). On the debate in the modern literature, see Meyer 1997.
[80] F 9. This passage is cited word for word by Harpokration (s.v. *archaiōs* and *kainōs*); it is one of the few direct quotations of Ephoros.
[81] Polybios 1.27.7 = FGrH 110. See qualifications by Schepens 1975. In this context, there is an important and characteristic remark by Thucydides (1.73.2), who names only 'bits of hearsay' (*akoai*) as 'witnesses' (*martyres*) for that which is 'very old', and contrasts it with the real perception, that is, the perception of that which is right before one, which he even calls literally 'seeing of that which is heard' (*opsis tōn akouomenōn*). In this sense even older poems would be 'witnesses' (see comment by Aristotle and n. 96), just as we nowadays still call our sources 'testimonia'. These witnesses, however, given the significance that autopsy and direct hearsay have, are associated with their own range of problems.

attitude, the focus of Ephoros' work is on recent and contemporary history. Eduard Schwartz (1959, 10) estimates that half of Ephoros' work is devoted to the fifty years before his time and a third of it to the thirty years before his time.

Nevertheless, Ephoros did not completely refrain from treating older epochs, including mytho-history. To that extent, he was writing – and in this he differed from Herodotos and Thucydides – very explicitly a universal history, universal even in a temporal sense. One might agree with Polybios[82] and see this as his great innovation and his continuing contribution to historiography. Given that there were other historians and mythographers in the fifth century BC, who treated older periods and whose work has not come down to us, this judgement might need to be modified or qualified.[83] Still, Ephoros occupies a special place as a representative of universal history. He not only exercised particular care on the literary composition of his work, but he also applied the whole extensive set of tools that had been developed in critical and theoretically reflective historiography since the sixth century BC in his own variant of the historical method, which also incorporated rhetorical techniques.

This is expressed in the decision about the principles to be followed, which he placed at the head of his history – beginnings, after all, are always especially tricky in history.[84] In the mytho-history of the Greeks, the really ancient stories about the origin of the world, the early reigns of the gods, and their struggles with each other and with various fantastic composite creatures – such as the Gigantomachy and the Battle against the Centaurs, which are cited as part of history in the *dissoi logoi* – are completely overgrown with miracles. Even as early as the sixth century BC, rationalist criticism of myth began to operate on this material; it objected to that which was implausible, physically impossible, and strikingly absurd in these tales, and in consequence it rejected them. This sort of thing – the implausible, the absurd, the monstrous – counted, as it were, as particularly 'mythic'; later the term '*mythologein*' came into use to describe it. However, objections to *mythologein* do not in any way imply a complete or principled rejection of myth as the telling of stories or as a part of history, that history was mytho-history. In fact, one simply used other terms to refer to the sort of thing that was to be excluded. Basically, what was to be avoided was what Thucydides and especially Isokrates conceptualised as '*to mythōdes*'.

---

[82] 5,33,2 = T7: *prōton kai monon . . . . ta katholou*; see also Schepens and Bollansé 2004b, 57–63.
[83] Ephoros' criticism of Hellanikos (T 30) implies that he had some precursors.
[84] On this, see for instance Timpe 1993.

This is the obvious reason, and Diodoros signals it, why Ephoros simply left this primordial early period, which was so rich in legends that its reality was almost invisible, out of his great work on history. He started with the return of the Heraclids, and thus with the heroic stories of the migrations in mytho-history,[85] that is, exactly with that material which came to be in the centre of interest in the period discussed above in Chapter 2. Ephoros became a classic in an area about which before poets and mythographers took pride of place. Even today, we can see to what extent he became an – in fact, *the* – authority.[86] Even the few fragments of the first books that are preserved illustrate this, including some concrete examples of the use of rational or rationalising criticism of myth (F 20.31).

For this very difficult project, Ephoros also made profitable use of a comparable intellectual discipline, which had also been developed during the second half of the fifth century BC, and in which sophists certainly played an important role. This was research into various local traditions, practices, properties, and peculiarities. We tend to summarise this under the title 'local history' or 'antiquarian literature'. As such, it is then treated as something distinct from proper historiography,[87] with which it, in another sense, certainly belongs.[88] For instance, even today we would surely consider Hippias' research on the list of Olympic victors[89] to be an eminently historical enterprise. In any case, we should try not to be excessively strict in drawing the boundaries of different genres.[90] Ephoros did not himself engage in any antiquarian or local historical research, but he did in general draw great profit from their results. The decision to publish a continuation of Jacoby's edition of the fragments of the Greek historians (FGrHist IV) opens up a huge potential domain for fruitful further research.[91]

---

[85] Diodor. 4.1.3; 16.76.5; T 8. 9.
[86] Polybios 9.1.4; 34.1.3f = T 18; see also Diodoros 4.1.3; 16.75.5; Busolt 1893, 156–8 works out the details (see also Kõiv 2003, 35f), and has re-constructed the history in an especially convincing way (223–9) with special reference to Messenia, an example that had great contemporary relevance for Ephoros. On this, see also Luraghi 2008, 209–48.
[87] The strict separation introduced by Momigliano (1950) became canonic here.
[88] On the antiquarian, see Schepens 2007, 49, 53, and generally also Bravo 2007; on local history, see Harding 2007, 181 and also the study by Clarke 2008.
[89] Which has been the subject of an excellent and illuminating recent study by Paul Christesen 2007. See also Ginzburg 2001, 52 with an important reference to Plat. Hipp. Ma. 285d.
[90] See the persuasive appeal by John Marincola 1999.
[91] On the edition itself, see Schepens 1997; 2000; 2006; Schepens and Bollansée 2004a. The volumes that have appeared up to the present include: Vol. IV A 1: *The Pre-Hellenistic Period* (G. Schepens, J. Engels, J. Bollansée, E. Theys, 1998), Vol. IV A 3: *Hermippos* (J. Bollansée, 1999); Vol. IV A 7: *Imperial and Undated Authors* (J. Radicke, 1999); Vol. IV A 8: *Anonymous Papyri* (S. Schorn,

There is copious evidence for Ephoros' commitment to applying the criterion of truth in pursuing his historical research, and for his commitment to the use of methods that would make his results satisfy that criterion.[92] Even the Stoic Strabo praises Ephoros in this respect. In fact, Ephoros engages in an articulated polemic[93] against 'deceptive tale-telling' (*pseudologein*), which is directed, as has already been mentioned, at, among others, his predecessor Hellanikos.[94] This is also where one should locate the criticism of music he makes, in the Prooimion to his work, because of its deceptive and enchanting properties (*apatē* and *goēteia*),[95] a formulation reminiscent of Gorgias.

As we have already mentioned in regard to the use of antiquarian material and local history, Ephoros consulted older traditions and authors, especially authorities like Homer, carefully, and he used them as sources for quotation.[96] Epigrams and inscriptions are cited as evidence (*dēloi*)[97] in the same way. Since it was not always possible in historiography to apply the principle of autopsy universally (particularly not when, like Ephoros, one was doing universal history), this kind of documentary testimony comes to have a special significance.[98]

The evidentiary value of this traditional material is assessed and re-assessed using the most rational and theoretically up-to-date procedures and applying appropriate techniques, methods of the kind that were characteristic of *elenchos*, for instance, etymological argument (F 22). One particularly important component of this process is the assumption that names and cult practices had a certain persistence – they remained relatively stable – an assumption that was operative in aetiological derivations, that is, in the explanations given of the original emergence of various cults.[99] This was associated with a serious attempt to get as clear and coherent a chronology as possible.[100]

Ephoros is also familiar with the scientific and philosophical geography that developed out of geometry in Ionia in the sixth century BC, and which had been linked since Hekataios with critical historiography. In Books 4 and 5 he gives an overview of the Oikoumene based on these ideas; his treatment enjoyed a high reputation even among ancient descriptive

---

J. H. Brusuelas, J. Obbink). See https://referenceworks.brillonline.com/browse/fragmente-der-griechischen-historiker-iv for the current state of publication.

[92] For appropriate references, see F 20.   [93] F 118, if that is a literal quotation.
[94] T 30 = Jos. C. Ap. 1.16 (Eus. Pr. Ev. 10.7).   [95] Polybios 4.20.5 = F 8.
[96] F 42, 119, 133f., 147, 149, 216. On poets and other prominent personalities as 'witnesses' in rhetoric, see Aristotle rhet. 1.15.1375b28–35.
[97] F 199, 122a.   [98] Schepens points this out very clearly (2007, 50f).   [99] F 20, 31, 118, 119.
[100] F 102, 223.

geographers.[101] He also uses the associated conceptions of space for his readings of historical events. His history even contains geo-political interpretations, as in the case of Boiotia, which he describes as an isthmus, whose position between two seas has made a deep mark on its history (F 119). This may seem peculiar to us nowadays because we have more refined cartographic tools, but this comment is an indication of Ephoros' basic orientation toward the 'science' available in antiquity.

One can thus cautiously conclude that Ephoros combined the achievements of ancient critical historiography à la Herodotos and Thucydides with a very up-to-date conception of rhetoric as a systematic, didactic discipline, which, in its own view of itself, was a comprehensive philosophy. He did this in a highly reflective way, in full knowledge of the dangers of rhetoric and its mode of arguing, but also of the opportunities its way of narrating the past provided. This amalgam is characteristic of the fourth century BC, up to the last third of it, as I shall now briefly illustrate using the example of the work of Theopompos (FGrH 115).[102]

Theopompos also bore the imprint of rhetoric in a special way. Here, too, the ancients noted a similarity to Isokrates, which also led to it being said that the relation between the two had been that of pupil and teacher. Dionysios of Halikarnassos even claimed that Theopompos had been Isokrates' most important pupil.[103] He was an even more drastic practitioner of Isokrates' doctrines, if one is to believe the saying attributed to Isokrates that he needed always to spur on Ephoros, but to rein Theopompos in.[104]

His particular association with rhetoric should be noted: Cicero, after all, cites him in the same breath as Isokrates when discussing successful *epideixis*.[105] In any case, he clearly shared with Isokrates the same general set of goals: the acquisition of 'culture' in and through rhetoric, philosophy, and the joy of learning (*philosophein, philomathein*).[106] His relation to philosophy seems also to have been like that of Isokrates, which perhaps explains the state of reciprocal polemics that existed between him and Platonists.[107]

---

[101] Even though much of what he has to say about Egypt is ridiculous (F 65).
[102] On Theopompos, see first of all Meyer 1909; Reed 1976; Pédech 1989; Shrimpton 1991; Flower 1994; Bleckmann 2006; Occhipinti 2013, and also the important surveys in Meister 1990, 90–3 and Marincola 2007c, 174–6.
[103] Dion. Hal. Ad Pompeium 6.1 (FGrH 115 T 20).
[104] Cic. Brutus 204; de orat. 3.36; Quint. Inst. 2.8.11.
[105] Cic. Orat. 207 (T37), see also Quint. Inst. 10.1.74: *oratori magis similis*.
[106] Phot. Bibl. 176.120b.   [107] Compare T 7 with T 48; F 259, 275, 294, 359.

As has already been suggested, the epideictic genre stood at the centre of all Theopompos' rhetorical projects. He went on tour as a public speaker for festive occasions through the Greek cities and sanctuaries, and acquired great renown for the quality of his speeches; an inscription containing a list of books in a library on the island of Rhodes (T 48) contains references to an Olympian and a Laconian Oration he composed, also eulogies to Korinth and Athens, and panegyrics of important rulers such as Philipp II and Maussolos. We can easily image these speeches as very much like similar speeches by Isokrates, perhaps even more dramatic than they are – think of the remarks about the need Isokrates felt to 'rein in' Theopompos. The striking resonances to speeches by Gorgias in the quotation from the Prooimion to Book 49 of Theopompos' *Philippika*, which is still preserved word for word,[108] certainly point in the direction of a highly dramatic style.

This rhetorical style is also a feature of Theopompos' main historiographic works, which, after an epitome of Herodotos (T 1; F 1–4), was: 'Greek Deeds' (*Hellēnikai Praxeis*)[109] and 'The Affairs of Philipp' (*Philippika*).[110] This work, too, as was customary in the genre, contained some comments on method: sometimes these were not just general remarks, but descriptions of one's own practice, such as a declaration of a commitment to fables or a reference to the importance of personal experience for a historian.[111]

The way in which Theopompos clearly focuses his major work on King Philipp of Macedonia shows that he had the intention of writing history with a political accent, but also that he felt he was capable of this. This would be particularly significant if Theopompos composed his work during the period when Alexander the Great was in power or thereafter (as is implied by the reference in the fragments to the year 324 BC) (F 330). This suggests that he did not allow himself to be dazzled by the greatness of the son, but rather made a conscious decision to attribute to the father a significant position in world history. This emphasis on Philipp as a monarch is criticised by Polybios (8.11.1ff) whose view of things is that of a politician with his roots in the Greek republics, but Polybios' defence of Philipp, of Alexander, and of their companions in arms against the objections that Theopompos levels against their personal morality (8.11.3ff) shows that his criticism of Theopompos' attachment to monarchy must be qualified: both of the two historians clearly were in essential agreement

---

[108] Polybios 8.9.6; Athen. 6.260d–261a (F 225).   [109] Pol. 8.11.3; Diod. 13.42.5 (T 13); F 5–23.
[110] Diod, 16.3.8: *peri Philippon historiai*. F 24–396.
[111] Strabo 1.2.35 (F 342); Polybios 12.27.8 (F 342).

about the general political significance of the Macedonian monarchy and they differed only in how they specifically characterised and evaluated it.

This is important because Theopompos' large work by no means limits itself to a treatment of Philipp and his time. Philipp left his imprint on historical events, but a number of very different incidents took place, and this very variety makes the epoch difficult to survey and summarise, although Theopompos did try to treat the whole wide spectrum of what happened. A later summary of Theopompos' history, which contained only the material about Philipp, was supposed to have contained only fifteen books, instead of the total of fifty-eight, that is, only about a quarter of the whole. So, Theopompos really did, as he claimed (F 25), undertake to treat 'the deeds of Greeks and barbarians' (*praxeis hellēnōn kai barbarōn*), that is, world history. The universal intent is signalled in the binary reference to Hellenes *and* barbarians.

In addition, this formulation is a reference to the similarity that exists between Theopompos and Herodotos, of whose work he, when still a young man, seems to have written a summary (*epitome*; T 1). In his first independent historical work, he starts, as Xenophon and others had done, where Thucydides leaves off, in the middle of the events of the war in the year 411 BC.[112] The work ends with the Battle of Knidos (394). The decision to stop here is, by the way, also a sign of his political sense. Even more important, though, is Theopompos' relation of Herodotos, who is the earlier historian whose conceptions leave the deepest impression on his later work, as we have seen, starting with the very wide definition of the historical subject matter that Theopompos adopts, namely 'the deeds of the Greeks and barbarians' ('*praxeis hellēnōn kai barbarōn*'). The composition of Theopompos' history is strongly reminiscent of Herodotos, with its focus on the growing power of an agent who has world historical potential – Philipp in the case of Theopompos, the Persians (collectively) for Herodotos. The work of the two historians shows similarities in structure: material that is not directly connected with the main thesis is arranged in digressions, often with a series of digressions one nested in the other, and in flashbacks, which allow Theopompos (for instance) to go

---

[112] I cannot enter the *quaestio vexata* of Theopompos' relation to the *Hellenica Oxyrhynchia*. Many scholars are rather optimistic about their ability to make an identification of the author (see Bleckmann 2006), but the fact that the debate never goes away shows that no certainty is possible here. Occhipinti 2013, 110f n. 159 gives a good overview of the state of the question. It is thus from a methodological point of view not conscionable to take *Hellenica Oxyrhynchia* as a work by Theopompos, much as one would love to have more of his work.

back into the past behind the official starting point of his work, the beginning of Philipp's rule.[113]

The digressions are sometimes of some length (T30), for instance, an extensive section of Books 39–43 is devoted to the history of the west, and inserted into this digression are three books (41–43) dealing with the tyrannies of Dionysios I and Dionysios II.[114] Theopompos goes into great detail in these books, with the result that the work looks a bit like a Russian *matryoshka* doll, with one digression embedded in another, as one can see if one looks at Photios' summary of the contents of Book 12.[115] Polybios criticises Theopompos' practice of 'jumping from one topic to the next',[116] but Theopompos has thought about his mode of proceeding carefully, and he adopts a method that is open to any historian who is trying to subject his possibly chaotic material to some principled order. He made a different choice from the one Ephoros made, but choosing Herodotos as the model for how to structure a narrative was certainly not an inherently absurd thing to do.

Anyone who samples it will notice that the *Philippika*, too, has been rhetorically spiced up in a similar way. The statement cited above, which used formulations like those of Gorgias, can be found in this work. The culinary metaphor applies not just to the general style of Theopompos' work, but the spicy wordplays and assonances seem also to have an impact on the content of what he says about individual people and events; they are what make some of his accounts particularly memorable. Thus, he claims that the companions of Philipp, and in fact all the members of his court, are completely effeminate, a bunch of 'pansies': 'They were called "comrades-in-arms" (*hetairoi*) but were actually whores (*hetairai*); they were by nature slayers-of-men, but in their mode of conducting themselves they were male prostitutes' (F 225). They were worse than the worst monsters of myth, Centaurs or Laistrygonians. Theopompos had in general a taste for pointed evaluations and drastic forms of criticism, and most of his criticism was directed at the private morals of some of the individuals he discussed. Alcoholism, addiction to gambling, sexual promiscuity, and greed were all standard charges he laid against those of whom he disapproved, but the effect that the constant repetition of these particular criticisms has on modern readers of the fragments is to make us inured to them, especially given that the ancient authors who cite him in this vein – that is, Athenaios

---

[113] Diod. 16.3.8 (T17). [114] Diod. 16.71.3, see also, in general, Occhipinti 2013.
[115] Phot. Bibl. 176.120a (F 103); see Occhipinti 2013, 101–3.
[116] Polybios 38.6.2–4 (F 28); on the relation to Theopompos, see Walbank 1957/1967/1979, volume three, 692 with further references.

in the first instance – were so clearly enjoying themselves when they recur again and again to the same sheet of charges. One must, however, resist the temptation to draw inferences from these isolated passages, apparently chosen with an agenda by figures like Athenaios, to the character of Theopompos' whole work.

These were clearly very special highlights that readers looked forward to with eager anticipation. This is probably connected with the pedagogic intention of ancient rhetoric, which, after all, understood itself as a type of philosophy. The work was shot through with emotionally highly coloured and linguistically ornamented expressions of praise and blame like those used in epideictic speeches of approbation or denigration. It is this philosophical aspect of rhetoric that gives it such a strong tendency to draw special attention to the mode of life and the moral orientation of the people it discusses.[117] On the other hand, Theopompos also very clearly makes a distinction between the category of the political and that of private morality. Interestingly enough, one can see this in the way in which Polybios treats what he takes to be Theopompos' excessive and gestural moralising. In the passage cited above (8.9–11), Polybios takes issue with the fact that Theopompos, at the beginning of his history, states that Europe had never seen a man like Philipp, but Theopompos then goes on to denigrate him morally in every respect. Polybios' criticism is directed at the discrepancy between these two things. This, however, presupposes that he admits that when Theopompos is giving his general evaluation of Philipp, he is basing that on an assessment of *to sympheron* – that which is advantageous (8.11.6); this, however, is an eminently political category.

One can find clear normative tendencies in other parts of the work, too, especially in matters of religion. Theopompos affirms that it is his intention to tell *mythoi*, but says he will do it better than Herodotos, Ktesias, Hellanikos, and the authors of Indica (F 381). From the rationalistic perspective of some other authors, this commitment to *mythoi* is not unproblematic. Polybios speaks of Theopompos' 'mythic and narrative digressions' (*mythikai kai diēgēmatikai parekbaseis*)[118] in a way that clearly indicates he thinks this is an issue. Theopompos is said to have placed the

---

[117] Dion, Hal. Ad Pomp. 6 (T20) 5f.
[118] Polybios 38.6.1, compare 16.12.9 (with the references to the monstrous) and Strabo 1.2.35 (where 'mythic' seems to stand as a synonym for 'not credible'). See also Dion. Hal. Ad Pomp. 6.11 (T 20a) (Theopompos tells childish and unbelievable stories); Porphyrios (Eus. Pr. Ev. 10.3.464d = F 70) says that Theopompos had been 'caught out as a liar'. The background for all of this is also the poetic-theatrical form of history-writing that was a feature of the Hellenistic world, see what follows.

miraculous centre stage in his history, and to have devoted a whole book, Book 8, to fairy tales. In general, though, these stories have to do with religious phenomena, as, for instance, when Theopompos reports that people are said to lose their shadows when they enter the inner sanctum (*abaton*) of the sanctuary of Zeus on Arcadian Lykeion. The religious component of this makes the use of legendary material permissible, however, even in the eyes of Polybios, if and when 'the piety of the mass of worshipers toward the divine' needed to be preserved (16.12.9). In the realm of the religious and the numinous, then, Theopompos seems to have held that normative considerations should be pre-eminent, and that would seem to cohere with his general stance, which was one of trying to inculcate the right moral attitudes into his audience.

There is, of course, a fundamentally literary component to this. A history is to express pleasure in inventing and telling stories in conjunction with a didactic element: *prodesse* and *delectare* are to form a unity. This is precisely what Dionysios of Halikarnassos points out (ad Pompeium 6.4) when he subsumes this kind of thing under the categories of 'the captivating of men's souls (*psychagogia*)' and 'the useful' (*ōphelia*). This is also an expression of a competitive streak vis-à-vis other authors, particularly Herodotos. This is why Theopompos makes a space for older history, discussions of which are integrated into the main text again and again in the digressions and flashbacks. One good example is the history of the amphictyony (F 63), but Theopompos was also in general attentive to stories about the events surrounding the foundation and early history of settlements.[119] In contrast to Ephoros, though, the centre of his interest was clearly occupied by history seen from the point of view of the present, as one can see by noting the way he begins his history at the point at which Thucydides ends his and the focus of his work on Philipp II.

Looking back at Theopompos' method and general orientation from our present historical perspective, though, we can and must sound a note of caution about using him as a source: he failed to maintain a proper distance to his subject and his tendency to engage in polemics was extreme. Polybios (12.25f.6) has also noted a carelessness about topographical features when Theopompos describes land battles, although this is perhaps a separate issue. On the other hand, Theopompos clearly states that the best person to describe military and political events would be someone who has some personal experience in these domains, just as is true in medical and navigational matters.[120] Polybios cites this without objecting to it.

---

[119] Dion. Hal. Ad Pomp. 6 (T 20), 4.   [120] Polybios 12.27.8 (F 342).

This statement by Theopompos is not simply an idle general comment he makes, but it reflects his own personal situation: he was at one point exiled for political reasons (he was accused of Laconism, that is, favouring collaboration with Sparta), and was correspondingly recalled when the political situation changed, and he was exiled again. So, he had great political experience and commitments, and he knew politics and politicians at first hand.

He was also able to put this political experience to fruitful use in his historiographic activities. He not only employed his own political experiences to make his historical judgement keener and more nuanced, but he also tried concretely to engage in research based on conversations with his contemporaries and with active politicians. He tried, if at all possible, to get eyewitness accounts, and generally he considered his activity as a philosophical rhetorician and historian to be something serious to which he was completely devoted. Not unlike Herodotos, he was constantly engaged in empirical research.[121] Athenaios (3.85a = T 28a) confirms that he was motivated by love of the truth and a strenuous attempt to 'investigate history with care', although this may perhaps finally go back to a bit of self-praise by the man himself. He tried to look behind the facades and reveal the hidden motives at work,[122] and one can find in his work also other virtues of 'classic' historiography, for instance, a sense for the importance of geography, and, like Thucydides, an awareness of the value of archaeological observations.[123]

It is not easy to arrive at a proper evaluation of Theopompos and his work, if one approaches it from the point of view of contemporary conceptions of how history should be done, and one can only agree with John Marincola (2007c, 176) that 'His *Philippica* seems to defy categorisation.' The ambivalence to which we have so often had occasion to refer is particularly highly developed in this work. On the other hand, he was a rhetorician and historian who had a definite interest in education and who was able to combine intensive research with an attractive and informative way of presenting his results. This is something even ancient critics partially admit. What we have here is clearly a case in which rhetoric and history-writing have come to be intimately linked, in a way that is not self-evidently

---

[121] Dion. Hal. Ad Pomp. 6.7f; Phot. Bibl. 176.120b; on similarity to Polybios in this regard, see Walbank 1957/1967/1979, volume two, 409.
[122] Dion. Hal. Ad Pomp. 6.7.
[123] On geography, see Occhipinto 2013, 91–7; on the ceramics of Chios and Thasos, see Strabo 7.5.9 (F 129).

deleterious to the methodical search for factual knowledge in the field of history.

It would be good to give this unity more recognition than it has had[124] (especially in view of the general suspicion of rhetoric that is part of so much of modern culture). One cannot understand Greek (that is, ancient) conceptions of the past on the basis of a simple antithesis between myth and history; neither can one play off historical truth, that is historiography, against rhetoric. What is essential here is the set of expectations that the audience, that is, listeners or readers, have. In the ancient world, they were accustomed to find out about history through the medium of a literature with a strong rhetorical element. This expectation was a kind of pact that existed between author and reader. Part of this pact was a certain assumption: the question of the correctness of the views expressed in the work, the agreement between the facts and what they were reported to be, should not be simply a secondary concern. Rhetoric, too, had its pretention to truth, but it also remained aware of how precarious and fragile claims to truth were, especially in the light of the methods and procedures it itself employed. *Ancient* listeners and readers were accustomed to having to deal with this. However, it represents a serious challenge to *our* conceptions. We should follow the rule Tracey Elizabeth Rihll (1999, x) proposed for the study of antiquity: 'Assume always that the ancient author makes sense.'[125] We should try to stick to this even if our ability to understand is put under even more stress than it has been in this discussion. With that, I wish to conclude.

The competitive and agonal mode that the Greeks adopted in developing their intellectual positions never led to clear progress in cognition, not at least to that type of progress which is claimed (since the Enlightenment) to be part of the inherent dynamic of our sciences. There were polemics in the ancient world and many, many new beginnings, but no cumulative approach to truth, even though, as we have seen, all the new beginnings circled continuously around truth in ever new ways. This is exactly what happened to the mainstream of historiography, which came under the influence of rhetoric in this period. This approach had hardly emerged properly, in the time of Macedonian expansion and Alexander the Great, when it already began to seem hopelessly tedious. The objections to it came, again, from one particular quarter, that of historical truth; what was demanded was description of the concrete event, an authentic presentation

---

[124] See, for instance, the verdict of E. Schwartz and F. Jacoby, p. 113; See also Bleckmann 2006.
[125] I owe my knowledge of this quotation to its use in a lecture by Alexander Meeus.

of what actually happened, which allowed one to visualise it clearly and in detail. One of the initiators of the new direction in history claimed that Ephoros and Theopompos essentially failed to provide this. They, he claimed, had devoted themselves to the literary side of history (*graphein*), not to the exact representation (*mimēsis*) of what had happened, and consequently to generating in the audience the pleasure (*hēdonē*) that was a concomitant of exact representation.

This initiator, Duris of Samos (FGrH 76), placed his censure of Ephoros and Theopompos exactly where authors had always preferred to place their criticism of their predecessors and competitors in the trade, in the Prooimion to his book of history. If one thinks back to the basic style of Theopompos, this seems an incredible objection – clearly a further instance of the often-overheated polemics that ancient historiographers directed at their predecessors, especially when they actually were going further down the paths which those predecessors had marked out. The successors did not wish to feel that they were dwarves on the shoulders of giants; rather, they wished to present themselves as the giants who overshadowed the dwarves who had come before them. In any case, one must not forget that Theopompos could not be totally summed up in his excesses, and he obviously did not appear to his younger contemporaries, who had their own experiences – experiences that were characteristic of their generation – to be dramatic enough. In any case, Duris represents a new approach.

This new, or at any rate purportedly innovative, form of historiography pursued the goals it had set itself – giving a concrete representation of events and producing an emotional reaction – chiefly by two means, and these were virtually the exact opposite of what the critical historiography thought, from the time of Hekataios to that of Ephoros, that it had put behind itself and had in fact actively opposed. The choice was construed as one between the use of the fabulous, *to mythōdes*, and direct, immediate representation. The new demand was that everything needed to be presented as if the listeners or readers were present at the event in question; history should be like theatre. Gorgias, the *dissoi logoi*, Plato, and Aristotle's *Poetics* were all in agreement about the possible effects of poetic treatment of any subject; it could radiate enchantment, but also deception. Up to the time of Duris, this was taken to be a danger for the decorous organisation of speech, and thus also for any work of history standing under the influence of rhetoric. It was an acceptable price to pay for attaining other goals, but it was recognised as a price. Suddenly, all this was reversed: something that had been dangerous and used with extreme caution became the central plank in the historian's credo, the focal point around which the presentation of the past was organised.

This is basically a return to the poetic origins of history, and the ambiguity that was there from the start – 'Is it true or is it an illusion?' – comes to be accentuated in a slightly different way, but it does not disappear. There is no necessary opposition between these two, rather, the poetic comes to the aid of what is factual, because it permits it to be adequately represented. Both advocates and critics of this approach agree that it operates by emphasising the dramatic – the weeping and gnashing of teeth, the things that cause gooseflesh and bring on tears – and it uses these as a special poetic means of giving what it takes to be an adequate representation of past events.[126] So, it is not completely without cause that this has been described as 'writing history as tragedy',[127] but, because of the complex discussions that that coinage has aroused, I would prefer to speak of a 'theatrical' mode of writing history. Quintilian's remark shows to what extent these poetic elements became and remained characteristic of historiography when he writes that written history (*historia*) is 'in some sense a poem in prose' (*quodam modo carmen solutum*).[128] It is no accident that this reminds one of Gorgias' definition of poetry as 'speech (*logos*) in metrical form'.

I think we can determine where this new approach to history was born with some precision: it was the expedition of Alexander the Great that broke down the boundaries of what could be imagined. It was thought that one could describe him and what he had wrought adequately only by appeal to the monstrous and miraculous, the paradoxical and incredible, even the impossible – all those things that one had struggled previously to excise carefully from the writing of history, using the rational criticism of myths. People had 'the impression that the Macedonian ruler had realised myth and that with him myth had become reality'.[129] It was therefore tempting to use all the poetic and literary means available, including those associated with the theatre and with drama, to try to give an adequate picture of all these fabulous events, and also to structure the sudden

---

[126] See Meister 2010, 155f and Flashar 2013, 155–7, 166–8 on these effects, which are already mentioned in Gorgias (B 11.9) in Plato's *Ion* (535b–e), and in Aristotle's famous definition of tragedy in terms of the generation of *phobos and eleos*.

[127] Walbank 1960/1985/2011, is fundamental (including its critical element). See also Gaertner and Hausburg 2013, 144–50 with further references.

[128] 10.1.31. On this aspect of Quintilian see Ax 1990b.

[129] Moggi 2013, 64 ('impressione che il sovrano macedone realizzasse il mito e che nello stesso tempo con lui il mito diventasse realtà').

revolution in world affairs that he brought about as a completely unexpected and unimaginable '*peripeteia*'.

This all also produces a change in the conceptual scheme and the connotations of the concepts used about history, as one can see in the criticism of this new type of historiography, a criticism that is largely inspired by philosophical objections to it. Given the state of the textual evidence, we actually know the work of the critics of this 'theatrical' approach to history better than we do the literature that they are attacking. 'Myth' is now re-defined so that it comes to mean something like what '*to mythōdes*' used to mean, that is, something not credible, something that was 'impossible for purely physical reasons' (*kata physin*).[130] It is sometimes also called an 'untrue' or 'false history' (*pesudēs historia*), which is invented. The contrast is 'true history' (*alēthēs historia*), which is supposed to be a simple report of what really happened. The critics claim that the new history is unrealistic because it puts such emphasis on the miraculous and monstrous (*thaumaston, teratologia*, etc.)[131] and on that which is improbable and unexpected (*paralogos, paradoxologia, peripeteia*).[132]

The general term that is used for these features is *kompos* (or the corresponding adverb *kompōdōs*).[133] Its basic sense is 'noise', but it is then used by extension for boasting, exaggeration, swagger. Here, it refers to a stylistic category: bombast or, as we might say, 'purple prose', but also with the connotation that the credibility of the whole account is diminished by the presence in it of so much exaggeration.[134] One could also call this 'poetic' or 'tragic'. It certainly serves to make an emotional impact on the audience, whether this is composed of listeners or readers, and it intends to shock, which is called '*ekplēttein*' ('startle'). In poetry, especially

---

[130] One could cite numerous passages to this effect, to mention a few of the more important: Polybios 3.47.9, 34.34.1–4; Asklepiades of Myrleia cited in Sextus Empiricus adversus mathematicos 1.252; Cic. inv. 1.27; Auct. Ad Her. 1.12f; Strabo 1.2.35; Quint. 2.42; Sex. Emp. Emp. Math. 1.263f, and see also Procop. BP 1.1.4. The remarks of Walbank 1960/1985/2011 are still very enlightening.

[131] See, for instance, Polybios 3.47.6, 15.34.1; Didymos in Demosth. col 12.50; Strabo 15.1.28.

[132] See, in the first instance, Polybios 2.56.13, 3.58.1, 10.2.6, 16.12.6, 9f; Dion. Hal. Ad Pomp. 6.11; Strabo 15.1.28.

[133] See P. Oxy LXXI 4808.9f.

[134] Stefan Schorn 2013, 115f. has recently demonstrated that quite clearly. The papyrus that is cited in the previous note P.Oxy. LXXI 4808 is a fragment of a collection of texts by historians who were critical of this theatrical approach to history. The remark cited here refers to Kleitarchos, one of the historians of Alexander. On *kompōdōs*, see L. Prandi in Moggi 2013, 84; F. Muccioli in Moggi 2013, 99 (whose references to FGrH 137 T 6 support the interpretation of Schorn).

in the theatre, this is perfectly legitimate, but not in any form of history committed to the truth.[135]

However, it is also perfectly easy to reverse this critical perspective and extrapolate to a 'poetic history' that used all of these terms in an innovative way and gave them a special positive value, adapting the poetic licence which is granted to 'invention' in literature to the representation of history and interpreting this as something good. Invention allows one to create a particular density of experience and to bring the audience as close as possible to historical events. What one is doing is not falsifying or deceiving, but providing an adequate – in fact, *the* adequate – impression of the events, so that the audience takes a direct part in it. The events really were colossal and unexpected, and what the historian is doing is simply making that palpable. This is just a matter of giving an appropriate interpretation of what happened. As we shall now see, there is reason to ascribe to some historians of this period an attempt to develop this kind of history.

Dramatic elements break through massively for the first time in the work of Kallisthenes (FGrH 124), who transforms incidents that occurred during Alexander's expedition into strange and alien events, which show the Macedonian king in a divine light. Later critics like Strabo and Plutarch, both of them intellectuals with a penchant for philosophy, say that Kallisthenes 'treated' the narrated events 'as if they were the sort of things that happen in a tragedy',[136] which is, by the way, the same thing they said about Duris. Kallisthenes, though, who also had a weakness for philosophy and was both the nephew and a collaborator of Aristotle's on historical and antiquarian matters, was himself almost certainly rather a devotee of the historiography in the style of Ephoros, rather than in that of Duris.[137] However, as a participant in Alexander's expedition he had the task of proclaiming the glory of the new hero, the descendant of Herakles and of Achilles, and finally, in fact, even of Zeus himself, to the Greek world. How could he have discharged this better than by expressing the truth while using the means provided by literature? This approach,

---

[135] On this, see especially Polybios 2.16.13–5, 2.56.7-13 (p. 130), 3.47.6, 15.34.1, 34.4.1-4; Strabo 1.2.35; Plut. Perikles 28.2, Alkibiades 32.5; Agatharchides de mari Erythraeo 8 (GGM I 117). In this context the word *plattein/plásma* ('form', 'shape' or anything formed or shaped – a sense that comes very close to that of 'fiction'), which in rhetoric and poetics can be used for the fashioning of a 'hypothetically true story' (*hōs alēthōs historia*) can acquire the negative sense of 'merely making up'(Walbank 1960/1985/2011). This is the way it is used by Hesych. (s.v. *Samiakos tropos*) in his criticism of Duris; see also Strabo 1.2.35.

[136] Strabo 17.1.43 (Kallisth. F 14), compare Plut. Perikles 28.2 (about Duris).

[137] On Kallisthenes, see especially Pédech 1984, 15–69; Prandi 1985; Zahrnt 2006; and the summary by Meister 1990, 104–7.

then, can probably be traced back to him, although as early as 327 BC he became a victim of the unbridled wrath of the great king, because he finally decided to remain loyal to his commitment to the freedom of the Hellenes.

There is no reason to be surprised that this approach was dominant for a while during the time of Alexander's expedition and also in the following, scarcely less dramatic, period of wars between Alexander's successors. Polybios gives a good account of this way of writing history, when discussing Phylarchos.[138] In order to brand the Macedonian Antigonos Gonatas and the Achaians, under Aratos, as particularly cruel, Phylarchos 'tried everything he could to provoke the pity (*eleos*) of the readers and make them feel the pain (*sympathies*) that the events inflicted'. That is why he describes women embracing altars, tearing their hair, and exposing their breasts, and also 'tears and lamentations of men and women, all confused together, carried off with their children and aged parents'.

In contrast to this, though, Polybios says, the historian should not spread terror by describing monstrous things (*ekplēttein ... terateuomenon*) and should not put invented speeches that recount the possible consequences of what has occurred into the mouths of the participants, 'as tragic poets do'. The reason is that the historian must concentrate on the truth in order to benefit those who wish to learn from history. Tragedy, however, is the domain in which 'the plausible' dominates, 'even if this plausibility is an illusion based on the deception of the viewer' (*to pithanon, k'an ēi pseudos, dia tēn apatēn tōn theōmenōn*, 12). With that, Polybios takes a position very like that of Aristotle in the *Poetics*, with its casuistic analysis of 'forms of deception'.[139]

The comments of Agatharchides in his treatise about the Red Sea (1.8 GGM I 117) point in the same direction. He speaks of the 'licences' (*exousiai*) of the writers who recount myths (*mythopoioi*), and stresses that the poets were more concerned with 'emotion' (*psychagōgia*) than with truth. But that was precisely what theatrical history-writing had intended to do. And in cases of doubt, emotional effect and success in deception (*apatē tōn theōmenōn*) were more important for historians in this tradition than was the factual correctness of what they recounted, that is, than the *alētheia* which had been so prized in the historiographic tradition (and also among rhetoricians).

---

[138] 2.56.7-10. On Phylarchos (FGrH 88), see in the first instance Kroymann 1956; Gabba 1957; Pédech 1989; Verhaegendoren 2010, and the short summary in Meister 1990, 100f.
[139] See Schmitt 2009, 203 on Aristot. Poet. 24.1460a12–1460b2 (see also Höffe 2009b, 21).

Polybios criticised all of this vigorously, but one must be cautious here in drawing conclusions.[140] Even Polybios must admit what the theatrical historians claim, namely that the historian's main concern must be to serve the cause of making historical narratives clear and vivid, because that is part of the task of representing reality. In addition, Polybios himself was fully aware to what extent vivid description was an integral part of history-writing. John Marincola (2013, 80–90) has recently stressed how close Polybios himself actually was to theatrical historiography, a fact that the traditional polemical intention of his remarks tends rather to make invisible. If one takes his explicit pronouncements at face value, Polybios is concerned in the first instance with truth, that is, with factual correctness, and that is why he takes such a definite position against uncontrolled exaggeration, the unrestricted use of dramatic means, and the priority given to effects and the calling forth of emotional reactions. But he also knew that one of the goals of the historian was to produce an attractive account (which would 'delight' the reader; *terpsis*) (15.36.1–10). So, the historian was not to be emotionally neutral (see, for instance, 2.56.13) – even if that were possible.

Polybios speaks explicitly of *energeia* and/or *enargeia*,[141] which means that past events must become present, must be made visible to our own eyes, and be 'close enough to touch'. What we have here, in my view, is something that goes beyond all the rich polemical debates about the proper way to write history. What becomes visible is a common feature of Hellenistic historiography, and in fact of Hellenistic literature and culture in general, what one might call its '*verism*'.[142]

Kunze describes the effect for which early and high Hellenistic art strove, by analysing the Toro Farnese, a group of figures sculpted by

---

[140] After all, as a matter of principle, one must note that Polybios himself is engaged in a competition with other historians, and this is part of his polemic. In particular, one must keep in mind that his criticism of Phylarchos is part of an attempt to defend Aratos and the Achaians against literary attacks on them.

[141] Which of these two words stand in the text cannot be unambiguously determined. The argument for *enargeia* is that this word is widely used in Hellenistic literature and literary theory (references in Kunze 2002, 235 n. 1383). On this question in general see Polybios-Lexikon s.vv. and Pédech 1964, 258 with n. 19 and especially Schepens 1975. One might, by the way, follow the usage of Agatharchides and speak of *pragmatikē enargeia* – the 'concreteness of the facts' as we might call it. See now Maier 2018 on *enargeia* in Agatharchides.

[142] The expression 'close enough to grasp' is taken from the title of a dissertation by Christian Kunze (2002). In ancient literature and literary theory, we know that various terms are used for this feature, such as *alēthinos*, *etymos* (see references in Kunze 2002, 233 n. 1360, and in general n. 1355), *akribes* (Theokr. 15.81), but sometimes the emphasis is still put on the deceptive, and illusory (*pseudos*) (Apoll. Rhod. 1.765). See also Queyrel 2010 with references to the connection between literature and the visual arts.

Apollonios and Tauriskos in about the first half of the second century BC. He uses for the specific and innovative forms of this work words that express exactly the same artistic intention as the one which we, on the basis of Polybios' critical account, can hypothetically ascribe to Phylarchos, the goal that animated this kind of history in the ancient world.

> The nature of the actions depicted unmistakeably reveals that the artist was trying to evoke strong and elemental emotions. What is presented are violent actions of superhuman-heroic energy, terrifying threats of the use of lethal force, and to increase the effect, in contrast the despairing pleading of the woman who is the victim, whose upper torso is exposed in a way designed to induce pity. What is noteworthy is that the myth is entirely transformed into concrete action. The punishment of Dirke ... is dramatised as an event that really takes place directly before the eyes of the viewer ... The viewer is forced to follow the action unfolding in such a dramatic way with keen attention, cannot keep it at a distance, and must succumb to its effect.[143]

---

[143] Kunze 2002, 36.

Concluding Perspectives

Greek historiography does not end at this point, in the Hellenistic era, but this is where my competence, which in any case has been subject to significant strain in writing this book, comes to an end. Still, I hope the reader will permit me a glance – perhaps a more than minimal glance – beyond the bounds I have set myself here. If we wish to take history as an element of culture (and not only of ancient culture), as I have done here, then we must also embrace the interlocking of that which is past and that which is present, of the factually correct and the deceptive, of the true and the poetic. We have taken account of the reservations of Polybios, but we have seen that these need to be qualified. So, it seems to me that recourse to rhetorical and theatrical means, the poetic and the literary in history-writing, are by no means *eo ipso* objectionable and to be rejected in principle. This is particularly the case when the project is to bring history closer to people, to make it sensibly palpable and accessible. This was probably also the intention of Duris and Phylarchos.

Christian Meier has recently stressed in a speech that was part of a ceremony of commemoration for Hermann Strasburger that this project is a dignified and worthy one, even if judged by the standards of today. Part of the inherent value of this approach lies in the fact that it increases our sensitivity to the perspective of the victims – *pathē* in the original sense. Without it, too, it would be impossible for us to experience ancient texts at all (Meier 2013, 35f.), and being able to experience them in an emotionally gripping way actually makes them, in a more all-encompassing sense, our sources. Angelos Chaniotis' remarks at Princeton were even more significant. Speaking of a visit of the Hollywood director Oliver Stone, he said:

> In his talk in Wolfensohn Hall, Stone focused on his film *Alexander*, a fourth version of which is in preparation. He shared with the audience his passion for the man who arguably and most radically changed the course of ancient history through his campaigns from his native Macedonia to India.

Following a great tradition that goes back to Johann Gustav Droysen's *History of Alexander the Great* (1833) – the book that laid the foundation for the study of Alexander – Stone narrated the story of a man driven by passion and vision. Inspired by mythical heroes, haunted by childhood memories, bereft of his greatest love, and surrounded by suspicion and betrayal. Listening to Stone speak, one could easily be seduced to believe that his is the narrative of an eyewitness, not a modern interpretation of ancient sources. This is where a cinematographic approach to history has clear advantages over that of the scholarly historical narrative; it creates in the audience the illusion of 'being there' and, in so doing, makes strong impressions, arouses empathy, provokes thoughts . . .

In the second century B.C.E. the historian Polybios criticized his fellow historian Phylarchos for writing in such a manner that his readers had the impression that they were eyewitnesses to what he was narrating. Eager to arouse pity and empathy among his readers, Phylarchos talked of women clinging to one another, tearing their hair and baring their breasts, and of the lamentations of women, children, and aged parents led away to captivity. Polybios resented all that, because he made a sharp distinction between the treatment of the past by the tragic poet, who seeks to thrill and charm an audience in the moment, and the historian, who seeks to educate for all time.

Polybios may be right in distinguishing between history and drama, but he is wrong in all other respects: in his assumption that empathy can be separated from cognition, and emotion from reason, and in his assumption that drama is less instructive than historiography. Twenty-two centuries later, audiences have the illusion that they are eyewitnesses of events, not thanks to the words of skillful narrators, but thanks to the moving images presented to them by the directors of feature movies and documentaries. The motion picture, the most popular form of dramatization, entertains, educates, and fills us with empathy. In this respect, it is an ally of the historian, not a rival. The dialogue of historians with Oliver Stone indicated the possibilities of interplay between scholarly history and the screen.[1]

However, at the latest, at this point one must not forget the ambiguity, for which the Greeks had a clear sense from the very beginning and despite all the metamorphoses and changes in their historiography and in their intentional history. The old problem was even made more profound and acute, by virtue of the fact that the deceptive, now neutrally called 'the fictive', as a medium for arousing emotional reactions, is not only grudgingly accepted as a price worth paying, but even welcomed with open arms. It is not for nothing that Phylarchos is cited. This permits one to draw the

---

[1] https://www.ias.edu/ideas/ancient-history-director's-cut.

conclusion that the old debates will continue to be relevant and will continue to be as sharply conducted as they were in antiquity.[2]

Precisely if one wishes to derive something positive from the intermingling of the poetic and theatrical, on the one side, and the true on the other, or thinks that it is in any case unavoidable, one is still confronted with the question of the proportions of the mixture: what weight does each of the two carry and where should the centre of gravity be? Should the attempt to present a vivid, immediately palpable truth outweigh the real, factual, 'pragmatic' truth? Should, in case of doubt, the striving for effect and illusions have preponderance? There is another possibility: one might take the decisive criterion – as it were, the qualification board which passes on admissibility of results – to be that the correct procedures have been followed and thus that the results presented are fully warranted; one could hold this view while at the same time by no means denying rhetoric and literary finish an important place in historiography.

For us, let Polybios stand as representative of this last possibility. The approach he developed, even though he sometimes exaggerated it when he was engaged in polemics, remained an important one in Hellenistic historiography.[3] The most significant components of this new approach were the renewed striving for sober, historical truth and a deep scepticism about sensationalism and the generation of myths. Agatharchides is committed to this position, as is Poseidonios (who was deeply influenced by Agatharchides), and the whole 'stoic' strand of historiography, including to some extent Diodoros, but especially Strabo. They developed very clear criteria for distinguishing correct from incorrect and truth from illusion. As a result, an epistemological grid became available, which retained its usefulness for the historiography of the Greeks for the whole period during which it flourished until far after the end of antiquity.

I will not be able to treat here the other major historians outside the mainstream who made notable contributions. Let me simply mention Timaios and Flavius Josephus. For them, too, reliability stood particularly

---

[2] Liebersohn 2010 has recently analysed the relevant critical debates about rhetoric that took place in the philosophical schools of antiquity.

Hayden White (1973) had a provocative effect on modern historians, but the debate about his position basically runs parallel to this ancient discussion. The main difference is that the modern discussion takes place after what is sometimes called 'the linguistic turn' in the post-modern milieu in which some were tempted to think that 'anything goes' was a good methodological principle. In response to this, historians have a tendency to circle the wagons, and to try to raise from the dead again the spirit of Leopold von Ranke (see Evans 1997).

[3] See the analysis of the approaches to history-writing in the Hellenistic period given by Pédech 1964, 74f who, to be sure, places the accents slightly differently.

high up in the scale of values for a historian.[4] We should not rashly subordinate this and similar achievements to the desire to bring the past back to life and make it easily visualisable. On the other hand, it will not do simply to anathemise from the very beginning any form of polished rhetorical and literary presentation of the past. If one did that, one would destroy completely our ability to see one of the essential properties of history, which is the narrative potential which it contains.

This is important because of the elemental connection that exists between narrative and human experience. Historiography can attain its own inherent, specific goal only when it has found literary form in a narrative. Only, that is, 'when it has ordered the past and configured it as narrative in ever changing, ever new ways. That is the only way to make experience of the past possible' (Stierle 1979, 118). There is, then, no place for an exclusive 'either/or', but only for a sensibility which recognise 'not only/but also'.[5] This is precisely the conclusion we should draw from studying the ancient obsession with, but also ambivalence about, the relation between truth and literary fiction. This is the quintessential result of my way of looking at Greek conceptions of history from the perspective of the cultural sciences.

If we consider Greek historiography relative to the standards that present professional historians and proponents of a critical science of history profess, and especially relative to their claims to objectivity, we may come to take the tension between facts and the imaginative elaboration of the facts, between real events and the rhetorical and literary treatment of such events, and the constant vacillation between the claim to truth and the evident pleasure humans take in illusion, in short, between fiction and truth, to be something to be suspicious about or even something to regret. However, we can learn from the Greeks, not least from their thinkers and poets, that despite our best efforts we will never be able to completely sever and separate 'that which belongs together'. So, we

---

[4] See Schepens 2007, 52f. on Timaios, who was often denigrated as mere 'armchair historian' and for his position. The revaluation of the direct testimony of eyewitnesses and of hearsay (Strabo 2.5.11) is also noteworthy. Casaubon saw in this change of valuation an implicit criticism of Polybios (see Radt on this passage). On Josephus and rhetoric, see, for instance c. Ap. 1.24–7 which contains a fundamental criticism of Greek historiography, which is said to be lacking because of the absence of early literacy in Greece (1.9–14), and also Sterling 2007, 234. See Hall 1996 and van Henten and Abusch 1996 on the influence of rhetoric on Josephus, and Gehrke 2016 on Josephus and the search for truth.

[5] See the important discussion of this topic in Daniel 2002, 432–43. The papers by Mann 1979 and Heuß 1979 on the close connection between history and narrative are still eminently worth reading. Recently Felix Maier (2012a, principally 319–34) has shown to what extent Polybios embodies these virtues in his history.

should not take this tension in the very nature of history-writing to be something negative, but, rather, as a bonus. Research is tremendously important, without a doubt essential, but there is something beyond it, and where does history become an active power in informing culture and life, if not in narrative? Narrative takes the distant truth to be its unreachable, imaginary object, and at the same time makes the past comprehensible by bringing it to life for people of the present.

References

Achilli, Ilenia (2012) 'Sullo scrittoio dello storico: in margine a D. Pausch (ed.), Stimmen der Geschichte: Funktionen von Reden in der antiken Historiographie', *Sileno* 38, 205–12.
Alcock, Susan E. (2002) *Archaeologies of the Greek Past: Landscape, Monuments, and History*, Cambridge.
Assmann, Aleida (1999) *Erinnerungsräume: Formen und Wandlungen des kulturellen Gedächtnisses*, Munich.
Assmann, Aleida and Friese, Heidrun (eds.) (1998) *Identitäten: Erinnerung, Geschichte, Identität*, 3rd ed., Frankfurt.
Assmann, Jan (1992) *Das kulturelle Gedächtnis: Schrift, Erinnerung und politische Identität in frühen Hochkulturen*, Munich.
Assmann, Jan (2003/1991) *Stein und Zeit: Mensch und Gesellschaft im alten Ägypten*, 3rd ed., Munich.
Ax, Wolfram (ed.) (1990a) *Memoria rerum veterum: Neue Beiträge zur antiken Historiographie und Alten Geschichte. Festschrift für Carl Joachim Classen zum 60. Geburtstag*, Stuttgart.
Ax, Wolfram (1990b) 'Die Geschichtsschreibung bei Quintilian', in Wolfram Ax (ed.), *Memoria rerum veterum: Neue Beiträge zur antiken Historiographie und Alten Geschichte. Festschrift für Carl Joachim Classen zum 60. Geburtstag*, Stuttgart, 133–68.
Backhaus, Knut (2007/2009) 'Lukas der Maler: Die Apostelgeschichte als intentionale Geschichte der christlichen Erstepoche', in Knut Backhaus and Gerd Häfner (eds.), *Historiographie und fiktionales Erzählen: Zur Konstruktivität in Geschichtstheorie und Exegese*, Neukirchen-Vluyn, 30–66.
Bal, Mieke (2002) *Kulturanalyse*, Frankfurt.
Barber, Godfrey Louis (1935) *The Historian Ephorus*, Cambridge.
Baumbach, Manuel, Petrovic, Andrej, and Petrovic, Ivana (eds.) (2010) *Archaic and Classical Greek Epigram*, Cambridge.
Berger, Peter L. and Luckmann, Thomas (1966) *The Social Construction of Reality*, Garden City, NY (German ed.: *Die soziale Konstruktion der Wirklichkeit: Eine Theorie der Wissenssoziologie*, Frankfurt, 1969).
Bernstein, Frank (2004) *Konflikt und Migration: Studien zu griechischen Fluchtbewegungen im Zeitalter der sogenannten Großen Kolonisation*, St. Katharinen.

Bertelli, Luigi (2001) 'Hecataeus: From Genealogy to Historiography', in Nino Luraghi (ed.), *The Historian's Craft in the Age of Herodotus*, Oxford, 67–94.
Bichler, Reinhold (2012) 'Über die Periodisierung griechischer Geschichte in der griechischen Historie', in Joseph Wiesehöfer and Thomas Krüger (eds.), *Periodisierung und Epochenbewusstsein im Alten Testament und seinem Umfeld*, Stuttgart, 87–119.
Bichler, Reinhold (2013) 'Die analogen Strukturen in der Abstufung des Wissens über die Dimensionen von Raum und Zeit in Herodots *Historien*', in Klaus Geus, Elisabeth Irwin, and Thomas Poiss (eds.), *Herodots Wege des Erzählens: Logos und Topos in den Historien*, Frankfurt, 17–41.
Bielfeldt, Ruth (2012) 'Polis Made Manifest: The Physiognomy of the Public in the Hellenistic City – with a Case Study of the Agora in Priene', in Christina Kuhn (ed.), *Politische Kommunikation und öffentliche Meinung in der antiken Welt*, Stuttgart, 78–122.
Bing, Peter (2009) *The Scroll and the Marble: Studies in Reading and Reception in Hellenistic Poetry*, Ann Arbor, MI.
Biraschi, Anna Maria (1989) *Tradizioni epiche e storiografia: Studi su Erodoto e Tucidide*, Naples.
Biraschi, Anna Maria (1996) 'Nostoi in Occidente ed esperienza "precoloniale" nella tradizione e nella coscienza antica: aspetti et problemi', in Francesco Prontera (ed.), *La Magna Grecia e il mare: Studi di storia marittima*, Taranto, 77–106.
Bleckmann, Bruno (2006) *Fiktion als Geschichte: Neue Studien zum Autor der Hellenika Oxyrhynchia und zur Historiographie des vierten vorchristlichen Jahrhunderts*, Göttingen.
Blösel, Wolfgang (2004) *Themistokles bei Herodot: Spiegel Athens im fünften Jahrhundert. Studien zur Geschichtsschreibung und historiographischen Konstruktion des griechischen Freiheitskampfes 480 v. Chr.*, Stuttgart.
Blumenberg, Hans (1990) *Arbeit am Mythos*, 5th ed., Frankfurt.
Boedeker, Deborah (1996) 'Heroic Historiographie: Simonides and Herodotus on Plataea', *Arethusa* 29, 223–42.
Boehringer, David (2001) *Heroenkulte in Griechenland von der geometrischen bis zur klassischen Zeit: Attika, Argolis, Messenien*, Berlin.
Borza, Eugene N. (1990) *In the Shadow of Olympus: The Emergence of Macedon*, Princeton, NJ.
Boschung, Dietrich, Busch, Alexandra W., and Versluys, Miguel John (2015) *Reinventing 'The Invention of Tradition'? Indigenous Pasts and the Roman Present*, Paderborn.
Bouchet, Christian and Giovannelli-Jouanna, Pascale (2015) *Isocrate : Entre jeu rhétorique et enjeux politiques*, Lyon.
Bowie, Ewen L. (1986) 'Early Greek Elegy, Symposium and Public Festival', *Journal of Hellenic Studies* 106, 13–35.

Bowie, Ewen L. (2001) 'Ancestors of Historiography in Early Greek Elegiac and Iambic Poetry?', in Nino Luraghi (ed.), *The Historian's Craft in the Age of Herodotus*, Oxford, 45–66.

Bowie, Ewen L. (2010) 'The Trojan War's Reception in Early Greek Lyric, Iambic and Elegiac Poetry', in Lin Foxhall, Hans-Joachim Gehrke, and Nino Luraghi (eds.), *Intentional History: Spinning Time in Ancient Greece*, Stuttgart, 57–87.

Bravo, Benedetto (2007) 'Antiquarianism and History', in John Marincola (ed.), *A Companion to Greek and Roman Historiography*, Oxford, 515–27.

Breglia, Luisa (1996) *Studi su Eforo*, Naples.

Bruner, Jerome S. (1998) 'Vergangenheit und Gegenwart als narrative Konstruktionen', in Jürgen Straub (ed.), *Erzählung, Identität und historisches Bewußtsein: Die psychologische Konstruktion von Zeit und Geschichte*, Frankfurt, 46–80.

Buchheim, Thomas (2012) *Gorgias von Leontinoi: Reden, Fragmente und Testimonien. Griechisch-deutsch*. Translated, edited, with an introduction and notes by Thomas Buchheim, Hamburg.

Burkert, Walter (1987/2001) 'The Making of Homer in the Sixth Century B.C.: Rhapsodes versus Stesichoros', in *Papers on the Amasis Painter and His World*. Colloquium sponsored by the Getty Center for the History of Art and Humanities and symposium sponsored by the J. Paul Getty Museum, Malibu, 43–62 (now in Walter Burkert, *Kleine Schriften I. Homerica*, Christoph Riedweg (ed.), Göttingen, 198–217).

Burkert, Walter (2004) *Babylon, Memphis, Persepolis: Eastern Contexts of Greek Culture*, Cambridge, MA.

Busolt, Georg (1893) *Griechische Geschichte bis zur Schlacht bei Chaeroneia. Vol. I: Bis zur Begründung des Peloponnesischen Bundes*, 2nd, enlarged, and completely revised edition, Gotha.

Calame, Claude (1996) 'Feste, riti e forme poetiche', in Salvatore Settis (ed.) *I Greci: Storia Cultura Arte Società. 2 Una storia greca. I. Formazione*, Turin, 471–96.

Calame, Claude (2006) 'La fabrication historiographique d'un passé héroïque en Grèce classique: *Archaia* et *palaia* chez Hérodote', *Ktema* 31, 39–49.

Calce, Renata (2011) *Graikoi ed Hellenes: storia di due etnonimi*, Pisa.

Cancik, Hubert (1986) 'Geschichtsschreibung und Priestertum im Vergleich von orientalischer und hellenischer Historiographie bei Flavius Josephus, contra Apionem, Buch I', in Ernst Ludwig Ehrlich, Bertold Klappert, and Ursula Ast (eds.), *Wie gut sind Deine Zelte, Jaakow ... Festschrift zum 60. Geburtstag von Reinhold Mayer*, Gerlingen, 41–62.

Candau Morón, José María, González Ponce, Francisco Javier, and Chávez, Antonio L. (2004) 'Crónicas, fundaciones y el nacimiento de la Historiografía Griega', in José María Candau Morón, Francisco Javier González Ponce, and Gonzalo Cruz Andreotti (eds.), *Historia y mito: El pasado legendario como fuente de autoridad*, Malaga, 13–29.

Candau Morón, José María, González Ponce, Francisco Javier, and Cruz Andreotti, Gonzalo (eds.) (2004) *Historia y mito: El pasado legendario como fuente de autoridad*, Malaga.

Canfora, Luciano (1971/1999/2011) 'Il "ciclo" storico', in *Belfagor* 26, 653–70 (then in *La storiografia greca*, Milan 1999, 61–91; English ed. in John Marincola (ed.) (2011) *Greek and Roman Historiography*, Oxford, 2011, 365–88).
Carr, Edward Hallett (1961) *What Is History?*, London (German ed.: *Was ist Geschichte?*, Stuttgart, 1963).
Castagnoli, Luca and Ceccarelli Paola (2019) *Greek Memories: Theories and Practices*, Cambridge.
Chaniotis, Angelos (2014) 'Mnemopoetik: Die epigraphische Konstruktion von Erinnerung in den griechischen Poleis', in Ortwin Dally, Tonio Hölscher, Susanne Muth, and Rolf Michael Schneider (eds.), *Medien der Geschichte: Antikes Griechenland und Rom*, Berlin, 132–69.
Christesen, Paul (2007) *Olympic Victor Lists and Ancient Greek History*, Cambridge.
Clark, Christopher (2012) *The Sleepwalkers: How Europe Went to War in 1914*, London.
Clarke, Katherine (2008) *Making Time for the Past: Local History and the Polis*, Oxford.
Classen, Carl Joachim (2010) *Herrscher, Bürger und Erzieher: Beobachtungen zu den Reden des Isokrates*, Hildesheim.
Cobet, Justus (2007) 'Das alte Ionien in der Geschichtsschreibung', in Justus Cobet, Volkmar von Graeve, Wolf-Dietrich Niemeier, and Konrad Zimmermann (eds.), *Frühes Ionien. Eine Bestandsaufnahme. Panionion-Symposion Güzelçamlı, 26. September – 1. Oktober 1999*, Mainz, 729–43.
Cobet, Justus, von Graeve, Volkmar, Niemeier Wolf-Dietrich, and Zimmermann Konrad (eds.) (2007) *Frühes Ionien. Eine Bestandsaufnahme. Panionion-Symposion Güzelçamlı, 26. September – 1. Oktober 1999*, Mainz.
Cohen, Shaye J. D. (1988) 'History and Historiography in the Against Apion of Josephus', in Ada Rapoport-Albert (ed.), *Essays in Jewish Historiography: in memoriam A.D. Momigliano* (History and Theory, Appendix 27), Middletown, 1–11.
Cohen-Skalli, Aude (2012) *Diodore de Sicile, Bibliothèque historique. Fragments. Tome I. Livres VI-X. Texte établi, traduit et commenté par Aude Cohen-Skalli*, Paris.
Connerton, Paul (1989) *How Societies Remember*, Cambridge.
Corcella, Aldo (2006) 'The New Genre and Its Boundaries: Poets and Logographers', in Antonios Rengakos and Antonios Tsakmakis (eds.), *Brill's Companion to Thucydides*, Leiden, 33–56.
Crielaard, Jan Paul (2009) 'The Ionians in the Archaic Period: Shifting Identities in a Changing World', in Ton Derks and Nico Roymans (eds.), *Ethnic Constructs in Antiquity: The Role of Power and Tradition*, Amsterdam, 37–84.
Dally, Ortwin, Hölscher, Tonio, Muth, Susanne, and Schneider, Rolf Michael (eds.) (2014) *Medien der Geschichte: Antikes Griechenland und Rom*, Berlin.
Daniel, Ute (2002) *Kompendium Kulturgeschichte: Theorien, Praxis, Schlüsselwörter*, 3rd rev. ed., Frankfurt.
Daux, Georges (1936) *Pausanias en Delphes*, Paris.

Deichgräber, Karl (1952/1984) 'Der listensinnende Trug des Gottes', in *Der listensinnende Trug. Vier Themen des griechischen Denkens*, Göttingen, 108–41 (now in Hans Gärtner, Ernst Heitsch, and Ulrich Schindel (eds.), *Ausgewählte Kleine Schriften*, Hildesheim-Munich-Zurich, 226–64).

Deichgräber, Karl (1958) 'Parmenides' Auffahrt zur Göttin des Rechts. Untersuchungen zum Prooimion seines Lehrgedichts', *Akademie der Wissenschaften und der Literatur Mainz. Abhandlungen der Geistes- und Sozialwissenschaftlichen Klasse*, 11, 631–724.

Detienne, Marcel (1967) *Les maîtres de vérité dans la Grèce archaïque*, Paris.

Diels, Hermann and Kranz, Walther (1952) *Die Fragmente der Vorsokratiker. Griechisch und deutsch*, 6th improved ed. (reprinted 1975), Berlin.

Di Gioia, Anna (2011) 'La duplicità di Phokos e l'identità dei Focidesi', in Luisa Breglia, Alda Moleti, and Maria Luisa Napolitano (eds.), *Ethne, identità e tradizioni: la 'terza' Grecia e l'Occidente*, Pisa, 197–218.

Dillery, John (2005) 'Sacred History', *American Journal of Philology* 126, 505–26.

Dilthey, Wilhelm (1983) *Texte zur Kritik der historischen Vernunft*. Edited and introduced by Hans-Ulrich Lessing, Göttingen.

Dougherty, Carol (1993) *The Poetics of Colonization: From City to Text in Archaic Greece*, Oxford.

Dräger, Paul (1997) *Untersuchungen zu den Frauenkatalogen Hesiods*, Stuttgart: Steiner.

Drews, Robert (1992) 'Herodotus 1. 94, the Drought ca. 1200 BC, and the Origin of the Etruscans', *Historia* 41, 14–39.

Eisenhut, Werner (1974) *Einführung in die antike Rhetorik und ihre Geschichte*, Darmstadt.

Erler, Michael (1997) '"Mythos und Historie" – Die Atlantisgeschichte als Platons Antwort auf die Frage: "Wie und wozu Geschichtsschreibung?" und Aristoteles' Reaktion', *Dialog. Klassische Sprachen und Literaturen* 31, 80–100.

Erskine, Andrew (2004) 'The Trojan War in Italy: Myth and Local Tradition', in José María Candau Morón, Francisco Javier González Ponce, and Gonzalo Cruz Andreotti (eds.), *Historia y mito. El pasado legendario como fuente de autoridad*, Malaga, 97–107.

Eßbach, Wolfgang (ed.) (2002) *wir/ihr/sie: Identität und Alterität in Theorie und Methode*, Würzburg.

Eucken, Christoph (1983) *Isokrates: seine Positionen in der Auseinandersetzung mit den zeitgenössischen Philosophen*, Berlin.

Eucken, Christoph (2003) 'Zum Konzept der politikoi logoi bei Isokrates', in Wolfgang Ort (ed.), *Isokrates: Neue Ansätze zur Bewertung eines politischen Schriftstellers*, Trier, 34–42.

Evans, Richard J. (1997) *In Defence of History*, London (German ed.: *Fakten und Fiktionen: Über die Grundlagen historischer Erkenntnis*, Frankfurt, 1998).

Falk, Harry (1993) *Schrift im alten Indien*, Tübingen.

Feldman, Louis H. and Levison, John R. (eds.) (1996) *Josephus' Contra Apionem: Studies in Its Character and Context with a Latin Concordance to the Portion Missing in Greek*, Leiden.

Fell, Martin (2004) 'Kimon und die Gebeine des Theseus', *Klio* 86, 16–54.
Figal, Günter (2000) 'Die Wahrheit und die schöne Täuschung. Zum Verhältnis von Dichtung und Philosophie im Platonischen Denken', *Philosophisches Jahrbuch* 107, 301–15.
Finnegan, Ruth (1988) *Literacy and Orality: Studies in the Technology of Communication*, Oxford.
Fittschen, Klaus (1969) *Untersuchungen zum Beginn der Sagendarstellungen bei den Griechen*, Berlin.
Flashar, Helmut (2013) *Aristoteles: Lehrer des Abendlandes*, Munich.
Flower, Michael A. (1994) *Theopompus of Chios: History and Rhetoric in the Fourth Century BC*, Oxford.
Fludernik, Monika and Gehrke, Hans-Joachim (eds.) (1999) *Grenzgänger zwischen Kulturen*, Würzburg.
Fornara, Charles W. (1983) *The Nature of History in Ancient Greece and Rome*, Berkeley.
Foster, Edith and Lateiner, Donald (eds.) (2012) *Thucydides and Herodotus*, Oxford.
Foxhall, Lin (1995) 'Monumental Ambitions. The Significance of Posterity in Greece', in Nigel Spencer (ed.), *Time, Tradition and Society in Greek Archaeology: Bridging the 'Great Divide'*, London, 132–49.
Foxhall, Lin, Gehrke, Hans-Joachim, and Luraghi, Nino (eds.) (2010) *Intentional History: Spinning Time in Ancient Greece*, Stuttgart.
Franchi, Elena (2016) *Die Konflikte zwischen Thessalern und Phokern. Krieg und Identität in der griechischen Erinnerungskultur des 4. Jahrhunderts*, Munich.
Franchi, Elena and Proietti, Giorgia (eds.) (2012) *Forme della memoria e dinamiche identitarie nell'antichità greco-romana*, Trento.
François, Étienne and Schulze, Hagen (eds.) (2001) *Deutsche Erinnerungsorte, I–III*, Munich.
Fränkel, Hermann (1960) *Wege und Formen frühgriechischen Denkens*, 2nd ed., Munich.
Fränkel, Hermann (1962) *Dichtung und Philosophie des frühen Griechentums: Eine Geschichte der griechischen Epik, Lyrik und Prosa bis zur Mitte des fünften Jahrhunderts*. 2nd rev. ed., Munich.
Fried, Johannes (2004) *Der Schleier der Erinnerung. Grundzüge einer historischen Memorik*, Munich.
Fuhrmann, Horst (1996) (with the collaboration of Markus Wesche), *'Sind eben alles Menschen gewesen'. Gelehrtenleben im 19. und 20. Jahrhundert, dargestellt am Beispiel der Monumenta Germaniae Historica und ihrer Mitarbeiter*, Munich.
Funke, Peter and Luraghi, Nino (eds.) (2009) *The Politics of Ethnicity and the Crisis of the Peloponnesian League*, Washington DC.
Gabba, Emilio (1957) *Studi su Filarco: le biografie di Agide e di Cleomede*, Pavia.
Gaertner, Jan Felix and Hausburg, Bianca C. (2013) *Caesar and the Bellum Alexandrinum: An Analysis of Style, Narrative Technique, and the Reception of Greek Historiography*, Göttingen.

Gehrke, Hans-Joachim (1985) *Stasis: Untersuchungen zu den inneren Kriegen in den griechischen Staaten des 5. und 4. Jahrhunderts v. Chr.*, Munich.

Gehrke, Hans-Joachim (1993) 'Thukydides und die Rekonstruktion des Historischen', *Antike und Abendland* 39, 1–19.

Gehrke, Hans-Joachim (1994) 'Mythos, Geschichte, Politik – antik und modern', *Saeculum* 45, 239–64 (English ed.: 'Myth, History, Politics – Ancient and Modern', in Marincola 2011, 40–71).

Gehrke, Hans-Joachim (1997) 'Gewalt und Gesetz. Die soziale und politische Ordnung Kretas in der Archaischen und Klassischen Zeit', *Klio* 79, 23–68.

Gehrke, Hans-Joachim (1998) 'Die Geburt der Erdkunde aus dem Geiste der Geometrie. Überlegungen zur Entstehung und zur Frühgeschichte der wissenschaftlichen Geographie bei den Griechen', in Wolfgang Kullmann, Jochen Althoff, and Markus Asper (eds.), *Gattungen wissenschaftlicher Literatur in der Antike*, Tübingen, 163–92.

Gehrke, Hans-Joachim (2000) 'Mythos, Geschichte und kollektive Identität: Antike exempla und ihr Nachleben', in Dittmar Dahlmann and Wilfried Potthoff (eds.), *Mythen, Symbole und Rituale: Die Geschichtsmächtigkeit der Zeichen in Südosteuropa im 19. und 20. Jahrhundert*, Frankfurt, 1–24 (English translation: 'Myth, History, and Collective Identity: Uses of the Past in Ancient Greece and Beyond', in Nino Luraghi (ed.), *The Historian's Craft in the Age of Herodotus*, Oxford, 286–313).

Gehrke, Hans-Joachim (ed.) (2001) *Geschichtsbilder und Gründungsmythen*, Würzburg.

Gehrke, Hans-Joachim (2003) 'Marathon: Von Helden und Barbaren', in Gerd Krumeich and Susanne Brandt (eds.), *Schlachtenmythen: Ereignis-Erzählung-Erinnerung*, Cologne, 19–32.

Gehrke, Hans-Joachim (2004) 'Was heißt und zu welchem Ende studiert man intentionale Geschichte? Marathon und Troja als fundierende Mythen', in Gerd Melville and Karl-Siegfried Rehberg (eds.), *Gründungsmythen, Genealogien, Memorialzeichen: Beiträge zur institutionellen Konstruktion von Kontinuität*, Cologne, 21–36.

Gehrke, Hans-Joachim (2005a) 'Die Bedeutung der (antiken) Historiographie für die Entwicklung des Geschichtsbewußtseins', in Eve-Marie Becker (ed.), *Die antike Historiographie und die Anfänge der christlichen Geschichtsschreibung*, Berlin, 29–51.

Gehrke, Hans-Joachim (2005b) 'Zur elischen Ethnizität', in Tassilo Schmitt, Winfried Schmitz, and Aloys Winterling (eds.), *Gegenwärtige Antike – antike Gegenwarten. Kolloquium zum 60. Geburtstag von Rolf Rilinger*, Munich, 17–47 (Italian ed.: 'Sull'etnicità elea', *Geographia Antiqua* 12, 2003, 5–22).

Gehrke, Hans-Joachim (2005c) 'Heroen als Grenzgänger zwischen Hellenen und Barbaren', in Erich S. Gruen (ed.), *Cultural Borrowings and Ethnic Appropriations in Antiquity*, Stuttgart, 50–67.

Gehrke, Hans-Joachim (2010) 'Representations of the Past in Greek Culture', in Lin Foxhall, Hans-Joachim Gehrke, and Nino Luraghi (eds.) *Intentional History: Spinning Time in Ancient Greece*, Stuttgart, 15–33.

Gehrke, Hans-Joachim (2011) 'Alfred Heuß und das 21. Jahrhundert: Analysen und – auch (auto)biographische – Betrachtungen', *Saeculum*, 61, 337–54.
Gehrke, Hans-Joachim (2013a) 'Heilige Texte in Hellas? Fundierende Texte der griechischen Kultur in ihrem soziopolitischen Milieu', in Andreas Kablitz and Christoph Markschies (eds.), *Heilige Texte: Religion und Rationalität*, Berlin, 71–86.
Gehrke, Hans-Joachim (2013b) '*Theoroi* in und aus Olympia. Beobachtungen zur religiösen Kommunikation in der archaischen Zeit', *Klio* 95, 40–60.
Gehrke, Hans-Joachim (2013c) 'Die Pentekontaëtie – ein Historiker macht Epoche', in Vincenz Brinkmann (ed.), *Zurück zur Klassik. Ein neuer Blick auf das Alte Griechenland. Eine Ausstellung der Liebieghaus Skulpturensammlung, Frankfurt am Main 8. Februar bis 26. Mai 2013*, Munich, 84–97.
Gehrke, Hans-Joachim (2014) 'Historiographie: Die Gegenwart in der Geschichte', in Ortwin Dally, Tonio Hölscher, Susanne Muth, and Rolf Michael Schneider (eds.), *Medien der Geschichte: Antikes Griechenland und Rom*, Berlin, 37–53.
Gehrke, Hans-Joachim (2016) 'Historical Truth and Historiography: The Case of Flavius Josephus', *Przegląd Historyczny* 107, 421–37.
Gehrke, Hans-Joachim, Hofmann, Kerstin P., Bernbeck, Reinhard, and Näser, Claudia (2011) 'Space and Collective Identities', *Reports of the Research Groups at the Topoi Plenary Session 2010, eTopoi. Journal for Ancient Studies, Special Volume* 1, 1–22.
Giangiulio, Maurizio (1989) *Ricerche su Crotone arcaica*, Pisa.
Giangiulio, Maurizio (ed.) (2005) *Erodoto e il 'modello erodoteo'. Formazione e trasmissione delle tradizioni storiche in Grecia*, Trento.
Giangiulio, Maurizio (2010a) *Memorie coloniali*, Rome.
Giangiulio, Maurizio (2010b) 'Collective Identities, Imagined Past, and Delphi', in Lin Foxhall, Hans-Joachim Gehrke, and Nino Luraghi (eds.), *Intentional History: Spinning Time in Ancient Greece*, Stuttgart, 121–35.
Giangiulio, Maurizo, Franchi, Elena, and Proietti, Giorgia (2019) *Commemorating War and War Dead: Ancient and Modern*, Stuttgart.
Gibson, Bruce and Harrison, Thomas (eds.) (2013) *Polybius and His World: Essays in Memory of F. W. Walbank*, Oxford.
Ginzburg, Carlo (2001) *Die Wahrheit der Geschichte: Rhetorik und Beweis*, Berlin.
Giuliani, Luca (2010) 'Myth as Past? On the Temporal Aspect of Greek Depictions of Legend', in Lin Foxhall, Hans-Joachim Gehrke, and Nino Luraghi (eds.), *Intentional History: Spinning Time in Ancient Greece*, Stuttgart, 35–55.
Giuliani, Luca (2014) 'Mythen- versus Lebensbilder? Vom begrenzten Gebrauchswert einer beliebten Opposition', in Ortwin Dally, Tonio Hölscher, Susanne Muth, and Rolf Michael Schneider (eds.), *Medien der Geschichte: Antikes Griechenland und Rom*, Berlin, 204–26.
Goethe, Johann Wolfgang von and Knebel, Karl Ludwig von (1851) *Briefwechsel (1774–1832)*, 2nd part, Leipzig.

Gotter, Ulrich (2002) 'Akkulturation als Methodenproblem der historischen Wissenschaften', in Wolfgang Eßbach (ed.), *wir/ihr/sie. Identität und Alterität in Theorie und Methode*, Würzburg, 373–406.

Graf, Fritz (1985) *Griechische Mythologie: Eine Einführung*, Munich (Engl., revised and augmented: Greek Mythology. An Introduction, Johns Hopkins U.P. 1993).

Grethlein, Jonas (2003) *Asyl und Athen: Die Konstruktion kollektiver Identität in der griechischen Tragödie*, Stuttgart.

Grethlein, Jonas (2005) 'Gefahren des *lógos*. Thukydides *"Historien"* und die Grabrede des Perikles', *Klio* 87, 41–71.

Grethlein, Jonas (2006a) *Das Geschichtsbild der Ilias: Eine Untersuchung aus phänomenologischer und narratologischer Perspektive*, Göttingen.

Grethlein, Jonas (2006b) 'The Manifold Uses of the Epic Past. The Embassy Scene in Hdt. 7.153–163', *American Journal of Philology* 127, 485–509.

Grethlein, Jonas (2008) 'Memory and Material Objects in the *Iliad* and the *Odyssey*', *Journal of Hellenic Studies* 128, 27–51.

Grethlein, Jonas (2009) 'How Not to Do History: Xerxes in Herodotus' *Histories*', *American Journal of Philology* 130, 195–218.

Grethlein, Jonas (2010) *The Greeks and Their Past: Poetry, Oratory and History in the Fifth Century BCE*, Cambridge.

Grethlein, Jonas and Rengakos, Antonios (eds.) (2009) *Narratology and Interpretation: The Content of Narrative Form in Ancient Literature*, Berlin.

Grimm, Jacob and Grimm, Wilhelm (1865) *Deutsche Sagen*, 2nd ed., Berlin.

Gruen, Erich (2013) 'Did Ancient Identity Depend on Ethnicity? A Preliminary Probe', *Phoenix* 67, 1–22.

Gutzwiller, Kathryn (2010) 'Heroic Epitaphs of the Classical Age: The Aristotelian Peplos and Beyond', in Manuel Baumbach, Andrej Petrovic, and Ivana Petrovic (eds.), *Archaic and Classical Greek Epigram*, Cambridge, 219–49.

Habicht, Christian (1961) 'Falsche Urkunden zur Geschichte Athens im Zeitalter des Perikles', *Hermes* 89, 1–35.

Haider, Peter (1996) 'Griechen im Vorderen Orient und in Ägypten bis ca. 590 v. Chr.', in Christoph Ulf (ed.), *Wege zur Genese griechischer Identität: Die Bedeutung der früharchaischen Zeit*, Berlin, 59–115.

Halbwachs, Maurice (1997) *La mémoire collective*. Critical ed. by Gérard Namer, Paris.

Hall, Jonathan M. (1997) *Ethnic Identity in Greek Antiquity*, Cambridge.

Hall, Jonathan (2002) *Hellenicity: Between Ethnicity and Culture*, Chicago.

Hall, Robert G. (1996) 'Josephus' Contra Apionem and Historical Inquiry in the Roman Rhetorical Schools', in Louis H. Feldman and John R. Levison (eds.) (1996) *Josephus' Contra Apionem: Studies in Its Character and Context with a Latin Concordance to the Portion Missing in Greek*, Leiden, 229–49.

Haller, Dieter (2012) *Die Suche nach dem Fremden: Geschichte der Ethnologie in der Bundesrepublik Deutschland 1945–1990*, Frankfurt.

Hammond, Nicholas G. L. and Griffith Guy T. (1979) *A History of Macedonia: Volume II. 550–336 B.C.*, Oxford.

Harder, Annette (1985) *Euripides' Kresphontes and Archelaos, Introduction, Text and Commentary*, Leiden.
Harding, Phillip (2007) 'Local History and Atthidography', in John Marincola (ed.) *A Companion to Greek and Roman Historiography*, Oxford, 180–8.
Hartmann, Andres (2010) *Zwischen Relikt und Reliquie: Objektbezogene Erinnerungspraktiken in antiken Gesellschaften*, Berlin
Hartog, François (2003/2012) *Régimes d'historicité: Présentisme et expériences du temps*, Paris.
Havelock, Eric A. (1982) *The Literate Revolution in Greece and Its Cultural Consequences*, Princeton, NJ.
Helly, Bruno (1995) *L'État thessalien: Aleuas le Roux, les tétrades et les 'Tagoi'*, Lyon.
Herda, Alexander (2006) 'Panionion-Melia, Mykalessos-Mykale, Perseus und Medusa. Überlegungen zur Besiedlungsgeschichte der Mykale in der frühen Eisenzeit', *Istanbuler Mitteilungen* 56, 43–102.
Hertel, Dieter (2003) *Die Mauern von Troia: Mythos und Geschichte im antiken Ilion*, Munich.
Hertel, Dieter (2008) *Das frühe Ilion. Die Besiedlung Troias durch die Griechen (1020–620/25 v. Chr.)*, Munich.
Heuß, Alfred (1946) 'Die archaische Zeit Griechenlands als geschichtliche Epoche', *Antike und Abendland* 2, 26–62 (now also in Alfred Heuß, *Gesammelte Schriften in 3 Bänden*, Stuttgart, I, 2–38).
Heuß, Alfred (1959) *Verlust der Geschichte*, Göttingen (now also in Alfred Heuß, *Gesammelte Schriften in 3 Bänden*, Stuttgart, III, 2158–236).
Heuß, Alfred (1979) 'Geschichtsschreibung und Geschichtsforschung. Zur "Logik" ihrer gegenseitigen Beziehungen', in Hartmut von Hentig (eds.), *Was die Wirklichkeit lehrt. Festschrift für Golo Mann zum 70. Geburtstag*, Frankfurt (now also in Alfred Heuß, *Gesammelte Schriften in 3 Bänden*, Stuttgart, 2250–88).
Heuß, Alfred (1984) 'Vom historischen Wissen', *Historische Zeitschrift* 239, 11–21 (now also in Alfred Heuß, *Gesammelte Schriften in 3 Bänden*, Stuttgart, III, 2116–27).
Heuß, Alfred (1995) *Gesammelte Schriften in 3 Bänden*, Stuttgart.
Higbie, Carolyn (2003) *The Lindian Chronicle and the Greek Creation of Their Past*, Oxford.
Himmelmann, Nikolaus (1994) *Realistische Themen in der griechischen Kunst der archaischen und klassischen Zeit*, Berlin.
Hirschberger, Martina (2004) *Gynaikōn Katalogos und Megalai Ēhoiai: Ein Kommentar zu den Fragmenten zweier hesiodeischer Epen*, Munich.
Höffe, Otfried (ed.) (2009a) *Aristoteles Poetik*, Berlin.
Höffe, Otfried (2009b) 'Einführung in Aristoteles' *Poetik*', in Otfried Höffe (ed.) *Aristoteles Poetik*, 1–27.
Hölscher, Tonio (1973) *Griechische Historienbilder des 5. und 4. Jahrhunderts*, Würzburg.
Hölscher, Tonio (1998) *Öffentliche Räume in frühen griechischen Städten*, Heidelberg.
Hölscher, Tonio (2014) 'Monumente der Geschichte – Geschichte als Monument?', in Ortwin Dally, Tonio Hölscher, Susanne Muth, and Rolf Michael Schneider (eds.), *Medien der Geschichte: Antikes Griechenland und Rom*, Berlin, 254–84.

Hölscher, Uvo (ed.) (1986) *Parmenides: Vom Wesen des Seienden. Die Fragmente griechisch und deutsch*. Edited, translated and annotated by Uvo Hölscher, with an afterword, Frankfurt.
Hölscher, Uvo (1989) *Die Odyssee. Epos zwischen Märchen und Roman*, 2nd rev. ed., Munich.
Hose, Martin (2002) *Aristoteles: Die historischen Fragmente*. Translated and annotated by Martin Hose, Berlin.
Hübner, Lars (2019) *Homer im kulturellen Gedächtnis: Eine intentionale Geschichte archaischer Homerrezeption bis zur Perserkriegszeit*, Stuttgart.
Hugh-Jones, Stephen (1979) *The Palm and the Pleiades: Initiation and Cosmology in Northwest Amazonia*, Cambridge.
Humphreys, Sally C. (1997) 'Fragments, Fetishes and Philosophers: Towards a History of Greek Historiography after Thucydides', in Glenn W. Most (ed.) *Collecting Fragments/Fragmente Sammeln*, Göttingen, 207–24.
Hunter, Richard (ed.) (2005) *The Hesiodic Catalogue of Women: Constructions and Reconstructions*, Cambridge.
Ioakimidou, Chrissula (1997) *Die Statuenreihen griechischer Poleis und Bünde aus spätarchaischer und klassischer Zeit*, Munich.
Irwin, Elizabeth (2006) 'The Transgressive Elegy of Solon?', in Josine H. Blok and André P. M. H. Lardinois (eds.), *Solon of Athens: New Historical and Philological Approaches*, Leiden, 36–78.
Iser, Wolfgang (1993) *Das Fiktive und das Imaginäre*, Frankfurt.
Jacoby, Felix (1949) *Atthis: The Local Chronicles of Ancient Athens*, Oxford.
Jacquemin, Anne (1999) *Offrandes monumentales en Delphes*, Athens.
Jördens, Andrea and Becht-Jördens, Gereon (1994) 'Ein Eberunterkiefer als "Statussymbol" des Aitolischen Bundes (IG XII 2,15). Politische Identitätssuche im Mythos nach dem Ende der spartanischen Hegemonie', *Klio* 76, 172–84.
Jung, Michael (2006) *Marathon und Plataiai: Zwei Perserschlachten als 'lieux de mémoire' im antiken Griechenland*, Göttingen.
Kablitz, Andreas (2003) 'Kunst des Möglichen: Prolegomena zu einer Theorie der Fiktion', *Poetica* 35, 251–73.
Kablitz, Andreas and Markschies, Christoph (eds.) (2013) *Heilige Texte: Religion und Rationalität*, Berlin.
Käppel, Lutz (1999) 'Artikel "Märchen"', *DNP* 7, 643–5, 647–9.
Kannicht, Richard (1980) '"Der alte Streit zwischen Philosophie und Dichtung". Zwei Vorlesungen über Grundzüge der griechischen Literaturauffassung', *Der Altsprachliche Unterricht* 23, 6, 6–37.
Kebric, Robert (1977) *In the Shadow of Macedon: Duris of Samos*, Wiesbaden.
Kern, Otto (1894) *Die Gründungsgeschichte von Magnesia am Maiander*, Berlin.
Kerschner, Michael (2006) 'Die Ionische Wanderung im Lichte neuer archäologischer Forschungen in Ephesos', in Eckart Olshausen and Holger Sonnabend (eds.), *'Troianer sind wir gewesen' – Migrationen in der antiken Welt*, Stuttgart, 364–82.
Knoepfler, Denis (2006) 'L'inscription de Naryka (Locride) au musée du Louvre : la dernière lettre publique de l'empereur Hadrien?' *Revue des Études Grecques* 119, 1–34.

Kocka, Jürgen and Nipperdey, Thomas (eds.) (1979) *Theorie und Erzählung in der Geschichte*, Munich.
Kohl, Karl-Heinz (2003) *Die Macht der Dinge: Geschichte und Theorie sakraler Objekte*, Munich.
Kõiv, Mait (2003) *Ancient Tradition and Early Greek History: The Origins of States in Early-Archaic Sparta, Argos and Corinth*, Tallinn.
Koselleck, Reinhart (1979) *Vergangene Zukunft: Zur Semantik geschichtlicher Zeiten*, Frankfurt.
Koselleck, Reinhart (2000) *Zeitschichten: Studien zur Historik*, Frankfurt.
Kowalzig, Barbara (2007) *Singing for the Gods: Performances of Myth and Ritual in Archaic and Classical Greece*, Oxford.
Krentz, Peter M. (2007) 'The Oath of Marathon, not Plataia', *Hesperia* 76, 731–42.
Kroymann, Jürgen (1956) 'Phylarchos', in *Paulys Realencyclopädie der classischen Altertumswissenschaft (RE)*. Supplement vol. 8, Stuttgart, 471–89.
Kühr, Angela (2006) *Als Kadmos nach Boiotien kam: Polis und Ethnos im Spiegel thebanischer Gründungsmythen*, Stuttgart.
Kullmann, Wolfgang (1960) *Die Quellen der Ilias*, Wiesbaden.
Kullmann, Wolfgang (1992) *Homerische Motive: Beiträge zur Entstehung, Eigenart und Wirkung von Ilias und Odyssee*, published by Roland J. Müller, Stuttgart.
Kullmann, Wolfgang (2002) 'Festgehaltene Kenntnisse im Schiffskatalog und im Troerkatalog der Ilias', in Antonios Rengakos (ed.), *Realität, Imagination und Theorie: Kleine Schriften zu Epos und Tragödie in der Antike*, Stuttgart, 9–26.
Kunze, Christian (2002) *Zum Greifen nah: Stilphänomene in der hellenistischen Skulptur und ihre inhaltliche Interpretation*, Munich.
Kyrieleis, Helmut (2012/2013) 'Pelops, Herakles, Theseus: Zur Interpretation der Skulpturen des Zeustempels von Olympia', *Jahrbuch des deutschen Archäologischen Instituts* 127/128, 51–124.
Landucci Gattinoni, Franca (1997) *Duride di Samo*, Rome.
Lane Fox, Robin (2008) *Travelling Heroes: Greeks and Their Myths in the Epic Age of Homer*, London.
Langewiesche, Dieter (2008) *Zeitwende: Geschichtsdenken heute*. Ed. by Nikolaus Buschmann and Ute Planert, Göttingen.
Le Goff, Jacques (1977/1988) *Storia e memoria*, Turin (French ed.: *Histoire et mémoire*, Paris, 1988; German ed.: *Geschichte und Gedächtnis*, Frankfurt; New York, 1992).
Liebersohn, Yosef Z. (2010) *The Dispute Concerning Rhetoric in Hellenistic Thought*, Göttingen.
Lohmann, Hans (2005) 'Melia, das Panionion und der Kult des Poseidon Helikonios', in Elmar Schwertheim and Engelbert Winter (eds.), *Neue Forschungen zu Ionien*, Bonn, 57–91.
Loraux, Nicole (1981/1993) *L'invention d'Athènes: Histoire de l'oraison funèbre dans la 'cité classique'*, Paris.
Lucius-Hoene, Gabriele and Deppermann, Arnulf (2004) *Rekonstruktion narrativer Identität*, 2nd edition, Wiesbaden.

Luhmann, Niklas (1977) 'Differentiation of Society', *Canadian Journal of Sociology* 2, 1, 29–53; doi:10.2307/3340510.
Lupi, Elisabetta (2019) *I pericoli dell'eudaimonia: La rappresentazione di Sibari nelle testimonianze letterarie di V-III secolo a. C.*, Freiburg.
Luraghi, Nino (2000) 'Author and audience in Thucydides' Archaeology: Some reflections', *Harvard Studies in Classical Philology* 100, 227–39.
Luraghi, Nino (ed.) (2001a) *The Historian's Craft in the Age of Herodotus*, Oxford.
Luraghi, Nino (2001b) 'Local Knowledge in Herodotus' Histories', in Nino Luraghi (ed.), *The Historian's Craft in the Age of Herodotus*, Oxford, 138–60.
Luraghi, Nino (2003) 'The Imaginary Conquest of the Helots', in Nino Luraghi and Susan E. Alcock (ed.), *Helots and Their Masters in Laconia and Messenia: Histories, Ideologies, Structures*, Cambridge, MA.
Luraghi, Nino (2006) 'Traders, Pirates, Warriors: The Proto-history of Greek Mercenary Soldiers in the Eastern Mediterranean', *Phoenix* 60, 21–47.
Luraghi, Nino (2008) *The Ancient Messenians: Constructions of Ethnicity and Memory*, Cambridge.
Luraghi, Nino (2010) 'The Demos As Narrator: Public Honors and the Construction of Future and Past', in Lin Foxhall, Hans-Joachim Gehrke, and Nino Luraghi (eds.), *Intentional History: Spinning Time in Ancient Greece*, Stuttgart, 247–63.
Maaß, Michael (1993) *Das antike Delphi: Orakel, Schätze und Monumente*, Darmstadt.
Maddoli, Gianfranco (1994) 'Die Konzeption von Wachstum und Großwerden in der griechischen Geschichtsschreibung des 5. Jh.', in Egert Pöhlmann and Werner Gauer (eds.), *Griechische Klassik: Vorträge bei der interdisziplinären Tagung des Deutschen Archäologenverbandes und der Mommsengesellschaft vom 24.-27.10.1991 in Blaubeuren*, Nuremberg, 129–39.
Maddoli, Gianfranco (2000/2013) 'Andate e ritorni nell' interpretazione delle tradizioni sui nostoi in Occidente', in *Homère chez Calvin: Figures de l'hellénisme à Genève. Mélanges Olivier Reverdin*, Geneva, 377–85; now also in Gianfranco Maddoli, *Magna Grecia: Tradizioni, culti, storia*, curated by Anna Maria Biraschi / Massimo Nafissi / Francesco Prontera, Perugia, 59–67 (quoted afterwards).
Maier, Bernhard (2012) *Geschichte und Kultur der Kelten*, Munich.
Maier, Felix K. (2012a) *'Überall mit dem Unerwarteten rechnen'. Die Kontingenz historischer Prozesse bei Polybios*, Munich.
Maier, Felix K. (2012b) 'Der Feldherr als Geschichtsschreiber: Polybios' Forderung nach Interdisziplinarität', *Rivista die Filologia e di Istruzione Classica* 140, 295–330.
Maier, Felix K. (2018) 'Wahrheitlichkeit im Sinne der *enargeia*: Geographie und Geschichte bei Agatharchides', in Thomas Blank and Felix K. Maier (eds.), *Die symphonischen Schwestern: Narrative Konstruktion von 'Wahrheiten' in der nachklassischen Geschichtsschreibung*, Stuttgart, 209–25.
Malkin, Irad (1994) *Myth and Territory in the Spartan Mediterranean*, Cambridge.
Malkin, Irad (1998) *The Returns of Odysseus: Colonization and Ethnicity*, Berkeley.

Mann, Golo (1979) 'Plädoyer für die historische Erzählung', in Jürgen Kocka and Thomas Nipperdey (eds.), *Theorie und Erzählung in der Geschichte*, Munich 40–56.
Mansfeld, Jaap and Primavesi, Oliver (eds.) (2012) *Die Vorsokratiker: Griechisch / Deutsch*. Selected, translated, and explained by Jaap Mansfeld and Oliver Primavesi, Stuttgart.
Marek, Christian (2010) *Geschichte Kleinasiens in der Antike*, Munich.
Marincola, John (1997) *Authority and Tradition in Ancient Historiography*, Cambridge.
Marincola, John (1999) 'Genre, Convention and Innovation in Greco-Roman Historiography', in Christina S. Kraus (ed.), *The Limits of Historiography: Genre and Narrative in Ancient Historical Texts*, Leiden, 281–324.
Marincola, John (ed.) (2007a) *A Companion to Greek and Roman Historiography*, Oxford.
Marincola, John (2007b) 'Speeches in Classical Historiography', in John Marincola (ed.) *A Companion to Greek and Roman Historiography*, Oxford, 118–32.
Marincola, John (2007c) 'Universal History from Ephorus to Diodorus', in John Marincola (ed.) *A Companion to Greek and Roman Historiography*, Oxford, 171–9.
Marincola, John (ed.) (2011) *Greek and Roman Historiography*, Oxford.
Marincola, John (2013) 'Polybius, Phylarchus, and "Tragic History": A Reconsideration', in Bruce Gibson and Thomas Harrison (eds.) *Polybius and His World: Essays in Memory of F. W. Walbank*, Oxford, 73–90.
Markschies, Christoph and Wolf, Hubert (eds.) (2010) *Erinnerungsorte des Christentums*, Munich.
Masaracchia, Agostino (2003) 'Isocrate e il mito', in Wolfgang Orth (ed.) *Isokrates: Neue Ansätze zur Bewertung eines politischen Schriftstellers*, Trier, 150–68.
Mavrogiannis, Theodoros (2003) *Aeneas und Euander: Mythische Vergangenheit und Politik in Rom vom 6. Jh. v. Chr. bis zur Zeit des Augustus*, Naples.
Meier, Christian (2013) 'Gedenkrede auf Hermann Strasburger anläßlich der hundertsten Wiederkehr seines Geburtstags', in Frank Bernstein and Hartmut Leppin (eds.), *Wiederanfang und Ernüchterung in der Nachkriegszeit: Dem Althistoriker Hermann Strasburger in memoriam*, Göttingen, 24–44.
Meinecke, Friedrich (1936) *Die Entstehung des Historismus*, Munich.
Meister, Klaus (1982) *Die Ungeschichtlichkeit des Kalliasfriedens und deren historische Folgen*, Wiesbaden.
Meister, Klaus (1990) *Die griechische Geschichtsschreibung: Von den Anfängen bis zum Ende des Hellenismus*, Stuttgart.
Meister, Klaus (2010) *'Aller Dinge Maß ist der Mensch': Die Lehren der Sophisten*, Munich.
Mertens, Dieter (2012) 'Die Agora von Selinunt', *Römische Mitteilungen* 118, 51–178.
Meyer, Doris (2005) *Inszeniertes Lesevergnügen: Das inschriftliche Epigramm und seine Rezeption bei Kallimachos*, Stuttgart.
Meyer, Eduard (1909) *Theopomps Hellenika*, Halle.

Meyer, Elizabeth A. (1997) 'The Outbreak of the Peloponnesian War after Twenty-Five Years', in Charles D. Hamilton and Peter M. Krentz (ed.), *Polis and Polemos: Essays on Politics, War, and History in Ancient Greece, in Honor of Donald Kagan*, Claremont, CA, 23–54.

Michaels, Axel (2013) 'Von Offenbarung zum Ritual: Der Veda in der Überlieferung', in Andreas Kablitz and Christoph Markschies (eds.), *Heilige Texte: Religion und Rationalität*, Berlin, 25–42.

Moggi, Mauro (2013) 'Un nuovo catalogo di storici ellenistici (*POXY* LXXI 4808). Tavola rotonda. Roma, Istituto italiano per la storia antica, 10 giugno 2011', *Rivista di Filologia e di Istruzione Classica* 141, 61–122.

Momigliano, Arnaldo (1950) 'Ancient History and the Antiquarian', *JWI* 13, 285–315 (also in Arnaldo Momigliano, *Contributo alla storia degli studi classici*, Rome, 1955, 67–106).

Most, Glenn W. (ed.) (1997) *Collecting Fragments/Fragmente Sammeln*, Göttingen.

Mühlmann, Wilhelm (1938) *Methodik der Völkerkunde*, Stuttgart.

Müller, Klaus E. (1987) *Das magische Universum der Identität: Elementarformen sozialen Verhalten; ein ethnologischer Grundriß*, Frankfurt.

Murray, Oswyn (2009) 'The Culture of the *Symposion*', in Kurt Raaflaub and Hans van Wees (eds.), *A Companion to Archaic Greece*, Oxford, 508–23.

Nafissi, Massimo (2010) 'The Great rhetra (Plut. Lyc. 6): A Retrospective and Intentional Construct?', in Lin Foxhall, Hans-Joachim Gehrke, and Nino Luraghi (eds.), *Intentional History: Spinning Time in Ancient Greece*, Stuttgart, 89–119.

Nagy, Gregory (1986) 'Pindar's Olympian 1 and the Aetiology of the Olympic Games', *Transactions and Proceedings of the American Philological Association* 116, 71–88.

Nagy, Gregory (1988) 'Mythe et prose en Grèce archaïque: *l'ainos*', in Claude Calame (ed.), *Métamorphoses du mythe en Grèce antique*, Geneva.

Nagy, Gregory (2009) *Homer the Classic*, Washington DC.

Nickau, Klaus (1990) 'Mythos und Logos bei Herodot', in Wolfram Ax (ed.), *Memoria rerum veterum: Neue Beiträge zur antiken Historiographie und Alten Geschichte. Festschrift für Carl Joachim Classen zum 60. Geburtstag*, Stuttgart, 83–100.

Nicolai, Roberto (1997) 'Pater semper incertus: Appunti su Ecateo', *Quaderni Urbinati* 56, 143–64.

Nicolai, Roberto (2001) 'Thucydides' Archaeology: Between Epic and Oral Traditions', in Nino Luraghi (ed.), *The Historian's Craft in the Age of Herodotus*, Oxford, 263–85.

Nicolai, Roberto (2004) *Studi su Isocrate: La communicazione letteraria del IV secolo a.C. e i nuovi generi della prosa*, Rome.

Nicolai, Roberto (2007) 'The Place of History in the Ancient World', in John Marincola (ed.), *A Companion to Greek and Roman Historiography*, Oxford, 13–26.

Nielsen, Thomas Heine (1997) '*Triphylia:* An Experiment in Ethnic Construction and Political Organisation', in Thomas Heine Nielsen (ed.), *Yet More Studies in the Ancient Greek Polis*, Stuttgart, 129–62.
Nietzsche, Friedrich (1980) *On the Advantage and Disadvantage of History for Life.* Translated, with an introduction, by Peter Preuss, Indianapolis.
Nora, Pierre (1984–1992) *Les lieux de mémoire*, Paris.
Nouhaud, Michel (1982) *L'utilisation de l'histoire par les orateurs attiques*, Paris.
Occhipinti, Egidia (2013) ' Teopompo e la Sicilia', *Klio* 95, 84–179.
Orth, Wolfgang (ed.)(2003) *Isokrates: Neue Ansätze zur Bewertung eines politischen Schriftstellers*, Trier.
Osmers, Maria (2013) *'Wir aber sind damals und jetzt immer die gleichen': Vergangenheitsbezüge in der polisübergreifenden Kommunikation der klassischen Zeit*, Stuttgart.
Pallantza, Elena (2005) *Der Troische Krieg in der nachhomerischen Literatur bis zum 5. Jahrhundert v. Chr.*, Stuttgart.
Parmeggiani, Giovanni (2011) *Eforo di Cuma: Studi di storiografia greca*, Bologna.
Patzek, Barbara (1992) *Homer und Mykene: Mündliche Dichtung und Geschichtsschreibung*, Munich.
Pédech, Paul (1964) *La méthode historique de Polybe*, Paris.
Pédech, Paul (1984) *Historiens compagnons d'Alexandre*, Paris.
Pédech, Paul (1989) *Trois historiens méconnus: Théopompe, Duris, Phylarque*, Paris.
Pohl, Walter and Wieser, Veronika (2019) *Ancient and Early Christian Narratives of Community*, Turnhout.
Pohlenz, Max (1937) *Herodot, der erste Geschichtsschreiber des Abendlandes*, Leipzig.
Pownall, Frances (2004) *Lessons from the Past: The Moral Use of History in Fourth-Century Prose*, Ann Arbor, MI.
Prandi, Luisa (1985) *Callistene: Uno storico tra Aristotele e I re Macedoni*, Milan.
Pratt, Louise H. (1993) *Lying and Poetry from Homer to Pindar: Falsehood and Deception in Archaic Greek Poetics*, Ann Arbor, MI.
Pretzler, Maria (2009) 'Arcadia: Ethnicity and Politics in the Fifth and Fourth Centuries BCE', in Peter Funke and Nino Luraghi (eds.), *The Politics of Ethnicity and the Crisis of the Peloponnesian League*, Washington DC, 86–109.
Primavesi, Oliver (2009) 'Zum Problem der epischen Fiktion in der vorplatonischen Poetik', in Ursula Peters and Rainer Warning (eds.), *Fiktion und Fiktionalität in den Literaturen des Mittelalters, Jan-Dirk Müller zum 65. Geburtstag*, I, 105–20.
Prinz, Friedrich (1979) *Gründungsmythen und Sagenchronologie*, Munich.
Proietti, Giorgia (2012a) 'Memoria collettiva e identità etnica: Nuovi paradigmi teorico-metodologici nella ricerca storica', in Elena Franchi and Giorgia Proietti (eds.), *Forme della memoria e dinamiche identitarie nell'antichità greco-romana*, Trento, 13–41.
Proietti, Giorgia (2012b) 'Prospettive socio-antropologiche sull'arcaismo greco: la storiografia erodotea tra tradizione orale e "storia intenzionale", in

Elena Franchi and Giorgia Proietti (eds.), *Forme della memoria e dinamiche identitarie nell'antichità greco-romana*, Trento, 181–206.

Queyrel, François (2010) 'Ekphrasis et perception alexandrine: la réception des œuvres d'art à Alexandrie sous les premiers Lagides', *Antike Kunst* 53, 23–47, pl. 6–8.

Queyrel, François (2012) 'Sculpture grecques et lieux de mémoire: nouvelles orientations de la recherche', *Perspective: La revue de l'INHA* 1, 71–94.

Raaflaub, Kurt (2002) 'Herodot und Thukydides: Persischer Imperialismus im Lichte der athenischen Sizilienpolitik', in Norbert Ehrhardt and Linda-Marie Günther (eds.), *Widerstand – Anpassung – Integration: Die griechische Staatenwelt und Rom*, Stuttgart, 11–40.

Radt, Stefan (2006) *Strabons Geographica*, vol. 5, Göttingen.

Ragone, Giuseppe (1996) 'La Ionia, l'Asia Minore, Cipro', in Salvatore Settis (ed.), *I Greci: Storia Cultura Arte Società. 2 Una storia greca. I. Formazione*, Turin 903–43.

Raible, Wolfgang (ed.) *Medienwechsel: Erträge aus zwölf Jahren Forschung zum Thema, 'Mündlichkeit und Schriftlichkeit'*, Tübingen.

Ranke, Leopold von (1844) *Die serbische Revolution: Aus serbischen Papieren und Mittheilungen*, 2nd ed., Berlin.

Reed, Kathleen (1976) *Theopompus of Chios: History and Oratory in the Fourth Century*, Berkeley.

Reichel, Michael (2005) 'Ist Xenophons Anabasis eine Autobiographie?', in Michael Reichel (ed.), *Antike Autobiographie: Werke – Epochen – Gattungen*, Cologne, 45–73.

Rengakos, Antonios (2006) 'Thucydides' Narrative: The Epic and Herodotean Heritage', in Antonios Rengakos and Antonios Tsakmakis (eds.), *Brill's Companion to Thucydides*, Leiden, 279–300.

Rengakos, Antonios and Tsakmakis, Antonios (eds.) (2006) *Brill's Companion to Thucydides*, Leiden.

Rengakos, Antonios and Zimmermann, Bernhard (eds.) (2011) *Homer-Handbuch: Leben – Werk – Wirkung*, Stuttgart; Weimar.

Ricœur, Paul (1985) *Zufall und Vernunft in der Geschichte*, Tübingen.

Ricœur, Paul (2004) *Gedächtnis, Geschichte, Vergessen*, Munich.

Ricœur, Paul (2005) *Vom Text zur Person: Hermeneutische Aufsätze*, Hamburg 2005.

Rihll, Tracey Elizabeth (1999) *Greek Science*, Cambridge.

Rogkotis, Zacharias (2006) 'Thucydides and Herodotus: Aspects of Their Intertextual Relationship', in Antonios Rengakos and Antonios Tsakmakis (eds.), *Brill's Companion to Thucydides*, Leiden, 57–86.

Rohde, Erwin (1899) *Psyche: Seelencult und Unsterblichkeitsglaube der Griechen*, 2 vols, 2nd ed., Freiburg (Reprint Darmstadt 1991).

Roisman, Joseph (2010) 'Classical Macedonia to Perdiccas III', in Joseph Roisman and Ian Worthington (eds.), *A Companion to Ancient Macedonia*, Oxford, 145–65.

Rollinger, Robert (2011) 'Der Blick aus dem Osten: "Griechen" in vorderasiatischen Quellen des 8. und 7. Jahrhunderts v. Chr. – eine Zusammenschau', in

Hartmut Matthäus, Norbert Oettinger, and Stephan Schröder (eds.), *Der Orient und die Anfänge Europas: Kulturelle Beziehungen von der Späten Bronzezeit bis zur Frühen Eisenzeit*, Wiesbaden, 267–82.
Rose, C. Brian (2008) 'Separating Fact and Fiction in the Aiolian Migration', *Hesperia* 77, 399–430.
Rössler, Martin (2007): 'Die deutschsprachige Ethnologie bis ca. 1960: Ein historischer Abriss', *Kölner Arbeitspapiere zur Ethnologie* 1, April.
Rossmann, Kurt (ed.) (1969) *Deutsche Geschichtsphilosophie: Ausgewählte Texte von Lessing bis Jaspers*, Munich.
Roth, Peter (2003a) *Der Panathenaikos des Isokrates: Übersetzung und Kommentar*, Munich.
Roth, Peter (2003b) 'Die Dialogszene im "Panathenaikos"', in Wolfgang Orth (ed.), *Isokrates: Neue Ansätze zur Bewertung eines politischen Schriftstellers*, Trier, 140–49.
Ruggieri, Claudia (2009) 'The Emergence of Pisatis', in Peter Funke and Nino Luraghi (eds.), *The Politics of Ethnicity and the Crisis of the Peloponnesian League*, Washington DC, 49–64.
Rumscheid, Frank (ed.) (2009) *Die Karer und die Anderen: Internationales Kolloquium an der Freien Universität Berlin, 13.-15. Oktober 2005*, Bonn.
Rüsen, Jörn (1990/2012) *Zeit und Sinn: Strategien historischen Denkens*, Frankfurt; digital revision 2012.
Rüth, Axel (2005) *Erzählte Geschichte: Narrative Strukturen in der französischen Annales-Geschichtsschreibung*, Berlin.
Rüth, Axel (2012) 'Narrativität in der wissenschaftlichen Geschichtsschreibung', in Matthias Aumüller (ed.), *Narrativität als Begriff: Analysen und Anwendungsbeispiele zwischen philologischer und anthropologischer Orientierung*, Berlin, 21–46.
Rutherford, Richard B. (2012) 'Structure and Meaning in Epic and Historiography', in Edith Foster and Donald Lateiner (eds.), *Thucydides and Herodotus*, Oxford, 13–38.
Sauer, Christoph (2011) *Valerius Flaccus' dramatische Erzähltechnik*, Göttingen.
Schade, Gerson (2011) 'Griechische Erinnerungsorte und Erinnerungsräume', *Hermes* 139, 112–19.
Scheer, Tanja (1986) 'Ein Museum griechischer, Frühgeschichte' im Apollontempel von Sikyon', *Klio* 78, 353–73.
Schepens, Guido (1970) 'Éphore sur la valeur de l'autopsie (*FGrHist* 70 F 110 = Polybe XII 27.7)', *Ancient Society* 1, 164–82.
Schepens, Guido (1975) '*Emphasis* und *enargeia* in Polybios' Geschichtstheorie', *Rivista Storica dell'Antichità* 5, 185–200.
Schepens, Guido (1977) 'Historiographical Problems in Ephorus', in *Historiographia Antiqua: Commentationes Lovanienses in honorem W. Peremans septuagenarii editae*, Leuven, 95–118.
Schepens, Guido (1997) 'Jacoby's FGrHist: Problems, Methods, Prospects', in Glenn W. Most (ed.) *Collecting Fragments/Fragmente Sammeln*, Göttingen, 144–72.

Schepens, Guido (2000) 'Probleme der Fragmentedition (Fragmente der griechischen Historiker)', in Christiane Reitz (ed.), *Vom Text zum Buch*, St. Katharinen, 1–29.
Schepens, Guido (2006) 'Storiografia e letteratura antiquaria: Le scelte di Felix Jacoby', in Carmine Ampolo (ed.), *Aspetti dell'opera di Felix Jacoby*, Pisa, 149–71.
Schepens, Guido (2007) 'History and Historia: Inquiry in the Greek Historians', in John Marincola (ed.) *A Companion to Greek and Roman Historiography*, Oxford, 39–55.
Schepens, Guido and Bollansée, Jan (2004a) 'Frammenti di politeiai, nomoi e nomima: Prolegomeni ad una nuova edizione', in Silvio Cataldi (ed.), *Poleis e politeiai: Esperienze politiche, tradizioni letterarie, progetti costituzionali. Atti del Convegno Internazionale di Storia Greca, Torino, 29 maggio – 31 maggio 2002*, Alessandria, 259–83.
Schepens, Guido and Bollansée, Jan (2004b) 'Myths on the Origins of Peoples and the Birth of Universal History', in José María Candau Morón, Francisco Javier González Ponce, and Gonzalo Cruz Andreotti (eds.), *Historia y mito: El pasado legendario como fuente de autoridad*, Malaga, 57–75.
Schmitt, Arbogast (2009) 'Epostheorie, Maßstäbe der Literaturkritik, zum Verhältnis von Epos und Tragödie (Kap. 23–26)', in Otfried Höffe (ed.), *Aristoteles Poetik*, Berlin, 195–213.
Schnapp, Alain (2011) 'Les ruines dans l'Antiquité classique', in Hans-Ulrich Cain, Annette Haug, and Yadegar Asisi (eds.), *Das antike Rom und sein Bild*, Berlin, 115–38.
Schorn, Stefan (2013) 'Überlegungen zu POXY LXXI 4808', *Rivista di Filologia e di Istruzione Classica* 141, 105–18.
Schott, Rüdiger (1968) 'Das Geschichtsbewußtsein schriftloser Völker', *Archiv für Begriffsgeschichte* 12, 166–205.
Schröder, Janett (2020) *Die Polis als Sieger: Kriegsdenkmäler im archaisch-klassischen Griechenland*, Berlin.
Schwartz, Eduard (1959) *Griechische Geschichtsschreiber* (Articles reprinted from RE), Leipzig.
Settis, Salvatore (ed.) (1996) *I Greci: Storia Cultura Arte Società. 2 Una storia greca. I. Formazione*, Turin.
Shrimpton, Gordon S. (1991) *Theopompus the Historian*, Montreal.
Sinn, Ulrich (2004) *Das antike Olympia: Götter, Spiel und Kunst*, Munich.
Stadter, Philip A. (2004) 'From the Mythical to the Historical Paradigm: The Transformation of Myth in Herodotus', in José María Candau Morón, Francisco Javier González Ponce, and Gonzalo Cruz Andreotti (eds.), *Historia y mito: El pasado legendario como fuente de autoridad*, Malaga, 31–46.
Stein-Hölkeskamp, Elke and Hölkeskamp, Karl-Joachim (eds.) (2006) *Erinnerungsorte der Antike: Die römische Welt*, Munich.
Stein-Hölkeskamp, Elke and Hölkeskamp, Karl-Joachim (eds.) (2010) *Die griechische Welt: Erinnerungsorte der Antike*, Munich.
Steinbock, Bernd (2013) *Social Memory in Athenian Public Discourse: Uses and Meanings of the Past*, Ann Arbor, MI.

Sterling, Gregory E. (2007) 'The Jewish Appropriation of Hellenistic Historiography', in John Marincola (ed.), *A Companion to Greek and Roman Historiography*, Oxford, 231–43.
Stierle, Karlheinz (1979) 'Erfahrung und narrative Form: Bemerkungen zu ihrem Zusammenhang in Fiktion und Historiographie', in Jürgen Kocka and Thomas Nipperdey (eds.), *Theorie und Erzählung in der Geschichte*, Munich, 85–118.
Strasburger, Hermann (1956/1965/1982) 'Herodots Zeitrechnung', *Historia* 5, 1956, 129–61 (afterwards also in Walter Marg (ed.), *Herodot: Eine Auswahl aus der neueren Forschung*, Second, revised, and expanded edition, Darmstadt, as well as in Hermann Strasburger (1982/1990) *Studien zur Alten Geschichte*, Vols. II/III, Walter Schmitthenner and Renate Zoepffel (eds.), Hildesheim, 627–75).
Strasburger, Hermann (1958/1968) 'Thukydides und die politische Selbstdarstellung der Athener', *Hermes* 86, 17–40 (then also in Hans Herter (ed.), *Thukydides*, Darmstadt, 498–530, as well as in Hermann Strasburger (1982/1990) *Studien zur Alten Geschichte*, Vols. II/III, Walter Schmitthenner and Renate Zoepffel (eds.), Hildesheim, 676–708).
Strasburger, Hermann (1977) 'Umblick im Trümmerfeld der griechischen Geschichtsschreibung', in *Historiographia antiqua: Commentationes Lovanienses in honorem W. Peremans septuagenarii editae*, Leuven, 3–52 (afterwards also in Hermann Strasburger, 1990, 169–218).
Strasburger, Hermann (1982/1990) *Studien zur Alten Geschichte*, Vols. II/III, Walter Schmitthenner and Renate Zoepffel (eds.), Hildesheim.
Straub, Jürgen (ed.) (1998a) *Erzählung, Identität und historisches Bewußtsein: Die psychologische Konstruktion von Zeit und Geschichte*, Frankfurt.
Straub, Jürgen (1998b) 'Geschichten erzählen, Geschichte bilden: Grundzüge einer narrativen Psychologie historischer Sinnbildung', in Jürgen Straub (ed.), *Erzählung, Identität und historisches Bewußtsein: Die psychologische Konstruktion von Zeit und Geschichte*, Frankfurt, 81–169.
Studnicka, Franz (1890) *Kyrene: Eine altgriechische Göttin*, Leipzig.
Svenbro, Jesper (1976) *La parole et le marbre: Aux origines de la poétique grecque*, Lund.
Thomas, Rosalind (2000) *Herodotus in Context: Ethnography, Science and the Art of Persuasion*, Cambridge.
Timpe, Dieter (1993) 'Über Anfänge in der Geschichte', in Jochen Bleicken (ed.), *Colloquium aus Anlaß des 80. Geburtstages von Alfred Heuß*, Kallmünz, 9–28.
Torraca, Luigi (1988) *Duride di Samo: la maschera scenica nella storiografia ellenistica*, Salerno.
Tsakmakis, Antonis (1995) *Thukydides über die Vergangenheit*, Tübingen.
Tuplin, Christopher (2007) 'Continuous Histories (Hellenica)', in John Marincola (ed.), *A Companion to Greek and Roman Historiography*, Oxford, 159–99.
Ulf, Christoph (ed.) (1996a) *Wege zur Genese griechischer Identität: Die Bedeutung der frükarchaischen Zeit*, Berlin.
Ulf, Christoph (1996b) 'Griechische Ethnogenese versus Wanderungen von Stämmen und Stammstaaten', in Christoph Ulf (ed.), *Wege zur Genese griechischer Identität: Die Bedeutung der frükarchaischen Zeit*, Berlin, 240–80.

Usener, Sylvia (1994) *Isokrates, Platon und ihr Publikum: Hörer und Leser von Literatur im 4. Jahrhundert*, Tübingen.

Usener, Sylvia (2003) 'Isokrates und sein Adressatenkreis: Strategien schriftlicher Kommunikation', in Wolfgang Ort (ed.), *Isokrates: Neue Ansätze zur Bewertung eines politischen Schriftstellers*, Trier, 18–33.

Van Henten, Jan-Willem and Abusch, Ra'anan (1996) 'The Jews as Typhonians and Josephus' Strategy of Refutation in Contra Apionem', in Louis H. Feldman and John R. Levison (eds.), *Josephus' Contra Apionem: Studies in Its Character and Context with a Latin Concordance to the Portion Missing in Greek*, Leiden, 271–309.

Vannicelli, Pietro (1993) *Erodoto e la storia dell' alto e medio arcaismo (Sparta – Tessaglia – Cirene)*, Rome.

Vannicelli, Pietro (2001) 'Herodotus' Egypt and the Foundations of Universal History', in Nino Luraghi (ed.), *The Historian's Craft in the Age of Herodotus*, Oxford, 211–40.

Vansina, Jan (1985) *Oral Tradition as History*, Madison.

Van Wees, Hans (1992) *Status Warriors: War, Violence and Society in Homer and History*, Amsterdam.

Van Wees, Hans (2006) '"The Oath of the Sworn Bands". The Acharnae Stela, the Oath of Plataea and Archaic Spartan Warefare', in Andreas Luther, Mischa Meier, and Lukas Thommen (eds.), *Das Frühe Sparta*, Stuttgart, 125–64.

Veit, Ulrich (2005) 'Kulturelles Gedächtnis und materielle Kultur in schriftlosen Gesellschaften: Anthropologische Grundlagen und Perspektiven für die Urgeschichtsforschung', in Thomas L. Kienlin (ed.), *Die Dinge als Zeichen – kulturelles Wissen und materielle Kultur: Internationale Fachtagung an der Johann Wolfgang Goethe-Universität Frankfurt am Main, 3.-5. April 2003*, Bonn, 23–40.

Verhaegendoren, Koen (2010) 'Outils de dramatization chez Phylarque', in Marie-Rose Guelfucci (ed.), *Jeux et enjeux de la mise en forme de l'histoire: Recherches sur le genre historique en Grèce et Rome* (Dialogues d'Histoire Ancienne, Suppl. 4.2), 421–38.

Vernant, Jean-Pierre (2007) *Mythe et pensée chez les Grecs*, now in Jean-Pierre Vernant, *Œuvres: Religions, rationalités, politiques*, Vol. I, Paris, 239–611.

Visser, Edzard (1997) *Homers Katalog der Schiffe*, Stuttgart.

Von den Hoff, Ralf (2010) 'Media for Theseus, or the Different Images of the Athenian Polis-Hero', in Lin Foxhall, Hans-Joachim Gehrke, and Nino Luraghi (eds.), *Intentional History: Spinning Time in Ancient Greece*, Stuttgart, 161–88.

Von Fritz, Kurt (1967) *Die griechische Geschichtsschreibung*. Vol. 1 (in two parts), Berlin.

Walbank, Frank W. (1957/1967/1979) *A Historical Commentary on Polybius*, Vol. I–III, Oxford.

Walbank, Frank W. (1960/1985/2011) 'History and Tragedy', in *Historia* 9, 216–34 (reprinted in Frank W. Walbank, *Selected Papers: Studies in Greek and Roman*

History and Historiography, Cambridge, 224–41 as well as now in John Marincola (ed.) *Greek and Roman Historiography*, Oxford, 389–412).

Walter, Uwe (1996) '"Common Sense" und Rhetorik: Isokrates' Verteidigung der politischen Kultur', *Geschichte in Wissenschaft und Unterricht* 47, 434–40.

Walter, Uwe (2010) '"Unser Altertum zu finden": Alfred Heuß' Kieler Antrittsvorlesung "Begriff und Gegenstand der Alten Geschichte" von 1949 (Einführung, Edition)', *Klio* 92, 462–89.

Węcowski, Marek (2004) 'The Hedgehog and the Fox: Form and Meaning in the Prologue of Herodotus, *Journal of Hellenic Studies* 124, 143–64.

Węcowski, Marek (2014) *The Rise of the Greek Aristocratic Banquet*, Oxford.

Wenskus, Reinhard (1961) *Stammesbildung und Verfassung: Das Werden der frühmittelalterlichen gentes*, Cologne.

Wesselmann, Katharina (2011) *Mythische Erzählstrukturen in Herodots 'Historien'*, Berlin.

West, Martin L. (1985) *The Hesiodic Catalogue of Women*, Oxford.

West, Martin L. (1997) *The East Face of Helicon: West Asiatic Elements in Greek Poetry and Myth*, Oxford.

White, Hayden (1973), *Metahistory: The Historical Imagination in 19th-Century Europe*, Baltimore.

Wiemer, Hans-Ulrich (2001) *Rhodische Traditionen in der hellenistischen Historiographie*, Frankfurt.

Wiemer, Hans-Ulrich (2013) 'Zeno of Rhodes and the Rhodian View of the Past', in Bruce Gibson and Thomas Harrison (eds.), *Polybius and His World: Essays in Memory of F. W. Walbank*, Oxford, 279–306.

Wilke, Brigitte (1996) 'De mortuis nihil nisi bene: Elaborierte Mündlichkeit in den attischen Grabreden', in Hans-Joachim Gehrke and Astrid Möller (eds.), *Vergangenheit und Lebenswelt: Soziale Kommunikation, Traditionsbildung und historisches Bewusstsein*, Tübingen, 235–55.

Zahrnt, Michael (2006) 'Von Siwa bis Persepolis: Überlegungen zur Arbeitsweise des Kallisthenes', *Ancient Society* 32, 143–74.

Zahrnt, Michael (2012) 'Was haben Apollonios' Argonauten auf dem Istros zu suchen?', *Klio* 94, 82–99.

Zajonz, Sandra (2002) *Isokrates' Enkomion auf Helena: Ein Kommentar*, Göttingen.

Zimmermann, Bernhard (2008) *Dithyrambos: Geschichte einer Gattung*, 2nd ed., Berlin.

Zimmermann, Bernhard (ed.) (2011) *Handbuch der griechischen Literatur der Antike: Erster Band. Die Literatur der archaischen und klassischen Zeit.* Handbook of Classical Studies, 7th section, 1st volume, Munich.

Zimmermann, Bernhard (2015) 'Der Macht des Wortes ausgesetzt, oder: Die Entdeckung der Fiktionalität in der griechischen Literatur der archaischen und klassischen Zeit', in Monika Fludernik, Nicole Falkenhayner, and Julia Steiner (eds.), *Faktuales und fiktionales Erzählen: Interdisziplinäre Perspektiven*, Würzburg, 47–57.

Zingg, Emanuel (2016) *Die Schöpfung der pseudohistorischen westpeloponnesischen Frühgeschichte: Ein Rekonstruktionsversuch*, Munich.

Zipfel, Frank (2001) *Fiktion, Fiktivität, Fiktionalität: Analysen zur Fiktion in der Literatur und zum Fiktionsbegriff in der Literaturwissenschaft*, Berlin.

Index

Ancient Authors and Artists
Agatharchides 130, 131, 135
Aischines 106
Apollodoros 46
Apollonios 132
Archilochos 29
Aristodama (of Smyrna) 12, 13, 27
Aristophanes 114
Aristotle 44, 80, 83, 90, 114, 126, 129, 130
Arrian 81
Athenaios 121, 122, 124

Bakchylides 26

Caesar 15
Cicero 19, 101, 112, 118

Demosthenes 106
Diodoros 51, 112, 113, 116, 135
Dionysios of Halikarnassos 118, 123
dissoi logoi 93, 99, 100, 115, 126
Dosiadas 24
Duris 126, 129, 133

Ephoros 30, 48, 51, 101, 102, 111, 112, 113, 114, 115, 116, 117, 118, 121, 123, 126, 129
Euripides 21, 25, 90
Ezekiel 72

Gorgias 93, 96, 97, 98, 99, 100, 102, 103, 105, 106, 117, 119, 121, 126, 127

Harpokration 114
Hekataios 18, 19, 49, 76, 77, 80, 82, 84, 87, 117, 126
Hellanikos 62, 63, 81, 115, 117, 122
Hellenica Oxyrhynchia 120
Herodotos 9, 17, 18, 30, 42, 50, 58, 62, 80, 82, 83, 84, 85, 86, 87, 88, 89, 90, 91, 95, 96, 97, 105, 114, 115, 118, 119, 120, 121, 122, 123, 124

Hesiod 16, 17, 45, 46, 48, 51, 52, 74, 94, 99
Hippias 116
Homer 16, 17, 20, 22, 23, 25, 28, 29, 32, 40, 45, 46, 49, 52, 54, 77, 90, 99, 117
Horace 34

Isokrates 97, 98, 101, 102, 103, 104, 105, 106, 107, 108, 109, 110, 111, 112, 113, 115, 118, 119

Josephus 33, 135

Kallisthenes 31, 51, 129
Kleitarchos 128
Ktesias 122

Mimnermos 11, 51, 52, 55, 66

Parmenides 79, 97
Photios 121
Phylarchos 130, 132, 133, 134
Pindar 24, 26, 27, 29, 30, 63
Plato 17, 103, 106, 118, 126
Plutarch 129
Polybios 33, 77, 83, 98, 112, 115, 119, 121, 122, 123, 130, 131, 132, 133, 134, 135

Quintilian 127

Sextus Empiricus 78
Simonides 29
Strabo 76, 117, 129, 135

Tauriskos 132
Theopompos 31, 51, 101, 102, 111, 118, 119, 120, 121, 122, 123, 124, 126
Thucydides 18, 21, 30, 81, 88, 89, 90, 91, 95, 96, 98, 101, 105, 106, 111, 113, 114, 115, 118, 120, 123, 124
Timaios 33, 83, 135
Tyrtaios 11, 25, 29, 49, 51, 52, 55, 66, 68

Xanthos 78
Xenophanes 77, 83, 106
Xenophon 88, 89, 101, 113, 120

Zeno of Elea 79

Modern Authors and Artists
Assmann, Jan 3, 19, 33, 80

Bauer, Otto 13
Berger, Peter L. 7, 8, 13
Bernstein, Frank 61
Blumenberg, Hans 43, 44
Bourdieu, Pierre 20
Büchler, Johann Lambert 7
Burckhardt, Jakob 19

Carr, Edward Hallett 4
Chaniotis, Angelos 133
Christesen, Paul 116

Dareste, Rodolphe-M. 15
Detienne, Marcel 16
Dilthey, Wilhelm 5, 7
Droysen, Johann Gustav 134

Giuliani, Luca 36
Goethe, Johann Wolfgang 21, 109
Goody, Jack 19
Grethlein, Jonas 30, 44, 88
Grimm, Jacob 2, 8
Grimm, Wilhelm 2, 8

Halbwachs, Maurice 2, 9
Hartog, François 73, 74
Heuß, Alfred 2, 64, 72, 136
Hölscher, Uvo 74
Husserl, Edmund 6

Jacoby, Felix 76, 113, 116, 125

Koselleck, Reinhard 2, 3
Kowalzig, Barbara 26
Kunze, Christian 131
Kyrieleis, Helmut 35

Loraux, Nicole 30, 92
Luckmann, Thomas 7, 8, 13
Luhmann, Niklas 20
Lupi, Elisabetta 86
Luraghi, Nino 87

Maier, Felix 136
Mann, Golo 136
Marincola, John 116, 124, 131

Meeus, Alexander 125
Meier, Christian 133
Mertens, Dieter 39
Meyer, Doris 34
Momigliano, Arnaldo 116
Mühlmann, Wilhelm 6

Nagy, Gregory 53
Nickau, Klaus 42
Nietzsche, Friedrich 2, 4, 13
Nora, Pierre 3

Primavesi, Oliver 16
Prinz, Friedrich 46, 49, 53, 54

Ranke, Leopold von 4, 16, 20, 135
Ricœur, Paul 9, 44
Rihll, Tracey Elizabeth 125
Rohde, Erwin 40
Rüth, Axel 43

Schepens, Guido 117
Schorn, Stefan 128
Schwartz, Eduard 113, 115
Stone, Oliver 133, 134
Strasburger, Hermann 85, 101, 133

Thomas, Rosalind 84

Weber, Max 4
Wenskus, Reinhard 6
White, Hayden 135

Zimmermann, Bernhard 74

Mythical and Historical Figures
Achaians (myth. Greeks) 54, 55, 57
Achilles 23, 39, 129
Agamemnon 107
Aigimios 60, 63
Aigyptos 57
Aiolians 46, 56, 62
Aiolos 44, 56, 62
Aitolos 62, 68
Ajax 37, 48
Alexander the Great 39, 78, 81, 102, 119, 125, 127, 129, 130, 134
Alkinoos 26
Amazons 35, 47, 92, 108
Amyntas 108
Andromache 48
Antigonos Gonatas 130
Aphrodite 28
Arabos 57
Aratos 130, 131

Index

Archelaos 21
Ares 28
Argives 85, 92
Argonauts 47, 57, 59
Artemis 32
Asarhaddon 72
Assyrians 72

Battos 66
Busiris 109

Centaurs 47, 93, 115, 121
Charmos 26
Cyclops 50, 62

Damarmenos 38
Demodokos 22, 23, 26, 28, 74, 83
Deukalion 46, 49, 53, 56
Diagoras 29, 30
Diomedes 37, 57
Dionysios I 108, 121
Dionysios II 113, 121
Dirke 132
Dorians 44, 46, 49, 50, 53, 54, 56, 62, 67, 68
Doros 44, 49, 54, 60, 62
Dymas 68

Endymion 56
Epeians 54
Epigones (of the Seven) 47
Erechtheus 53
Erinyes 71
Eumolpos 92
Eurystheus 58, 60, 108

Gelon 113
Glaukos 37
Gyges 83

Hecuba 48
Hektor 34, 37
Helen 45, 48, 90, 97, 105
Helios 30
Hellen 48, 49, 54, 56
Hephaistion 39
Hephaistos 28
Heraclids 47, 49, 55, 56, 58, 59, 60, 66, 68, 108, 116
Herakles 11, 30, 35, 47, 56, 57, 58, 59, 60, 92, 108, 129
Hieron I 63
Hipparchos 26
Hyllos 60, 68

Ion 44, 62
Ionians 44, 46, 50, 54, 56, 60, 62, 67, 68, 69, 107

Jason 47

Kadmos 45, 63, 76
Kandaules 83
Kastor 47
Keyx 60
Kleisthenes of Athens 28
Kleisthenes of Sikyon 53
Kroisos 50
Kronos 11, 45, 46
Kypselos 31, 66

Labdakos 63
Laios 63
Laistrygonians 121
Lapiths 47, 93
Latinos 52
Lelegians 57
Leokrates 25, 31
Lykurgos of Athens 25, 31
Lykurgos of Sparta 63, 113
Lysander 113

Maussolos 119
Menelaos 48
Minyans 59, 64
Mnemosyne 16
Muses 16, 73, 74, 78, 99

Nausithoos 62
Neleids 63
Neleus 56, 62, 63
Nestor 56

Odysseus 23, 48, 57, 72, 74, 82, 99
Oidipous 45, 63
Oinomaos 37
Orestes 38, 47, 48
Oxylos 66

Palamedes 99
Pamphylos 68
Patroklos 39
Peirithoos 47
Peisistratides 26
Pelasgians 50, 51, 57, 85
Pelops 11, 36, 37, 38, 51, 53
Penelope 74
Periander 113
Perikles 113
Perinthos 68

Phaiakians 62
Phemios 23, 98
Philipp II 119, 120, 121, 122, 123
Philoktetes 48
Phoinix 57
Phokos 63, 68
Polydeukes 47
Polyneikes 63
Poseidon 53, 67, 69
Pyrrha 46, 49

Sanherib 72
Sargon II 72
Selene 56
Seven against Thebes 47, 92, 93

Tantalus 37
Teisamenos 38
Telamon 47
Telemachos 47
Teukrids 108
Thales 77
Theopompos 11
Theras 68
Theseus 36, 38, 47, 107, 108
Thracians 77, 92, 108
Tiglat-Pilesar III 72
Tlepolemos 30, 59, 65
Trojan War Heroes 46, 48, 57, 63
Trojans 17, 50
Tydeus 47

Xerxes 85

Zaleukos 113
Zeus 11, 24, 35, 45, 46, 123, 129

Places and Political Entities
Achaia, Achaians 54, 66, 68, 130, 131
Aegean 54
Aitna 63
Aitolia, Aitolians 12, 38, 56, 62, 66, 68
Arcadia, Arcadians 35, 50, 123
Argos, Argives 85, 108
Asia 11, 51, 55, 56, 57, 58, 67, 68
Athens, Athenians 25, 26, 28, 30, 31, 35, 38, 47, 50, 51, 53, 55, 56, 60, 67, 82, 91, 92, 93, 103, 104, 107, 108, 109, 119

Boiotia 118

Chaleion 12, 14
China 15
Chios 124
Cilicia 72

Crete, Cretans 24, 50, 54, 113
Cyprus 108

Delphi 35, 38, 65, 66
Doris 54, 60, 62, 67
Dryopis 54

Egypt, Egyptians 33, 80, 118
Elis, Eleans 35, 37, 38, 53, 56
Eretria 38
Erineos 11
Etruscans 57
Europe 122

Helike 68, 69
Herakleia at Latmos 56
Hestiaiotis 54

Ionia 62, 77, 117

Karians 57, 58, 72
Kolophon 11, 14, 66, 77
Korinth 66, 113, 119
Kroton 86, 90
Kyrene 58, 59, 60, 61, 64, 65, 66, 70

Lamia 12
Latmos 56
Lindos 29, 38
Locris, Ozolian 12
Lydia, Lydians 50
Lykeion 123

Macedon, Macedonians 21, 125, 127
Magnesia 32
Melos 54
Messene, Messenia 11, 116
Miletos, Milesians 113
Mykale 67

Okeanos (Ocean) 46
Olympia 29, 37, 38, 56, 119

Panionion 67
Paros 29
Peloponnese 49, 51, 54, 55, 58, 60
Perinthos 68
Persia, Persians 85, 93, 113, 120
Phoenicians 50, 58
Phokis, Phokians 35, 53, 63, 66, 68
Phrygia 72
Phthia, Phthiotis 53
Pindos 54
Plataiai, Plataians 108

Priene 18
Pylos 11, 54

Rhodes 29, 30, 38, 59, 119

Salamis 26
Samos 18
Scheria 62
Selinus 39
Sicily 91
Smyrna 11, 12, 27
Sparta, Spartans 11, 14, 26, 29, 31, 35, 38, 51, 59, 64, 66, 67, 104, 108, 124
Stoa Poikilē 35
Sybaris 86, 90

Tegea, Tegeans 82
Thasos 124
Thebes, Thebans 45, 47, 58, 92, 93, 108
Thera 54, 58, 59, 60, 61, 63, 64, 65, 68
Thessaly, Thessalians 12, 66
Trachis 58, 60
Troy 38, 39, 45, 47, 48, 57, 97, 107

General Terms, Concepts, Events
aetiology 70, 71, 117
agon 19, 26, 79, 111, 125
agora 22, 26, 32, 39
Aiolian Migration 56
alētheia, alēthes etc. 9, 18, 74, 97, 99, 107, 128, 129, 130
amazonomachy 35, 47, 92, 108
amphictyony 26, 123
ancestors (cult / worship of) 12, 24, 25, 30, 31, 37, 39, 40, 48, 49, 52, 53, 56, 57, 59, 60, 63, 64, 104, 108, 109
antiquarian literature 116, 129
asylum 60

Boiotian Migration 56
Brahmans 15

Calydonian Boar 38
Catalogue of Ships 50
centauromachy 93, 115
colonisation 39, 55, 58, 61, 62, 63, 64, 65, 71, 72
community of descent 8
community of fate 13, 68
competition 19, 20, 26, 28, 34, 79, 80, 81, 99, 104, 123, 125, 131

decree of honour 31
Dekeleian War 104
Delian League 108
displacement 54, 59, 60, 61, 71, 85

Dorian Migration 49, 50, 51, 53, 54, 55, 58, 62, 65, 107
druids 15

eleatic 106
elenchos, elenctic method 79, 80, 88, 90, 97, 105, 117
epideictic 30, 92, 93, 96, 97, 103, 105, 112, 118, 119, 122
eponymy 44, 52, 62, 63, 64
ethnic, ethnology etc. 5, 6, 8, 19, 39, 44, 51, 66, 67
ethnos (Gr.) 12, 51, 54, 66
euhemerism 51

fairy-tale motifs 17, 66, 70, 123
festival 26, 27, 30, 69, 89, 92, 110, 119
forensics 30, 79, 87, 90, 97, 98, 105, 106, 111
founder (hero) 30, 39, 40, 59, 62, 63, 64, 66, 68, 76
friendship 37, 58, 62

genealogies 21, 48, 49, 52, 57, 59, 62, 63, 67, 76, 77, 80, 108
geography 77, 85, 117, 124
gigantomachy 93, 115
grave (cult) 38, 39, 40, 56
great divide 22

heroes 38, 39, 40, 41, 45, 46, 47, 48, 51, 52, 56, 57, 59, 62, 63, 64, 66, 68, 71, 74, 76, 107, 129, 134
Himera, Battle of 113
historiē 18, 77, 83, 85, 87, 96
historism 4

ideal type 1, 4, 5, 95, 96
identity, identities 5, 6, 7, 11, 12, 35, 36, 38, 42, 43, 44, 49, 51, 52, 64, 68, 70, 95
Ionian Migration 11, 51, 55, 56, 65, 107

kinship 21, 48, 55, 56, 58, 59, 62, 64, 67, 85
kleos 22, 23, 24, 25, 33, 34, 74, 76, 84, 97

Lindos, temple chronicle of 38
local history 116, 117

Marathon, Battle of 35, 40, 108
Megarean Decree 113
miasma 65
migration 11, 48, 49, 50, 51, 52, 53, 54, 55, 56, 57, 58, 59, 60, 61, 62, 65, 66, 68, 69, 70, 71, 107, 116
mnēmones 14
monument(alisation) 24, 29, 31, 32, 33, 34, 35, 86, 92

neo-historism 4
nostoi 47, 57

Olympic victors, list of 116
oracles 31, 38, 65
ostracism 26

panhellenism 26, 35, 109, 113
Parthenon 36
Peloponnesian League 60
Peloponnesian War 88, 93, 108, 113
Pentekontaetia 88
performance 20, 22, 23, 26, 27, 28, 29, 30, 32, 33, 40, 41, 44, 95
Persian Wars 17, 31, 93, 104, 106, 108
phylē, phylai (tribes) 28, 67, 68
Plataia, Battle of 31, 40, 82
Platonists 106, 118
polis 12, 19, 27, 28, 32, 39, 40, 62, 67, 87
progenitor 30, 56, 62, 63, 64
public space 27, 31, 32, 33, 35, 36, 39

reification 7, 8, 13
relics 38, 40
revenge 28, 47, 58
Rhetra, Great 31

rites / rituals 10, 14, 16, 36, 40, 41, 60, 62, 72, 95
ruins 39

sacrality 15, 16, 28, 36, 38, 62, 64, 65, 69, 72, 89, 110, 123
saddle-time 4
Salamis, Battle of 25
singers 20, 22, 23, 27, 29, 32, 49, 52, 63, 64, 69, 73, 74, 77, 78, 98
sites of memory 3, 38, 39
sophism 93, 106, 116
stasis 61
Stoics, stoic 117, 135
symposium 22, 26, 69
syssities 24, 26

Thessalian Migration 56
tribes (Gr.) 49, 64, 66, 67, 68
Trojan War 35, 38, 45, 46, 47, 48, 49, 50, 51, 55, 93, 106, 107
truth 13, 16, 18, 20, 33, 44, 73, 74, 77, 78, 79, 82, 87, 88, 91, 93, 94, 95, 96, 97, 98, 99, 100, 101, 102, 103, 104, 105, 107, 109, 110, 111, 117, 124, 125, 127, 128, 129, 130, 131, 133, 135, 136, 137

violence 54, 55, 59, 60, 65, 71, 72, 132

For EU product safety concerns, contact us at Calle de José Abascal, 56–1°,
28003 Madrid, Spain or eugpsr@cambridge.org.